BEYOND THE
Windswept Dunes

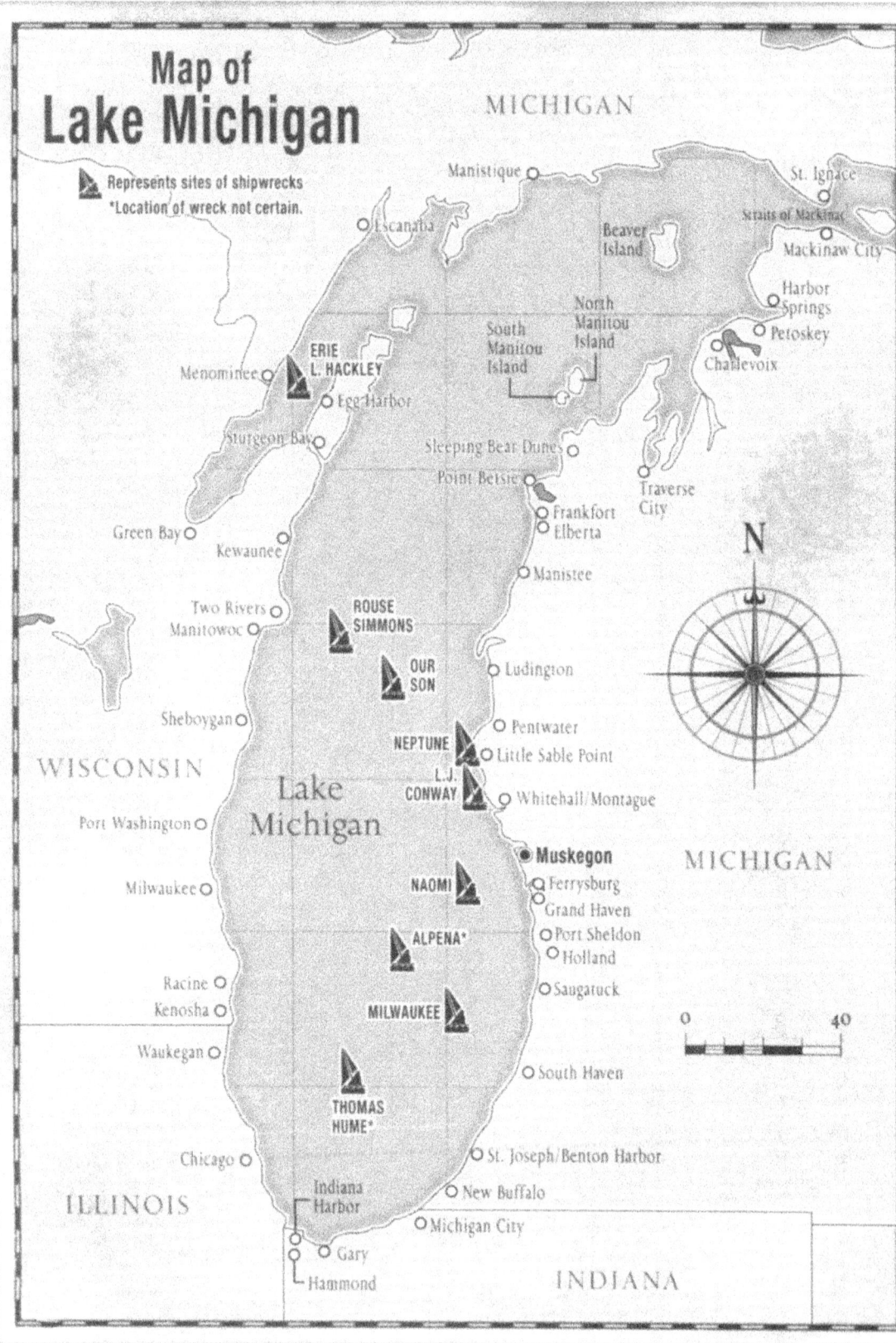

BEYOND THE
Windswept Dunes

The Story of Maritime Muskegon

———◇———

ELIZABETH B. SHERMAN

WAYNE STATE UNIVERSITY PRESS   DETROIT

Great Lakes Books

A complete listing of the books in this series can be found at the back of this volume.

Philip P. Mason, Editor
Department of History, Wayne State University

Dr. Charles K. Hyde, Associate Editor
Department of History, Wayne State University

Copyright © 2003 by Wayne State University Press,
Detroit, Michigan 48201. All rights are reserved.
No part of this book may be reproduced without formal permission.

07 06 05 04 03   5 4 3 2 1

Library of Congress Cataloging-in-Publication Data

Sherman, Elizabeth B.
Beyond the windswept dunes : the story of maritime Muskegon / Elizabeth B. Sherman.
    p. cm. — (Great Lakes books)
Includes bibliographical references and index.
ISBN 0-8143-3127-0 (Paper : alk. paper)
1. Muskegon Region (Mich.)—History, Naval. 2. Muskegon Region (Mich.)—Commerce—History. 3. Muskegon Region (Mich.)—Economic conditions. 4. Shipping—Michigan—Muskegon Region—History. 5. Lumber trade—Michicagn—Muskegon Region—History. 6. Inland navigation—Michigan—Muskegon Region—History. 7. Navigation—Michigan, Lake—History. 8. Shipwrecks—Michigan—Muskegon Region—History. 9. Shipwrecks—Michigan, Lake—History. I. Title. II. Series.
F574.M9S54 2003
977.4'57—dc21   2003002567

∞The paper used in this publication meets the minimum requirements of the American National Standard for Information Sciences—

This book is dedicated to my mother,
Margaret M. Sherman,
who instilled in me a love of books
and a greater love of learning.

CONTENTS

List of Maps and Illustrations ... xi
Preface ... xiii
Acknowledgments ... xv

1. Hewn from the Wilderness: Muskegon's Earliest Days ... 1

Trapper, Trader, Soldiers, Spy: The Visit by the HMS *Felicity* ... 4

2. Lumber Days on Muskegon's Waterfront ... 7

"Dreadful Endurance": The *Neptune* and Other Early Shipwrecks of Muskegon ... 24

A Tragic Homecoming: The Wreck of the *Granada* ... 27

Safe in the Sand: The *Trial* and the *Annie Nelson* ... 28

Semper Paratus: The Muskegon Lifesaving Crew and the Wreck of the *R. B. King* ... 29

"So Terrible a Reality": The Wrecks of the *South Haven*, the *Helen*, and the *L. J. Conway* ... 32

Legend and Mystery: The Fate of the *Rouse Simmons* and the *Thomas Hume* ... 38

"Frenchman, he don't lak to die": The Wreck of the *Waukesha* ... 44

The Charmed Life of the *Lyman M. Davis* ... 48

3. Steamships and Car Ferries of Muskegon ... 53

Sailing Blind: The Wreck of the *Wabash Valley* ... 69

Lost to the Depths: The Wreck of the *Alpena* ... 70

A Steamer for All Seasons: The *Alabama* ... 74

Up Against the Big Guns: The *Charles H. Hackley* — 80
"Carelessness Becomes a Mortgage to Danger": The Wreck of the Steam Barge *Milwaukee* — 83
Trials by Fire: The *Naomi* and the *Nyack* — 89
"They Will Probably Send Me to Hell": The Wreck of the *Muskegon* — 91
Adrift in Changing Times: The Story of the *Illinois* and the *Missouri* — 98
The "Queen of the Great Lakes": The *Milwaukee Clipper* — 101
All Dressed Up and Nowhere to Go: The *Aquarama* — 104
"A Monster of Its Kind": Muskegon's First Car Ferry — 106
The *Shenango* Legacy: The Grand Trunk Car Ferries — 108

4. Maritime Muskegon in the Twentieth Century — 113

Bad Luck Comes in Threes: The Wreck of the *Salvor* — 117
Psychic Intervention: The Wreck of *Our Son* — 124
Breakwater Blues: The Wreck of the *Henry W. Cort* — 126
Tragedy Averted: The Near-Wreck of the *Fred W. Green* — 132
Coming Full Circle: The *Highway 16/LST 393* — 133
Laid-Up Lakers: Steel Strikes of the 1950s — 136
Breakwater Blues Reprise: The Ordeal of the *Makefjell* — 139
Museum Ships: The USS *Silversides* and the USCGC *McLane* — 143
The *Halcyon*'s Days in Muskegon: From Seaside to Scrapheap — 146

5. Muskegon Today: New Ships and Old — 151

Poem: The Good Captain — 155

Appendix A: Angus Linklater/The *Granada* — 157
Appendix B: Capt. J. D. Dunbar/The *R. B. King* — 159
Appendix C: Frank Dulach/The *Waukesha* — 161
Appendix D: Frank Dulach Reiterates — 165
Appendix E: *Toronto Evening Telegram*/The *Lyman M. Davis* — 167
Appendix F: Frank Blakefield/The *Erie L. Hackley* — 169
Appendix G: "Doc" Ray Cooke/The *Alabama* — 171

Contents

Appendix H: Guy E. Jones/The *Naomi* — 175
Appendix I: Capt. Edward Miller/The *Muskegon* — 177
Appendix J: Lyman Nedeau/The *Salvor* — 181

Notes — 185
Glossary — 193
Bibliography — 197
Index — 207

MAPS AND ILLUSTRATIONS

Map of Michigan   ii
Map of Muskegon Area Shipwrecks   22
1. Charles H. Hackley   11
2. The schooner *Kate Lyons*   12
3. Captain Seth Lee   13
4. Mason Lumber Company with schooners at the dock   15
5. Booming tugboat *Third Michigan*   19
6. Harbor tug *R. P. Easton* towing the *Lyman M. Davis*   21
7. Muskegon Channel, 1882, and the Nelson lumber mill   23
8. Unidentified shipwreck   30
9. The scow schooner *Helen*   35
10. Hackley and Hume lumber mill   40
11. The *Rouse Simmons*   41
12. The schooner *Waukesha*   45
13. Frank Dulach   49
14. Schooner *Lyman M. Davis*   50
15. The side-wheel steamer *Huron*   59
16. Steamers *C. J. Truesdell* and *Laketon*   60
17. The harbor of Muskegon   61
18. The Goodrich dock, the *Alabama*, and the *Virginia*   62
19. Crosby's steamer *Nyack*   64
20. Coastal steamer *Carrie A. Ryerson*   65
21. The steamer *Erie L. Hackley*   66
22. The *Favorite*   68
23. The side-wheel steamer *Alpena*   71
24. Painting of the *Alpena*   73
25. The *Alabama*   75
26. Main cabin of the *Alabama*   76
27. The *Georgia* works to free the *Alabama*   77

Maps and Illustrations

28. Captain Gerald Stufflebeam   79
29. The steamer *Charles H. Hackley*   82
30. The *Charles H. Hackley* racing the *Atlanta*   84
31. The steam barge *Milwaukee*   85
32. Crosby steamer *Naomi*   90
33. The burning of the *Naomi*   91
34. The burned-out *Nyack*   92
35. The Crosby steamer *Muskegon*, 1919   94
36. Viewing the wreckage of the passenger steamer *Muskegon*   96
37. The *Muskegon's* pilothouse washed ashore   99
38. The engine from the *Muskegon* in the channel   100
39. The steamer *Juniata*   102
40. The *Milwaukee Clipper*, c. 1941   103
41. The *Aquarama*   106
42. The car ferry *Muskegon*   109
43. Grand Trunk car ferry *Madison*   111
44. Aerial view of the Mart dock with the *Milwaukee Clipper*, *Highway 16*, and *Aquarama*   116
45. Aerial view of Muskegon Channel   118
46. The stone barge *Salvor*   120
47. The A-frame of the shipwrecked *Salvor*   122
48. The *Our Son*   125
49. The wreck of the whaleback *Henry W. Cort*   128
50. The *Cort's* crew   131
51. The freighter *Fred W. Green*   134
52. The *LST 393* as the auto carrier *Highway 16*   135
53. Freighters at sunset, 1956   138
54. Six ore boats, 1959   139
55. The Norwegian freighter *Makefjell*   141
56. Tugs attempting to pull the *Makefjell* free   144
57. The submarine USS *Silversides*   146
58. The USCGC *McLane*   147

PREFACE

I did not intend to write a book. The original plan was to write several articles on ships that frequented Muskegon from the lumber days on and see if the *Muskegon Chronicle* or a maritime journal would be interested in publishing them. However, as I dug into the books and microfilm in the basement of Muskegon's Hackley Public Library, I realized there was a tremendous wealth of information, stories, and other "dirt"—much more than could be adequately covered in a couple of articles. To do justice to the topic—by now expanded to include all major ships, shipwrecks, and various maritime people, incidents, and developments—I decided a book was the only appropriate format.

As a Muskegon native, raised on Muskegon Lake and someone who often played along the Lake Michigan shore, I'm ashamed to admit I grew up knowing next to nothing about Muskegon's maritime history. Of course, the *Milwaukee Clipper* and *Highway 16* were familiar sights on the lakes, as were the various foreign ships that visited the port. From my childhood, I can recall the lineup of big ore carriers in the harbor during the steel strikes of 1956 and 1959, although at that time I didn't know why the boats were just sitting there. Of the old lumber schooners, I had heard of the *Lyman M. Davis* and the story that my grandfather, Thomas M. Sherman, had once taken a trip to Chicago and back on that popular schooner. (More recently, I learned that he actually sailed on the ship as a cabin boy.) The significance of that piece of family history was lost on me until later years. Such was about the extent of my youthful understanding of this topic. I'm sure others who grew up around or worked on the vessels are more enlightened about Muskegon's shipping history, but by and large the stories I found are not common knowledge, even to many local residents.

Those living in other areas around the Great Lakes are very aware of their maritime heritage as evidenced by the maritime museums, lighthouse preservation efforts, and underwater preserves where scuba divers can explore the remains of a number of lost vessels. In addition, several well-known authors have written books documenting exciting tales of Great Lakes ships and shipwrecks, in some cases focusing on a strategic coastline or major shipping port rich in lake lore. But Muskegon tends to be overlooked or given just a sidelong glance. It's time to take a closer look at what has happened in the waters around the Port City.

A few points of clarification need to be made. During my research, I found that several local writers have written about Muskegon's shipping history, and their articles were published at various times in the *Muskegon Chronicle* from the 1940s to around 1970. Unfortunately, in the spinning of a good yarn, the facts were sometimes treated loosely or typos were made that confused the facts, and I found these accounts less than trustworthy. For me, it wasn't enough just to relate these great stories; I was determined to tell them based on the facts. Often these articles discussed a particular ship or incident, but I turned to other sources for more accurate information.

The reader will find that some of the sections provide great detail concerning a particular ship or event, while other accounts are less fully developed. This is primarily due to the amount of information available. The city's newspaper, the *Muskegon Chronicle,* started publication in 1869, and copies of it on microfilm date from around that time. From the 1880s on, the local newspaper reporters covered maritime activities and incidents more fully since, by then, the city had grown and was heavily dependent on the shipping of lumber and other cargo. Thus, I found a surfeit of detailed information on ships and lake activities from the late nineteenth century to the present. However, there were a number of early Muskegon shipwrecks about which we have only the vaguest information, the details unrecorded or unknown. Sometimes all that is known is the name of the ship, the year, general vicinity and cause of the wreck, and possibly the number of casualties (if any). I have mentioned some of these in the book, giving the reader just a sketchy outline while wishing I could present a fuller picture.

This book is not intended to be an exhaustive detailing of every aspect of Muskegon's maritime history. Obviously, there are some areas I chose to avoid; with a focus on the larger commercial vessels, I have not included a discussion of recreational boating or commercial fishing. Within the chosen framework, I wanted to provide readers with a fairly comprehensive and informative overview, including major events, certain "firsts," and, whenever possible, a good story. I hope these become a part of the common knowledge for the people of the Muskegon area and a solid addition to all the other tales of the Great Lakes enjoyed by those who love the Inland Seas.

ACKNOWLEDGMENTS

I am indebted to a number of people who assisted and encouraged me in the writing of this book. First of all, I wish to thank my aunt, Sue Wierengo, who suggested I turn my early research into a more extensive article or series of articles. At the time, neither of us knew what would evolve.

There are a few people whom I came to rely on for assistance on a number of issues or who had access to little-known facts that I needed. Many thanks to Barbara Martin, archivist at the Muskegon County Museum, for giving me access to valuable materials and photographs, as well as answers to numerous questions; to Mike Spears for his contributions of hard-to-find information on the *Neptune* wreck, the *Algoma*, and other pieces of Muskegon's early history; and to Robert Graham, archivist at the Historical Collections of the Great Lakes, for locating rare photos and the information I needed when I had exhausted all other avenues of research.

Two individuals were instrumental in providing me with personal accounts and details that helped set the record straight for their respective stories: Lyman Nedeau, one of the survivors of the *Salvor* wreck, who gave me his first-hand account of the incident, and Robert Stufflebeam, the son of Captain Gerald Stufflebeam, who provided accurate information concerning his father's career and the *Alabama*. I am deeply grateful for their support on this project and helpful reading of the *Salvor* and *Alabama* sections.

My thanks go to the readers of the manuscript's preliminary draft for their suggestions and corrections: Karen Carty, Jerry Crowley, Dr. Mary Dereski, Janet Fisk, and Dr. Steven D. Rodgers. The time and care they took in critiquing the draft are greatly appreciated. I'm also grateful for Joann and Lee Murdock's helpful comments on a later draft of the manuscript.

Others who have given me invaluable information and direction in the course of my research are Jeanine Masak, projects archivist at Michigan State University's Archives and Historical Collections; Bob Morin, Sr., and John Waite of the Great Lakes Naval Memorial and Museum (formerly the USS *Silversides* and Maritime Museum); Thomas W. O'Bryan, P. E. and Jim Hopp of the Grand Haven Area Office of the U.S. Army Corps of Engineers; Dan Bloom of the West Michigan Dive Center; Sandy Planasek of the Great Lakes Lighthouse Keepers Association; author David Swayze; Scott Peters of the Michigan Historical Museum; John Polacsek, director of the Dossin Great Lakes Museum; Molly Biddle of the Wisconsin Maritime Museum; Davis Elliott of the Navy Department Library; and Heather Wilson, research specialist for Intellisearch/Toronto Reference Library. My thanks to all.

Acknowledgments

I wish to acknowledge the dedication of the late Jean Hume Browning, who preserved valuable documents concerning the Hackley and Hume Lumber Company. This collection is now housed at Michigan State University. In those personal archives I found little-known, informative details concerning the ships owned by the firm. In addition, and in this regard, a big thank-you to my sister, Helen Sherman, for digging up the letter from Thomas Hume concerning the loss of the schooner *Thomas Hume* (a piece I missed on an earlier visit to the MSU archives) as well as for finding other documentation on Muskegon's maritime history.

Special thanks go to Lynda and Bill Charles, who helped introduce me to Lyman Nedeau. I also want to express my appreciation to the staffs at the Hackley Public Library, the Norton Shores Public Library, the Burton Historical Collection of the Detroit Public Library, the Great Lakes Marine Collection of the Milwaukee Public Library, and the Chicago Historical Society for their help and patience as I conducted my research, and to Linda Thompson, *Muskegon Chronicle* librarian, for assistance in finding exclusive photographs in the newspaper's archives.

In the later stages of the book's development, a number of individuals and groups lent their support and to them all I am very grateful. In particular I wish to thank Malcolm McAdam and other members of the Great Lakes Maritime Institute's board of directors for their help and advice, and to Dr. Philip Mason, both as a member of GLMI's board and as editor of the Great Lakes Books Series of Wayne State University Press, for his enthusiasm and personal interest in guiding my efforts in this endeavor. Many thanks to author Joe Grimm for his advice and map artist Fred Fluker for his wonderful illustrations.

Finally, many family members and friends provided me with encouragement and support as I worked on this project over the past few years, and to them all, I am deeply grateful.

CHAPTER 1

Hewn from the Wilderness

Muskegon's Earliest Days

The early French explorers and voyageurs of the Great Lakes discovered on their travels that the coastlines of the Inland Seas presented an ever-changing panorama. From the marshy wetlands of western Lake Erie and the St. Clair River flats, to the rocky outcroppings of Lake Huron's Georgian Bay and the forbidding, yet fantastic Pictured Rocks of Lake Superior, a rich variety of landscapes met their gaze as they paddled their birchbark canoes. Along the way, they envisioned the immense potential offered by the virgin wilderness. In some areas they found fertile soil well suited for growing crops and fruit trees. Game was plentiful in the dense forests and open fields, fish were abundant in lakes and rivers. In time, other valuable resources would be discovered or realized and ultimately exploited—copper and iron from the lands along Lake Superior, and the tall pine from the primeval forests that covered extensive tracts in both Michigan peninsulas.

While coasting along the Lake Michigan shorelines, the early explorers focused on the Wisconsin side since it appeared to hold the most promise. Jean Nicolet, who in 1634 was eager to find a passage to China and, later, Louis Jolliet and Father Jacques Marquette, who went in search of the Mississippi in 1673, pursued their goals along the lake's lee side. However, those who traveled along the western shoreline of Michigan's Lower Peninsula, including Father Marquette on his last voyage, followed a sandy strand nearly three hundred miles long—a forbidding terrain that attracted little interest. Here, the westerly winds blowing in from the northern plains build up the big lake's waters, creating the breakers that pound rock to sand, and these same winds then sculpt the desert-like landscape, shaping and reshaping it over the course of a season or a century. Golden dunes rise up from the beach and roll back from the water's edge, with tufted sand reed grasses and the coarser marram grasses helping to stabilize the terrain. Stunted, tenacious trees, such as jack pine and cottonwood, dig in a short distance back from the water's edge and feel the brunt of the harsh winter winds. Further back, hills are crowned with dense forests of white pine, beech, and oak.[1] Some stretches of dunes lie low and undulating. Others, such as those further north, soar four hundred feet high.

CHAPTER I

Compared to other shores around the Great Lakes, this terrain appeared particularly desolate to the first Europeans. Even as late as 1845, the west Michigan shoreline left a poor impression on those who viewed it. A Norwegian traveling by ship to Milwaukee made these comments on sighting the long and barren expanse: "The northern shore of Lake Michigan reveals on that side an ugly and poor landscape. High sandhills rise several hundred feet from the surface of the lake. As far as I could see, there was no sign of vegetation except a few scrubby pines in the valleys and some brown heather.... Long sandbars extend several miles out from the shore so that no ship can land."[2] Who would want to settle in this harsh land?

The French voyageurs and *coureurs des bois*[3] did not settle the region but roamed the wilderness freely, trading with the natives, primarily the Ottawa, and loading their canoes with valuable furs to be sent back east. As they explored further inland, they found a particular scenario repeating itself along the length of this shoreline. A river—maybe fifty, maybe two hundred miles long—flows from the interior of the Lower Peninsula westward, some waterways coursing down from the vast pine forests of the north-central uplands, some rising from the rolling country in the south-central regions, but all finding an outlet in the expansive waters of Lake Michigan. As it nears the big lake, the river fills a smaller lake basin just east of the ridge of dunes. The waters, less forceful but still determined, push on, creating a channel that cleaves the sandy stretch between the two, allowing the river waters to finally reach their deepwater destination. In time, many of the towns and cities of western Michigan—Manistee, Ludington, Pentwater, Whitehall and Montague, Muskegon, Grand Haven—would be built along the protected waters where they met the dunes and Lake Michigan, providing safe ports for the ships that traveled the length of the big lake.

The area around what would become Muskegon—the name originated from the Ottawa Indian term "Masquigon" meaning "marshy river" or "swamp"—did not appear to be an ideal place for a large settlement.[4] The Muskegon River, the longest in the peninsula, wending two hundred miles southwest from its source at Higgins Lake in the north-central region, forks into two branches at its mouth, then spreads out to form a lake approximately five miles long and two-and-a-half miles across at its greatest width. To the east, the head of Muskegon Lake is bounded by mosquito-infested marshes, the western mouth by the barren dunes where a shallow, meandering channel feeds the lake's waters to Lake Michigan. Just south of the channel at that time rose a massive three-hundred-foot-high sand dune that dominated the harbor entrance. Because thousands of passenger pigeons inhabited the dune, the region's settlers named it Pigeon Hill. The smaller Bear Lake lies to the north of Muskegon Lake, connected to it by a narrow channel. Further back from the shores spread miles of dense woodland.

The sandy soil and marshlands were not conducive to farming. However, the area teemed with a variety of game—beaver, mink, muskrat, otter, deer—which thrived in the wetlands and forests. Outside the native Ottawa population, only a few individuals well suited for the rugged and isolated conditions called Muskegon home in the last half of the eighteenth century and into the early nineteenth century, and for them the fur trade was

Muskegon's Earliest Days

the main commercial activity. While the French voyageurs and *coureurs des bois* traveled and traded in the area from the late 1600s until the 1750s, their impression on the region was as transient as the wakes made by their canoes. However, the fur traders who worked for the British interests and, later, the American fur companies made their presence more permanently felt with the establishment of trading posts around Muskegon Lake and other west Michigan waterways.

As they were elsewhere in the Great Lakes region, these lakes and rivers were the lifeblood for those making a livelihood there, providing the main routes for transportation, commerce, and communication. They cradled the dugouts, birchbark canoes, and flat-bottomed bateaux that carried basic trade items—the fur pelts so highly valued in the eastern states and abroad, and the guns, utensils, trinkets, and supplies prized by the natives and vital to the earliest settlers. In time, the river and lake harbor would prove to be even more valuable assets to Muskegon, essential for the town's growth as a major lumbering and shipping port on the lakes.

Control of the Great Lakes passed to the British when they defeated the French in the French and Indian War (1754–60). A few years later, when the resistance by Pontiac and his Ottawa followers in what was called "Pontiac's Rebellion" was quelled in 1763, the region's lucrative fur trade came fully under British control.

The American Revolution barely touched the Lake Michigan wilderness so far removed from the struggles in the colonies. However, the British military presence dominated Lakes Huron and St. Clair, as England was intent on maintaining the fur trade activities on the lakes and checking any possible rebel infiltration in the region. At this time, no ships of size were allowed to engage in commercial trade; the British feared that rebels might commandeer such a vessel, fitting her out for an armed engagement.[5] However, between their strongholds at Detroit and Michilimackinac, the British transported troops and supplies on vessels belonging to what was called the Provincial Marine.[6] These small ships—primarily sloops and schooners—carried armaments and patrolled the lakes, alert to any possible encroachment by rebel forces.

During this period, the closest threat to England's control of the Great Lakes came in 1778 when a Virginian, George Rogers Clark, took a contingent of Kentucky riflemen and pushed west into northern Illinois. They managed to capture the British Fort Sackville, near Vincennes. The news reached Detroit and a force led by Lt. Col. Henry Hamilton set out across lower Michigan and recaptured the fort. Clark's men retreated, but they returned during the harsh winter of 1779, and with the aid of some French settlers and the townspeople of Vincennes the Americans once again took Fort Sackville.[7] This seemingly small victory was a foot in the door and marked the Northwest Territories for further expansion by Americans. In 1783, when the Treaty of Paris was signed, the door to the Great Lakes region was flung open to settlers as they moved inland from the eastern states.

Americans took over the fur-trading activities from the British, although England did not entirely leave the lakes until 1796 when the terms of Jay's Treaty effectively pushed them out. In the Muskegon area, beginning in the early 1800s, a handful of fur-trading

CHAPTER I

posts were established around Muskegon Lake and the surrounding shorelines, some representing John Jacob Astor's powerful American Fur Company, others operating under independent entrepreneurs. The first one on Muskegon Lake was founded in 1810 near the channel to Lake Michigan by a man named Lamorandie. Another early trader, Pierre Constent, set up a post nearby soon afterward. In 1812, a French-Canadian, Jean Baptist Recollect, established one on Bear Lake Channel, and around 1818, the American Fur Company employed a trader named Pierre Lassallier, whose post was located further up on the Muskegon River.[8]

The fur-trading canoes and bateaux of these early years were well suited to the waterborne activities of Muskegon. However, as the traders gave way to the lumber speculators, lumberjacks, and early settlers, larger sailing vessels passed through the port until hundreds came to call, turning a backwoods settlement into a major shipping center for the region's huge lumber industry.

Trapper, Trader, Soldiers, Spy: The Visit by the HMS *Felicity*

On the afternoon of October 31, 1779, a small British sloop sailed along the eastern shore of Lake Michigan. Off the port side, the desolate sand dunes and dense forests stretched along the horizon; off starboard, nothing interrupted the vast grey-green waters of the inland sea. The vessel had endured a rough ten-day passage through choppy waters kicked up by winds laced with sleet and snow.[9] It was around 5:00 when the crew dropped anchor about a half mile offshore, opposite to where a winding waterway connected a large inland lake to Lake Michigan. The sloop's master, Captain Samuel Robertson, sent out a small boat to take a an interpreter, Charles Gautier, and two Frenchmen to a nearby trading post with orders to bring back Black Peter. The mysterious Black Peter, one of the first non-native settlers in the region and owner of the trading post near the channel, was found, and the party returned to the ship with the trader and three Ottawa natives. Once onboard, goods were exchanged, the British providing the locals with rum, tobacco, bread, and pork and accepting a supply of venison in return. More important, information was exchanged. Captain Robertson had been given orders by the British Lieutenant Governor Patrick Sinclair, stationed at Michilimackinac, to take the HMS *Felicity* and cruise the length of Lake Michigan, gathering corn and any provisions the British could use and that otherwise might fall into the hands of the American rebels. Black Peter, who is believed to have been a paid agent for the British, informed him of several recent corn shipments, but confirmed he had no knowledge of any rebel activity in the area.[10]

After the locals were returned to shore, the ship continued her voyage along the Michigan shoreline to track down a corn shipment allegedly sent up the Grand River, twelve miles farther south. Captain Robertson, a Scotsman with years of experience on saltwater, noted in the ship's log that they encountered rough seas and hazy conditions as the sloop sailed around the head of the lake and northward along the Wisconsin shoreline. The *Felicity*'s two-week cruise ended when she safely arrived back at the Straits of Mackinac on November 6.[11]

The HMS *Felicity*—a single-masted vessel rigged fore and aft—was one of several small British ships used not only in the Great Lakes fur trade, which the British then controlled, but also in patrolling the lakes at the time of the American Revolution. For this role, she was armed with four to six swivel guns. The fifty-seven-foot, forty-five-ton sloop was built in the King's Shipyard at Detroit in 1773 or 1774, and remained in service for many years. On her regular route between Detroit and the Straits of Mackinac, she carried troops, supplies, and trade items (including rum, brandy, and furs), as well as official government communications.[12] However, on this particular voyage in the fall of 1779, she became the first ship to visit the site where the city of Muskegon would grow from a few small trading posts to a major Great Lakes port.

CHAPTER 2

Lumber Days on Muskegon's Waterfront

The village grew gradually from 1840 through the early 1850s into a frontier town known as Muskeego.[1] In about 1840, with the fur trade all but dead, the small number of fur traders gave way to another breed of men—a highly transient lot predominantly made up of land speculators and lumbermen who were tempted by the huge expanse of forested land that covered the northern half of the Lower Peninsula. The speculators followed the rivers deep into the wilderness, searching for prime stands of timber. They found that

> an extensive hardwood forest covered much of the southern portion of the state. North of a line running roughly from Muskegon to Saginaw, the character of the forest changed markedly with the appearance of extensive stands of soft woods, either in pure stands or mixed with hard woods. The swamp lands of northern Michigan abounded in tamarack and yellow cedar of excellent quality. There were also extensive tracts of less valuable Norway pine and jack pine in the area. But the timber interests of the country were drawn to the extensive stands of white pine.[2]

The lumbermen were mostly of Yankee stock, men who had wielded axe and peavey in the trade in Maine, New York, and Pennsylvania. Joining them were a number of French Canadians, skilled woodsmen well seasoned in such work. Immigrants arrived, and if they had no experience as lumberjacks or mill hands, they soon got it.[3] Ambitious entrepreneurs saw great wealth in the forests and, backed by financial support, built lumber mills in the boomtowns that grew up at the river mouths, expecting to make their fortune from the seemingly endless supply of timber. A number of them succeeded.[4] The men who came to this wilderness were young and single, well suited for the rough and dangerous work in the lumber camps and the wild life in the towns, and able to move on if more profitable employment beckoned them. The newly established (in 1805) territory of Michigan provided them with a fresh beginning and unlimited opportunities in the frontier settlements along the shores of Lakes Huron and Michigan.

While other communities along the west Michigan shore saw similar growth based on lumber, Muskegon boasted a number of advantages that gave it a distinct edge. As the timber grew scarce near the towns where it was cut and milled, it became necessary to search further inland for the pine to keep the sawmills operating. Speculators for the lumbering interests had only to follow the Muskegon River—at two hundred miles, the longest in the Lower Peninsula—to find extensive tracts of the tall white pine in the heart of the state, timber that could be floated to the distant mills around Muskegon Lake. Not only did the size of Muskegon Lake accommodate the numerous mills built along its shores, it also formed one of the best natural harbors on Lake Michigan—a destination for the hundreds of vessels that brought in men, equipment, and supplies, and eventually shipped out millions of board feet of lumber. In addition to these natural features, the town enjoyed considerable leverage through its proximity to the major lumber markets—Chicago in particular. As Chicago expanded and towns sprang up further out on the prairies and western plains, the demand for lumber became incessant, and Muskegon, along with other west Michigan towns—in particular, Grand Haven, White Lake, Manistee, Ludington, and Traverse City—was able and eager to meet those demands.

Lake transportation was essential for bringing in supplies from larger cities to the small settlement on the southeastern shore of Muskegon Lake—everything from food, clothes, tools, and household utensils to furniture and even lumber to build the first frame houses arrived by boat. Small schooners—often called "sailing stores"—visited the settlements around Lake Michigan to deliver the goods along with news from the outside world. According to local lore, the first such ship bringing supplies to Muskegon went out of control while approaching the dock adjacent to Thomas Dill's general store and her bowsprit rammed into the store's front window. It is reported that the crash and tinkle of broken glass drew dozens of gawkers to the scene.[5]

The men who came to Muskegon in search of jobs and possibly a place to settle more often than not booked passage on one of the sailing ships. Many first immigrated to one of the Wisconsin ports or Chicago and, upon hearing of job opportunities in Muskegon, would then ship out on a schooner, often working their way across the lake.[6] In the January 26, 1901 edition of the *Muskegon Daily Chronicle,* one early arrival, Dennis Garvey, described what the town was like fifty years earlier. "It looked like poverty and misery in Muskegon the day I sailed into this harbor in the late 1840s," he recalled. "Muskegon was the most lonesome place one could imagine. I was only 21 years of age when I came, and I don't know how I stood it as I did." At that time, the town of several hundred residents primarily consisted of a few sawmills, along with company stores for the mill employees, boardinghouses where most working men lived, general stores, saloons, and log cabin homes for some families. In his account, Garvey remembered some of the early sailing vessels that visited the port: "The schooners which came to Muskegon were the *Muskegon,* owned by C. Davis & Co., the *George R. Roberts,* owned by Ryerson & Morris, the *Honest John* and *Henry Clay,* the *W. C. Walton,* and occasionally the *Illinois* and the *New Hampshire* would run up from Grand Haven. Most of the early settlers came in on the *Roberts.*"[7]

Local businessmen relied on these ships to occasionally take them to the larger Lake Michigan cities of Chicago and Milwaukee where they could purchase inventory for their stores, buy special equipment for their mills, and transact business deals. Such a trip could take a few days to several weeks depending on the weather and lake conditions. Despite the hazards, a voyage by ship was preferable to a slow journey by land via woodland trails or barely passable roads.

However, ships could only make it through when there was open water. Thus, winters isolated the small community and proved particularly harsh when snow lay deep, ice grew thick, and provisions ran low. Early Muskegonite Henry Egelston recalled the winter of 1857, when the town ran out of necessities: "In '57 they were all out of provisions in Muskegon, even out of horse feed and they sent over to Chicago for the first boat to bring provisions. The boat came in here to the mouth and this lake was full of ice. Everybody turned out and sawed a road through the ice and got the boat up here to the dock to find to their surprise that it was loaded with whiskey and feed."[8]

The exporting of lumber from the region officially began in the mid-1830s as a modest enterprise. At that time, the Pennoyer mill, located a short way up the Muskegon River in Newaygo County, was busy sawing logs into lumber. In 1837, some of the manufactured lumber was rafted down to the river's mouth, where it was loaded onto the schooner *Celeste*. The ship then sailed for Chicago, delivering the first lumber cargo transported through the Muskegon waterway.[9]

The year 1837 also marks the birth of the city of Muskegon and, coincidentally, the birth of the city's lumber era. In that year the first sawmill on Muskegon Lake was built by Benjamin H. Wheelock of the Muskegon Steam Mill Company. That August, another entrepreneur, Jonathan H. Ford of the Buffalo and Black Rock Company, started construction of a water mill at the mouth of Bear Lake. A year later, the Ford mill was ready for business in Muskegon's fledgling lumber trade. The first lumber sawed there was transported to the mouth of Muskegon Lake and loaded onto the schooner *Victor*. It was February 1839, and due to ice conditions on Lake Michigan, the *Victor* reached Chicago only after a ten-day voyage.[10]

In the years that followed, Muskegon harbor became home to a growing number of lumber schooners. These shallow-draft vessels usually carried two or three masts and were rigged with fore-and-aft sails. In length, they could range from sixty to two hundred feet. A standard feature on most Great Lakes schooners was a centerboard (also known as a slip keel or drop keel), which gave them greater stability in open water but could be retracted when plying the shallower channels or harbors. A schooner needed only a small crew, often fewer than ten men. Several variations of the schooner were the clipper schooner, which combined the sharp lines and speed of a seagoing clipper ship with the flat-bottom design and cargo-carrying capacity of a schooner, and the scow schooner, which had a more boxy appearance and a shallower draft, enabling it to carry more cargo but also making it hard to handle in rough seas.[11]

The *Victor* and *Wave* were two of the earliest of these vessels to make regular visits. In 1848, Theodore Newell built the schooner *Muskegon* in Milwaukee specifically to transport lumber from Muskegon to Kenosha, Wisconsin, and other Lake Michigan ports. Sailing ships based in other ports also made regular visits to the harbor, adding

CHAPTER 2

to the bustle of activity on the lake. For an otherwise isolated community, they provided the necessary business and social contacts and a steady transportation system for men and goods to help Muskegon grow. It was on one of these vessels, the two-masted clipper schooner *Challenge,* that on April 17, 1856, a young man sailed into Muskegon, having worked his way across from his home town of Kenosha. In Muskegon he would rise to the challenge presented by the lumber business in the thriving young town, eventually becoming one of the city's leading lumber barons and philanthropists. This enterprising man of action was Charles H. Hackley.

When Charles Hackley arrived in Muskegon, his father, Joseph Hackley, who had come to the town in 1855 to work as a carpenter, arranged for him to take employment at the Durkee, Truesdell and Company mill. Over the next fifty years, through a combination of wise investments, various partnerships, a determined work ethic, and sterling reputation for fair dealing, Charles Hackley achieved great prosperity through the lumber industry and left his distinctive mark on his adopted hometown.

It is beyond the scope of this book to discuss the activities and accomplishments of the number of lumber barons based in Muskegon during the heyday of the industry. However, a focus on the lumber business owned by Hackley and his partners,[12] especially with regard to their shipping practices, can offer a window on one successful operation, including the economic changes and trends the firm faced that impacted its maritime activities, both during the lumber era and in its aftermath. It should be noted that the business concerns Hackley dealt with were shared by other lumbermen of Muskegon, and his approach in handling them influenced others. In addition, his career and personal life are well documented. Thus, the man and his enterprise provide an excellent model of a successful lumber baron of nineteenth-century Michigan. As Muskegon moved from its role as a major lumbering port to a city struggling to find its place in a world of greater industrial diversity, Hackley was a prominent player in these events.

In 1870, Charles Hackley and his partner at that time, James McGordon, acquired three-fourths interest in three lumber schooners: the *Kate Lyons,* the *Rouse Simmons,* and the *H. C. Albrecht* (which later became the *Thomas Hume*). The captains of the respective vessels owned the remaining quarter interest. By 1881, the fleet had grown to include the schooners *Andrew Jackson* and the *Cape Horn.* In addition, Hackley owned several harbor tugs—the *J. H. Hackley* and the *James McGordon*—built specifically for the company.[13] The business of the harbor tugs was very competitive, with schooner captains choosing tugs with the lowest towing rates to take them through the channel. Since the rates could not be dictated by the individual mills, Hackley and presumably other lumbermen who owned tugs found this aspect of the business less profitable than originally anticipated. However, by maintaining their own fleet of lumber schooners, Hackley and McGordon could be assured that their ships would be available during the peak of the shipping season.[14] They also were reacting to the Chicago Vessel Owner's Association's recent increase in freight charges; by operating their own fleet, they knew they could realize a small profit. However, with the dramatic increase in the number of ships sailing the Great Lakes in the 1880s, and the resulting competitive freight rates

Muskegon lumberman and philanthropist Charles H. Hackley ([P87–232] Muskegon County Museum).

offered, this margin of profitability also shrank. The case of the schooner *Rouse Simmons* clearly illustrates this predicament. In 1883, she returned an annual profit of $1,682.51; the next year, profit fell to $406.74. From that time on, the *Simmons* earned no more than $500 annually for the company.[15] Although Hackley would occasionally charter other ships, he predominantly relied on the company's fleet, accepting orders for lumber based on the capacities of his vessels.

The captains hired by the lumbermen to sail the schooners were given freedom to use their discretion in managing the ship's affairs during the shipping season, from hiring their crew (usually four to six men) to paying for necessary expenses (equipment and repairs) and collecting freight receipts at the time the cargo was unloaded.[16] In the 1850s, according to Dennis Garvey, sailors made the same wages as mill hands—$16 per month, or approximately fifty cents a day.[17] By the end of the nineteenth century, a sailor might earn close to $2 per day. *Waukesha* survivor Frank Dulach mentioned he had $14 in wages coming, and that was for his seven days of work aboard the ill-fated schooner. Captains' salaries were determined at the end of the season when they would forward their financial records to the firm's office. Once an audit was done, they would be paid.

CHAPTER 2

The schooner *Kate Lyons,* owned by Charles Hackley and sailed by Captain Seth Lee ([P86–134] Muskegon County Museum).

The salary for a season depended on the profits of a lumber firm. In the early 1880s, when Muskegon's lumber business was near its height, the captains of the Hackley and Hume firm earned an annual salary of $1,800. However, by the 1890s, with the boom ending, the drop in profits meant a drop in salaries; in the 1890 season, they made only $600.[18]

One captain for the Hackley and Hume Lumber Company became a close personal friend of Charles Hackley. In 1872, Hackley and Captain Seth Lee went in together on the purchase of the *Kate Lyons,* and Lee, who had years of experience sailing the Great Lakes, was master of the schooner for the next three years.[19] Between 1875 and 1880, he worked as superintendent of the dry dock and tugs for the Muskegon Booming Company. Lee went on to operate a ferry service between Muskegon and North Muskegon on his small steam vessel, the *Erie L. Hackley.*

Captain Lee saw his share of dangers during his years on the lakes, and on at least one occasion his heroic actions saved lives. In late October 1875, a violent gale struck Lake Michigan as the coal-laden schooner *Hubbard* was making her way to Chicago.

Captain Seth Lee ([P94-011] Muskegon County Museum).

The vessel had sprung a leak and Captain James Adams decided to head for the safety of Muskegon's harbor forty-five miles away. Just at the channel's mouth, the surging breakers tossed the schooner onto a sandbar about one thousand feet below the piers where she lay stranded, subjected to the pounding waves. Lee responded to the crisis and managed to rescue Adams and his crew. Unfortunately the local newspaper account does not detail this brave exploit but simply states, "The men were rescued by Captain Seth Lee, of this city."[20]

In his later years Lee worked at several non-maritime occupations, but in all his endeavors he enjoyed the support of the Hackley and Hume firm, which provided him with certain benefits, including the free services of the company's bookkeeper for his own businesses.[21] The captain, his wife, Kittie, and two children lived in a house near Hackley's elaborate home, and because of his estrangement from his own wife, Hackley became a frequent visitor at the Lee household, enjoying the warmth of their friendship to the extent that he was given his own room there. When Captain Seth Lee died in 1900, Hackley was made trustee of his estate.[22]

CHAPTER 2

In 1850, six lumber mills—three on the north side and three on the south side of Muskegon Lake—produced approximately 60,000 feet of lumber per day. By 1857, the number of mills had grown to sixteen, most of them stretched along the south shore of Muskegon Lake, from the river's mouth to the channel at Lake Michigan. More and more lumbering establishments were built around the lakeshore until the boom peaked in the 1880s. By 1888, the lakefront on both sides boasted forty-seven sawmills which, in that decade, cut an average of over 600 million board feet of lumber per year. All told, during the nineteenth century Muskegon's mills produced a staggering amount of lumber—over 30 billion board feet—making them the most productive on Lake Michigan and second only to the mills of the Saginaw River Valley on the state's east side.[23]

The processed lumber was loaded onto carts—both hand-drawn and horse-drawn—and taken out to the long docks adjacent to the mills where it was stacked as high as twenty feet, ready for the "dockwallopers" to load onto the schooners or, in later years, the lumber barges. The well-known phrase "time is money" was keenly understood in the lumber towns; with the amount of lumber produced and the high demand for it, the cargo had to be moved fast. Lake and weather conditions were beyond human control and could either speed or delay a ship on its voyage, or prevent it from entering the harbor for several days on end, but manual and mechanical labor could be driven to high levels of production. In Muskegon, the dockwallopers—longshoremen who operated as an independent unionized group—gained a reputation as the fastest cargo loaders on the Great Lakes.[24] Working in gangs of approximately twenty-four, they competed with other groups of dockwallopers to load a schooner as quickly and efficiently as possible. The record for loading one vessel in Muskegon, using a twenty-four-man gang, was 350,000 board feet of lumber in five hours.[25]

The typical lumber schooner could hold between 200,000 and 250,000 board feet, with most stowed belowdecks and a portion of the cargo transported on the main deck. The mill owners found that green lumber weighed more than seasoned lumber and thus displaced more water when loaded onto the ships. For their own part, Hackley and his partners preferred to ship seasoned lumber to the markets. Any green lumber cut at the mill was stacked on the dock in a cross-piling formation that allowed air to circulate through the pile and dry out, or season, the wood.[26] The process usually took about sixty days unless heavy rains or high humidity interfered.

The shipping activity around the harbor kept pace with the amount of lumber cut and waiting to be loaded. During the 1881 navigation season, more than 2,800 vessels arrived in the port. In June alone, the records show 469 ships arriving and 470 clearing the harbor. It was not unusual for over twenty sailing ships to clear Muskegon harbor in less than two hours. The figures nearly doubled within a few years. In June and July 1885, 975 ships came into the port and 939 cleared.[27] By 1889, of the many busy ports around Lake Michigan, Muskegon came in third, behind Chicago and Milwaukee respectively, in terms of shipping tonnage.[28]

Throughout the lumber era on Lake Michigan, Chicago was the prime recipient of west Michigan's lumber, although other towns at the southern end and the western side

Mason Lumber Company with schooners at the dock, train in the foreground, c. 1879 ([P85–177] Muskegon County Museum).

of Lake Michigan imported a good share of the wood products. These cities—Chicago, Milwaukee, Kenosha, and Michigan City—represented not only destinations for the lumber shipped there; they were also key in helping expand the market. The railroad lines found these cities well suited as hubs for the expanding stretches of rail, and thus the lumber sent by water could continue the journey to points further west and help build settlements that sprang up to the south and west of the Great Lakes region. In viewing it from this perspective, Muskegon and other west Michigan lumber towns stood on a line that marked the boundary of the old frontier (the Northwest Territories) and the new frontier of the Great Plains and the West.

In September 1838, Lt. James T. Homans of the U.S. Navy conducted a survey of the harbors along Michigan's western shore. He found a number of good harbors and sent a highly favorable report to John M'Donnell of the Collectors Office in Detroit. In his account, part of which appeared in the *Detroit Daily Advertiser*, he made the following comments:

> My tour thus far has been a truly satisfactory one, and will prove acceptable to the people of your state, from my being able to report so many good harbors on its western shore. Plats river, aux Betseis, Manistu, Pere Marquette, White and Pentwater rivers, are capable of being made most excellent harbors, by removal of slight obstructions at their entrances; . . . Muskegon river is the best harbor on Lake Michigan, at this moment there being twelve feet of water on the bar, and the channel being straight opening into a lake eight miles long by four wide; and with our vessel, we went in there during a heavy gale of wind blowing on shore, without any pilots, and the same gale which wrecked the steamboat *W. F. P. Taylor* at Michigan City.[29]

Lieutenant Homans's ship was very lucky to have made it safely into Muskegon harbor under such conditions and when the channel happened to be most accessible. As a rule, sailing vessels on the Great Lakes needed assistance to maneuver their way through

CHAPTER 2

the many rivers, channels, and crowded harbors. Schooner captains came to rely on the sturdy harbor tugs to tow their ships safely to and from the docks. When Muskegon's lumber era was in its infancy, the schooners plying the channel had to do so on their own as long as there was a favorable breeze. If the wind died out, a rowboat with two strong oarsmen was prepared to come out and give the vessel a tow. In 1847 the first tugmen, Captain William Mees and Captain John Witherell, provided Muskegon with regular tug service. The early tugboats that used side-wheel propulsion were replaced by more powerful steam-driven tugs by the 1860s. By 1881, the city's tug fleet had grown to twenty-two; of these, fifteen were used for towing, with the other seven used as ferries.[30]

Witherell had a long career in Muskegon's harbor. His father, a building contractor in New York state, moved his family first to the Chicago area, then to Muskegon in 1847 when John was twelve years old. The elder Witherell built three of the earliest lumber mills in the Muskegon area, and for himself he built and operated a water mill at the head of what is now Mona Lake. However, the family suffered hard times when the dam broke and their mill was heavily damaged. To help out, young John ended his schooling and went to work on the Muskegon waterfront. He started out on a tug owned by Captain Mees and became so adept at handling the boat that Mees would leave seventeen-year-old John as acting captain if he needed to be absent. This marked the auspicious beginning of Captain Witherell's long career on a variety of local vessels. Over the years he commanded a number of tugboats, among them the *Alice Getty;* the *H. Warner;* the *Hackley* and the *McGordon* for the Hackley and Hume Lumber Company; the *Pony* for the Muskegon Booming Company (see below); and the *O. M. Field* for the Crosby Transportation Company. Later he captained some of the small ferryboats that criss-crossed Muskegon Lake, from Muskegon to North Muskegon or to the Bay Mill on the western end of the lake. His final years were spent on small steamers that served the resorts on Mona Lake. Witherell retired from sailing just two years before his death in 1907 at the age of seventy-two.[31]

During the lumber heyday, the tugs hustled constantly to handle the heavy schooner traffic, towing the vessels from the channel entrance to one of the mills around Muskegon Lake, or from the dockside through the channel and back into the open waters of Lake Michigan. The long hours could be brutal for the men on the tugs as they operated around the clock at the busiest times of the shipping season. An incident in Witherell's career on a harbor tug highlights the potential risk for the men to "fall asleep at the wheel":

> So extended and arduous were the hours of lake traffic that once he and his men worked so long without sleep that they literally fell over. They were returning from taking a vessel out to the big lake when Captain Witherell noticed something wrong. Upon stepping down to the engine he found that the engineer and fireman had both fallen back asleep. He himself could hardly wait to bring the boat up to the first dock so that he could follow their example.[32]

As in many Great Lakes ports, fierce competition developed among the tugboat owners to be the first to reach an inbound schooner. There was good money to be made:

the charge for a tow was between $10 and $25 per vessel, depending on the tonnage and distance of the tow. The tugs would wait inside the harbor piers for one or more schooners to approach the channel and then the race was on to see who could get to them first. A single tug often took several schooners in tow. On one occasion, the tug *McGordon*, with Witherell at the helm, set a local record, bringing in seven ships through the channel in one tow.[33]

Another fleet of tugs, owned by the Muskegon Booming Company, was used to transport logs to the lumber mills. Before 1850, mill owners had to make their own arrangements to somehow get their rafts of logs from the river mouth to their own booming pens. They might hire boom hands to pole the logs to the mills or have teams of horses walk along the shore pulling a boom of logs. But as more and more logs were floated down the river to Muskegon Lake, lumbermen came up with more efficient methods of handling them, primarily through the use of steam-driven boats. Two of the several early vessels engaged in log booming activities were the *Rattlesnake* and the *Algoma*. The *Rattlesnake* was a scow owned by George Ruddiman, one of Muskegon's earliest lumbermen. She was fitted with a steam wheel driven by a small engine and could handle 300–400 logs at a time. The *Algoma* was a single-masted side-wheel steamer built in Mishikawa, Indiana, in 1845. The sizeable 71-ton craft measured 127 feet long with a beam of nearly 16 feet. In 1853, she came under the ownership of Daniel Ball of Grand Rapids. However, the vessel found employment as a booming tug for Muskegon lumbermen Robert W. Morris and Martin Ryerson, and they bought the vessel around 1858. Later, in the 1860s, she was acquired by the Muskegon Booming Company. Years of hard work no doubt took their toll on the boat. In addition, the tougher, steam-driven tugs built specifically for booming huge rafts of logs rendered the *Algoma* obsolete. In the late 1800s, the vessel's derelict hull could be found at the mouth of Bear Lake Channel.[34]

Efforts were made to improve booming operations, but the situation remained less than satisfactory until finally in 1864 the state legislature passed a law regulating the activity of booming companies. That year, the Muskegon Booming Company was formed to comply with the new regulations and took over the immense job of handling the logs from the time they hit the river far upstream to their arrival at one of the sawmills. The company, most of whose stockholders were prominent area lumbermen, purchased tugs and other equipment necessary to run the extensive operation on Muskegon Lake. The booming grounds were strategically located along the lake's south shore at the mouth of the Muskegon River. Logs floated down the river were sorted by brand into the company's booming pens, then chained in huge rafts to be towed. These powerful tugs could deliver rafts of up to 10,000 logs to the mills. The number of trips a tug could make in a day depended on the distance traveled; the mills near the head of the lake could expect five or six tows to arrive daily, whereas the mills further west might get only two per day. The booming company's operation ran on a tight schedule, with each tug assigned to a specific route. In addition, several tugs had special duties. The *Boss* was used by the foreman to deliver orders to the other tugs, while the *McGraft* and *Pony* were assigned to pick up the rafting and tow chains at the mill sites and return them to the booming company dock.[35]

CHAPTER 2

Fire was a constant threat in the lumber towns. With tons of board lumber, shingles, and sawdust along the docks and the density of the mill sites along the water's edge, a spark could start a conflagration that could threaten a city and any vessel at the docks. Fire sources were everywhere; the mills each had smokestacks and refuse burners. Open-pit fires were commonly found scattered throughout the mill sites, surrounded by cross-piles of the drying lumber up to twelve feet high. Prior to 1887, tugs burned wood slabs and the resulting sparks would often ignite fires in the acres of sawdust lying thick on the ground. Sparks from the tugboat *Nellie* were thought to have caused a massive fire at the Hackley and Hume mill property on the night of December 3, 1888. The blaze destroyed 7.5 million board feet of lumber worth $75,000.[36] Muskegon saw its share of fires that claimed individual lumber mills, as well as two devastating fires—the first in 1874 (the Pine Street Fire) and another in 1891—which destroyed many blocks of the city's downtown. While the city of Muskegon had a large fire station and individual mills were equipped with pumps and hoses, the Muskegon Booming Company also took on some responsibility along the waterfront. Three of its tugs—the *Ira O. Smith*, the *Third Michigan*, and the *Comet*—carried extensive firefighting equipment. The crew members virtually lived on these tugs, always at the ready to handle the pumps and a thousand feet of hose should fire threaten the dockside.[37]

Productive times for the Muskegon tugs ended by the turn of the century. Beginning in the 1880s, schooners were increasingly replaced by steam barges, which could transport more lumber at lower cost and did not require a tow through the channel. In addition, the railway lines carried lumber to market year-round. The Muskegon Booming Company gradually ended its operations as fewer logs came down the river and the local economy turned to other products. It finally dissolved in 1894.

A number of port cities around the Great Lakes had extensive shipyards, which turned out the big schooners, steamers, tugs, and other lake vessels. Muskegon, however, in spite of its large, deep harbor, with miles of waterfront, never developed into a major shipbuilding center. One likely reason for this is that as immigrants moved into the Great Lakes region from the eastern states and abroad, other ports that had already established shipbuilding facilities—Black River (present-day Lorain), Ohio, Detroit, and Bay City/Saginaw, among others—attracted men with the necessary skills. Shipwrights who made their way further west were drawn to the larger cities of Chicago and Milwaukee and the port of Manitowoc, Wisconsin, which, from its earliest days until well into the twentieth century, enjoyed a distinctive reputation as a premier shipbuilding and repair port. When the west Michigan territory was opened up, the types of workers early Muskegon required were lumberjacks, speculators, and mill hands, not shipwrights or others with diverse skills, and thus the town missed the opportunity to attract such craftsmen.

Another factor can be found in the general immigration trends around Lake Michigan. Most settlers coming to the region were drawn to the Wisconsin shore and that region's population quickly grew. As early as 1835, the Milwaukee area showed considerable promise as a strategic port halfway between the early trading centers of Green Bay and

Booming tugboat *Third Michigan* ([P86–125] Muskegon County Museum).

Chicago. Those traveling between these port cities chose to go by water rather than by the rough land route, and as a result other settlements—Sheboygan, Racine, Kenosha, Waukegan—grew up along the Wisconsin and Illinois shorelines, attracting immigrants from Norway, Sweden, and Germany, among other countries, who brought with them a variety of skills, including shipbuilding. In addition, those who planned to move further west across the continent were naturally drawn to Chicago and the towns along Lake Michigan's lee shore as the starting points for their land journey. Milo M. Quaife, in his book *Lake Michigan,* compares the development of the Wisconsin and Michigan shorelines:

> So it came about that the Wisconsin coast of Lake Michigan was dotted with aspiring metropolises while along the Michigan coast there was no comparable development; and since trade and population go hand in hand, the routes of the vessels which came to Lake Michigan ran down the Wisconsin coast. This convenience of access to the Wisconsin shore thus provided a further reason for intending western settlers to locate in Wisconsin rather than in western Michigan.[38]

Still, shipbuilding and repair work did find a place in Muskegon, albeit on a small scale. A few operations appear and then quickly disappear from maritime records, but the two most well-known shipyards on Muskegon Lake lasted long enough to build some notable craft. The first shipyard in Muskegon was founded in 1868 by Captain Joseph P. Arnold for the Muskegon Booming Company, and was located along Ottawa

CHAPTER 2

Street west of the booming company's pens. A small business, the Arnold shipyards repaired vessels and built boats such as tugs and dredges.[39] The tugs *Avery Newell, Comet, R. P. Easton, G. P. Kingsbury, North Muskegon, John Torrent,* and the small propeller *Erie L. Hackley* were all built by the Arnold Company, with the *Comet* and the *Easton* commissioned by the Muskegon Booming Company. The boats constructed by Arnold may have been small, but they were well crafted and proved to be staunch vessels. This high-quality workmanship may have induced the Mason and Davis lumber firm to commission the Arnold Company to build a lumber schooner, the *Lyman M. Davis,* which rose in status well above many similar ships on the Great Lakes (see "The Charmed Life of the *Lyman M. Davis*" at the end of this chapter). Another shipbuilder, Henry J. Footlander, operated a shipyard at the foot of Terrace Street where he built vessels such as the forty-ton schooner *Jessie Martin,* the thirty-two-ton schooner *Annie F. Morse,* along with the tugs *Cora Fuller* and *Kelly Bros.*, and the small propeller *Carrie Mather.*[40]

Muskegon today covers the whole south side of Muskegon Lake, having incorporated the smaller communities that grew up around the mill sites and at the harbor entrance. But in the early days, each had its own identity. As the city grew, the dense wilderness dividing the settlements was cut down and the narrow track of road along the lakefront became a major connector, later named Lake Shore Drive. West of the village of Muskegon was "Pinchtown," so named because it was a narrow strip of settlement pinched between Muskegon and the next official village of Lakeside. Lakeside itself in 1870 was little more than a few shanties and small houses along the main road.

Because of their strategic waterfront locations, two villages—Port Sherman and Bluffton—formed the cornerstone of Muskegon's maritime community. At the mouth of Muskegon Lake, Port Sherman had several sawmills but also became the center of the local commercial fishing industry.[41] The harbor's lighthouse was located here as was, from 1905 on, the Life Saving Station (later the U.S. Coast Guard Station). Summertime saw Chicago vacationers come to stay at the Sherman House, a popular resort established in 1874 by Captain E. B. Fuller. Muskegon residents also made excursions—often on one of the small local steamers—to the Sherman House for dinner and dancing. Further east, on the strip of land bounded by Muskegon Lake and Lake Michigan, lay Bluffton, where the Muskegon area's first post office was built (in 1838). The village also was the original location for the city's customs office. When the office was moved further east to Muskegon proper around 1879, ship captains protested the inconvenience of making the longer trip to get their clearance papers. Thus, when shipping traffic was heaviest, a substation was established at Bluffton.[42] Both Port Sherman and Bluffton were home to fishermen, sailors, members of the Life Saving Service, the lighthouse keepers and their families, and others who made a livelihood on the big lake.[43]

Muskegon Lake offers a safe harbor for vessels coming into the port. While windy weather can kick up choppy, white-capped waves on the lake, these are mere ripples compared to the huge, foaming breakers that batter the eastern shoreline of Lake Michigan during an autumnal gale. However, vesselmen on both schooners and steamships quickly learned that the channel at Muskegon represented both a passage to safety and

Harbor tug *R. P. Easton* towing the *Lyman M. Davis* out of the harbor, 1903 ([P86–137] Muskegon County Museum).

a dangerous—even deadly—waterway to transit in foul weather. Other channels along the west Michigan shore could also be hazardous, but Muskegon's gained a reputation of being the worse to enter in stormy weather, with a wicked combination of heavy surf and hidden sandbars at the entrance that could knock a ship off course in the narrow straits and toss it onto the pier, or threaten to strand a vessel some distance from more protected waters.

With the busy traffic in and out of Muskegon's harbor and thus the greater likelihood of shipwrecks, local businessmen realized that improvements had to be made to the channel and harbor entrance. In 1851, a small lighthouse was built a short distance south of the channel. This was abandoned when a larger lighthouse, complete with quarters for the lighthouse keeper, was constructed closer to the waterway in 1871. The light from the main lighthouse shone a steady white beacon visible to ships up to fourteen miles away. In addition, a red light, which could be seen ten miles out on the lake, was erected atop four posts a short way out on the south pier. Range lights also marked the channel entrance.[44]

The channel itself, so vital to the city's commerce, proved it could also be very fickle. In Lieutenant Homans's account of 1838, he described it as being straight with a depth of

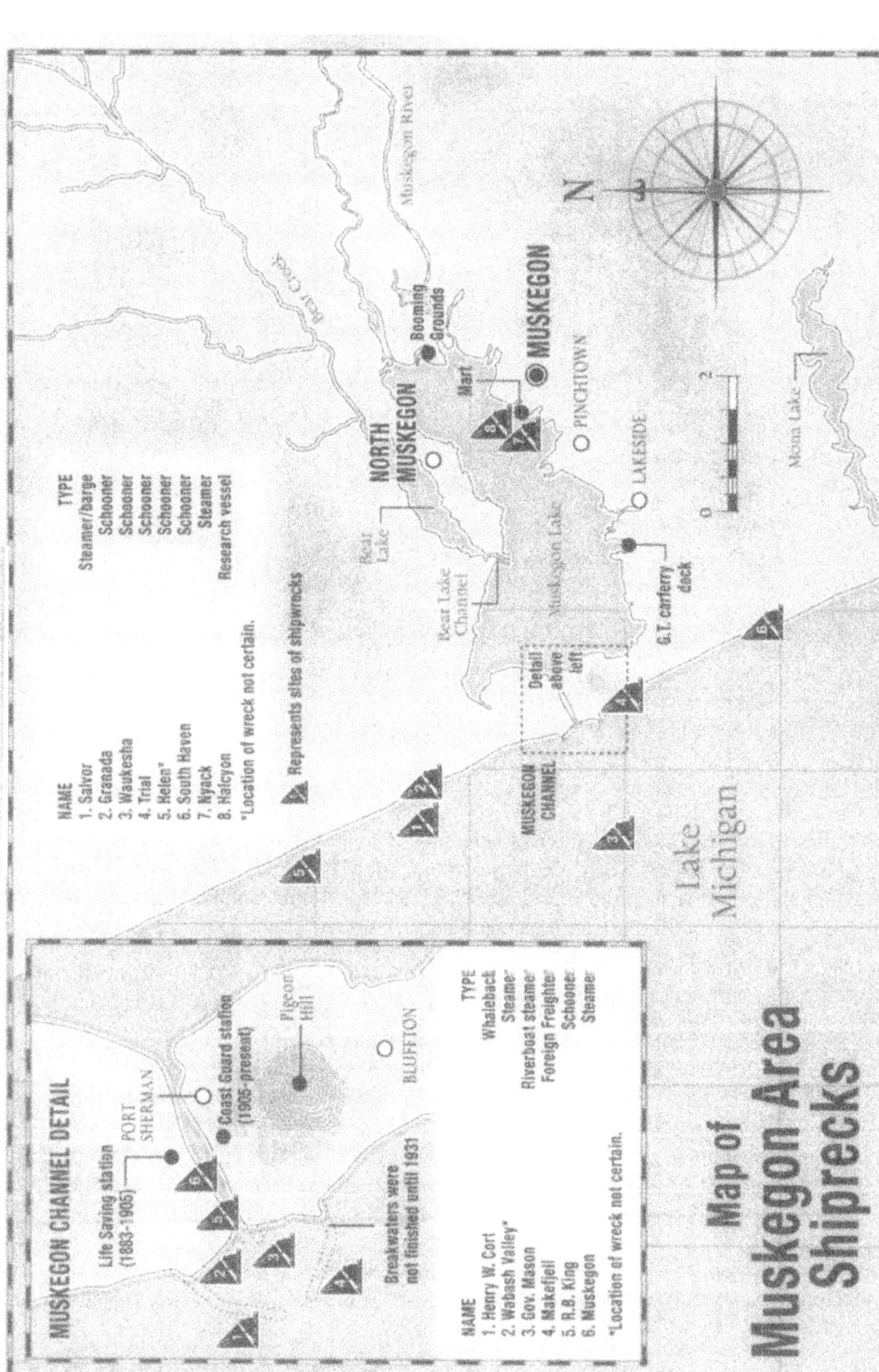

Early view (1882) of Muskegon Channel with the Nelson lumber mill at Port Sherman ([P85–170] Muskegon County Museum).

twelve feet. Apparently, he caught it at a good time. Most of the time, in its natural state, the waterway was relatively narrow and its winding course shifted with the currents. The water depth would vary, sometimes running as shallow as four to six feet. On the Lake Michigan end, the waves, blown by westerly winds, often created the sandbars that made it difficult for a vessel to enter or depart the harbor without the risk of running aground.

Starting in the 1850s, a committee of twelve influential lumbermen, intent on improving ways to get their product to market, tried to alert Congress to the importance of Muskegon's role as a major harbor and its need for a straight and deeper channel, but their requests for federal aid were ignored. However, in 1857, they managed to obtain $50,000 from the state for use in harbor improvements. The monies, raised through a special tax on Muskegon County, went toward dredging the channel and gradually widening it to 150 feet. In 1861, a state law was passed that allowed local groups to make improvements to their harbors, and the Muskegon group decided to do just that. In 1862, they formed the Muskegon Harbor Company. Work commenced the following year with the construction of slab piers along both sides of the one-and-a-half-mile-long channel, with the pier on the south side at 1,500 feet and the pier on the north side at 500 feet. Both piers were extended out into Lake Michigan over the next several years.[45]

While this work straightened the channel, it did nothing to deepen it. Apparently the dredging done in 1857 was not sufficient. In early spring 1864, the lumbermen grew frustrated when thirty-two of their ships, laden with lumber and shingles, were compelled to wait twelve days for natural forces to deepen the channel waters—a mere four feet at the time—and allow the ships to leave port.[46] The shallow depths also had kept out all inbound vessels. That year Lyman G. Mason, one of the lumber barons and then supervisor of the harbor committee, hired the captain of the propeller *Caldwell* to undertake the job of boring his way through the channel to increase its depth. This was done by forcing the ship backward through the channel from Lake Michigan. Once done, the captain found that the sand had filled in behind the propeller, and to get back to Lake Michigan he had to turn around in Muskegon Lake and bore through the channel again. This double boring created the desired effect and from then on the steady current through the channel maintained it at an adequate depth, with occasional dredging needed to accommodate the increasingly larger ships.[47]

In 1867, Congress realized the value of Muskegon's harbor and provided the necessary funding to further improve the channel. The slab piers were replaced with pile piers. A beacon light was built on the south pier, now extended even further from shore. To make the lighthouse keeper's duty of maintaining the beacon easier even in stormy weather, a ten-foot-high catwalk was built on top of the south pier. The extension of both south and north piers continued periodically until the late 1800s when they stretched some distance into Lake Michigan—350 feet on the south side and 250 feet on the north. A foghorn was built at the end of the south pier in 1898, replacing the bell which had hung in a frame to warn ships during periods of low visibility. In 1903, the current lighthouse was constructed on the south pier. Originally painted white (and later bright red), the steel-sided cylindrical tower standing forty-eight feet high was equipped with a fourth-order Fresnel lens, the light from which could be seen for a distance of up to fourteen miles. The south pier light was automated in the 1940s.

The first U.S. Life Saving Station in Muskegon was built in 1878 on the north side of the channel, about halfway between the two lakes. However, it was moved to a site further west in 1883. With plans to widen the channel, the decision was made in 1905 to move the Life Saving Station to the present location of the U.S. Coast Guard Station (now the National Oceanic and Atmospheric Administration Field Station) on the channel's south side. The old station was purchased in 1917 by a local man, loaded onto a scow, and transported to Bluffton where it served for some years as a grocery store.[48] Today, the north side of the channel shows no trace of the early Life Saving Station grounds.

"Dreadful Endurance": The *Neptune* and Other Early Shipwrecks of Muskegon

Since 1679, when the explorer La Salle's small ship *Griffon* went missing on her maiden voyage, the Great Lakes have claimed thousands of ships. While not notorious as a "graveyard" of the lakes, the shores near Muskegon have seen a number of vessels founder, broken apart and lost, often within a short distance of the channel and the safe harbor. One of the earliest casualties occurred in 1839 when the brig *Neptune* was blown ashore during a late November storm. Although the shipwreck occurred thirty miles north of Muskegon at what is now Little Sable Point, the people of Muskegon responded to help the three survivors, who suffered so severely from the bitter cold that two of them had to have their legs amputated.

The *Neptune* had left Cleveland (one account says Buffalo) and was bound for Chicago with supplies when the gale overtook her. Seventeen of the twenty on board drowned, but the captain, John H. Sims, and two others—the captain's brother and the mate, named Webster—managed to reach the uninhabited shore. Captain Sims left to go in search of help, walking south along the shoreline. A few days later he arrived in Muskegon, hungry and suffering from frostbite. While he received treatment, some men from the settlement set out to locate the wreck, salvage what goods they could, and bury the dead. At the wreck site they found the other two crewmen, who had just barely survived for nine days on the cold and desolate beach, and transported them back to Muskegon.

The first published account of the *Neptune* disaster appeared in the December 10, 1839 edition of the *Detroit Daily Advertiser*. The correspondent, writing to the paper's editor from Grandville (near Grand Rapids) on December 3, reported the following:

> Dear Sir:—The Brig Neptune went ashore near Point Solitude[49], on Monday of last week, and 19 of the 20 souls on board were either drowned or frozen to death. The Captain, the only survivor, got as far as Muskegon Thursday. He says that the vessel was very little injured when he left her. Two others reached the above with the Captain, but soon froze to death. The Captain has both feet badly frozen. It is from the messenger who came to Grand Haven for a physician that we learned this much. Not knowing the owner or where the vessel belongs, I drop this to you that the owner may be advised of his loss.[50]

Another letter, written by someone in Muskegon and dated November 29, appeared in the December 10 issue of the *Detroit Daily Free Press*. Under the headline "Dreadful Shipwreck and Loss of Life," the editor noted: "We received by the last western mail, the following letter giving an account of a melancholy shipwreck and loss of life on Lake Michigan." The writer provided other details of the disaster:

> Sir.—The Brig Neptune, John H. Sims, Master, was driven on shore at Little Point au Sable, about 30 miles north of Muskegon river in the gale of Monday the 25th inst. There was on board in all, NINE of the crew and ELEVEN passengers, all drowned and perished with the cold, except Capt. Sims, who, with two others, reached the shore. One, the brother of the captain, and Webster, the mate, the two who ventured to leave the wreck with the captain, perished immediately on reaching the shore. The brig was full freighted from Buffalo for Chicago, principally with merchandize. Capt. Sims, who was without eating or anything to eat from Monday morning till Friday morning, came out to the settlement yesterday. He is badly frostbitten, but in good spirits. The people from this place go out tomorrow to bury the dead, and save what they can from the wreck.[51]

CHAPTER 2

More details of the *Neptune* shipwreck and aftermath appeared in the April 9, 1840 edition of the *Detroit Daily Advertiser*. The editor had received a letter from a man in Port Sheldon—apparently the writer of the earlier account to that paper—who provided the following information:

> Our readers will recollect that the brig Neptune was wrecked last fall and 17 of the 20 persons on board drowned. The following extract from a letter, from a gentleman at Port Sheldon, in this State gives some melancholy particulars on the fate of the three survivors:
> "On my return I met the unfortunate individual the Captain of the Neptune, at a shanty on the Grandville road. He left Port Sheldon this morning and is on his way to Cleveland, where his family reside. Our people have been very kind to him, and I think he will never forget this attention. He repeated to me over and over again his thanks and hearty wishes for the success of our operations. He was attended by Mr. Ward, a merchant of Cleveland.
> "Since writing to you on this subject, two more persons belonging to the Neptune have been found alive; the mate, and an old tar. The mate was in a most deplorable condition, and obliged to lay down in the bushes, being entirely helpless from frozen limbs—The other was not much better off. They were nine days in this condition before they were discovered; the old sailor keeping his messmate alive on whiskey and apples, which had been washed from the wreck, and for which he had to crawl over the ice and snow to the beach, a distance of a quarter of a mile. These poor fellows are now at Muskegon, and both have been obliged to have their legs amputated. The mate's life is still despaired of. I understand they are made as comfortable as their situation will allow, but will see for myself in a few days." These, it will be remembered were the only survivors of twenty, who were on the brig. Much has been said of the suffering of those who were saved from the Lexington[52]; but we can for no idea of more dreadful endurance that this case exhibits; and those acquainted with the fiercely cold scenes exhibited on the frozen beach of our northern lakes in a winter's storm, with the surf dashing against covered mountains of ice, heaped in huge masses along the shore, must be astonished, that these poor fellows, thrown wet and nearly naked upon their icy summits, without a human being near to assist them could have lived an hour.[53]

On May 3, 1840, just six months after the *Neptune* tragedy, a sudden squall drove the riverboat *Governor Mason* onto the sandbars near the mouth of Muskegon Channel, where she caught fire before the pounding waves quickly broke her up.[54] The *Governor Mason*, built in 1837 to join a fleet of shallow-draft riverboats that plied the Grand River around the young town of Grand Rapids, had fallen on hard times. Her owners decided to set her on a new route that might prove more lucrative—ferrying passengers and cargo between Grand Haven and Muskegon. What started out as a fair spring day turned foul, and the vessel—hardly suited for the rough waters of Lake Michigan—never completed her maiden voyage on the big lake. Details of the wreck are sketchy, but it is recorded that several lives were lost.

Another early Muskegon wreck involved the wooden passenger and freight steamer *Wabash Valley*, which was lost when overtaken by a blinding snowstorm on November 22, 1860. She was headed from Milwaukee to Grand Haven when the storm hit, and in the whiteout the captain lost his bearings. Heavy seas were running and the breakers carried the ship onto the beach. All of those aboard—passengers and crew—made it safely to shore, but the ship, broken in half, was destroyed by the waves as she lay stranded on the Muskegon shoreline (see "Sailing Blind: The Wreck of the *Wabash Valley*" in this volume).

A Tragic Homecoming: The Wreck of the *Granada*

"I would rather cross the ocean twenty times, at this season of the year, than make one trip from the St. Lawrence River to Chicago on the lakes," said Capt. Ira Brown, an old Lake Erie skipper to a New York *Sun* reporter. "The unusual loss of life and property on the lakes is proportionately very much greater than it is on the Atlantic Ocean, and you may always expect to hear of disasters on the Great Lakes following the reports of every severe storm. Lake skippers will take risks that would appall the bravest ocean sailor. They will start from port with vessels that are hardly seaworthy in the calmest weather, and more of them are afloat during the most dangerous part of the year than during any other time. This is because the months of October and November are the most profitable to vessel owners, cargoes then being plenty and rates highest."[55]

On October 15, 1880, the 229-ton lumber schooner *Granada* left Muskegon bound for Chicago with a load of lumber. The ship, in the employ of the McGraft and Montgomery Lumber Company of Lakeside, was a family-run enterprise, with Captain Robert Linklater and his brother Angus heading up a crew made up of five other men. They left the port in fair and mild weather, but halfway to Chicago the ship was overtaken by a monstrous storm that plunged Lake Michigan into chaos. The tempest brought winds howling from the southwest at sixty-five to seventy-five miles per hour. Temperatures plummeted to below freezing and blinding snow enveloped the ships unfortunate enough to be caught out on the lake.[56] The *Granada*'s crew had no time to rig the vessel for the onslaught, and when the rudder was snapped off and the steering vane lost, the schooner was left to the mercy of the huge waves.

The storm pushed the helpless vessel, shattered and snow covered, to the northeast, where she finally grounded on the sandbars several hundred yards offshore of her home port of Muskegon. Two crewmen had died from the bitter cold on the open lake. When the remaining crew, nearly frozen, sighted shore, they were heartened by the hope of being rescued soon. Some locals had gathered along the beach two miles north of the channel and spotted the stranded ship. In a brave attempt to save the men, the lifesaving crew tried to launch a lifeboat, but the violent breakers defeated their efforts; those onshore could only watch the tragedy unfold. The Linklater brothers and surviving crew, one of them badly injured, realized their only hope was to somehow make it to shore on their own. Those who could constructed makeshift rafts of what remained of the lumber cargo and pieces of the broken vessel. Mate William Bissett and another sailor, known only by his first name, Matt, were the first to leave the wreck.

> About half past three the mate, Wm. Bissett, made a raft and started. He was several times washed off, but fought for dear life. Every board that came near he would seize and put under

him, and thus kept on building till near the shore, when he was rescued. He could barely walk, and his first words were: "For God's sake, boys, get a line to them poor fellows!"[57]

Captain Linklater and his brother next set off on a raft they built. But the craft broke apart and the captain drowned, despite his brother's desperate efforts to save him. (See appendix A for Angus Linklater's personal account.) Angus Linklater, William Bissett, and Matt were the only ones who survived the ordeal.

Muskegon's newly formed Life Saving Service came under severe criticism from the newspaper for failing to reach the men of the *Granada* and possibly save more lives. The reporter for the *Muskegon Daily Chronicle* made these scathing comments: "There certainly was very bad management on the part of the Lifesaving Crew, or their commander, as there was bungling work made of it. The crew is a new one, just put in this month. Volunteers were plenty, however. This is the first time the crew has had an opportunity to do active work, and they failed, for some reason or other."[58] The lifesaving crew consisted of local mariners, some of rank and with years of sailing experience: Captain A. C. Majo, master of the tug *Newell Avery*; Byron Beerman, the tug *Torrent's* engineer; Charles Foster, the *Torrent's* fireman; Captain Dick Aims of the scow *Seabird*; and two crew members and the cook of the *Seabird*.[59] It may have been that for all their skills as individual seamen, the men's lack of regular lifesaving drills and the resulting close teamwork left them open to criticism when they faced their first test. On the other hand, the storm's severity and the wreck's distance from shore might have been enough to thwart the rescue attempts of any surfmen—new or seasoned.

Still, Angus Linklater described the volunteer group's actions as "gallant." Eventually the local paper came around to this view. In 1903, in an interview with Captain Majo, the *Muskegon Daily Chronicle* recognized the *Granada*'s rescue crew as "heroic" and their effort as "perhaps the bravest ever effected at this port."[60]

Today, the broken remains of the *Granada* lie buried in the sands somewhere offshore of Muskegon State Park.

Safe in the Sand: The *Trial* and the *Annie Nelson*

The *Granada* tragedy had all the ingredients of a major newspaper story—death and drama, the heroic struggle of man against the raging sea. But not all shipwrecks bear such hallmarks. At Muskegon and other places along the west Michigan shoreline, it was relatively common for a schooner caught in a storm to be deliberately run up on the beach. The captain might decide it was too risky to enter a harbor channel and opt instead to beach his vessel. While this is not to dismiss the dangers involved, these episodes usually ended with the captain and crew safe on the shore.

Former Muskegon County sheriff and local historian Peter Cardinal wrote about this practice in his account "Saga of the Seas": "Beaching was a common practice in those days [late 1800s]. With heavy seas and a narrow harbor, it was difficult for a sailing vessel to maneuver. So they would drop all their canvas except a jib sail and head for the shore. As they crossed the first sandbar, they pulled the sea plug and let the ship begin to fill with water. As she rode on in, she took on more and more water until when it reached the beach, it was literally sunk."[61]

These incidents were reported in the Muskegon newspaper, but with (by today's standards) frustratingly little detail. In mid-November 1883, a gale swept Lake Michigan and roughed up several small schooners off the harbor. The entire article, which appeared in the Friday, November 16 edition of the *Muskegon Daily Chronicle* under the simple headline "Beached," reads thus:

> At 11 o'clock yesterday morning the little hooker "Trial" ran on the beach high and dry at this port. She left Milwaukee Monday morning and had been out on the lake ever since. The crew, consisting of three men, were rescued by the Muskegon Life Saving Crew. The captain, an aged man, was almost overcome with the cold when taken from the boat.
>
> The small schooner "Annie Nelson" left Manitowoc for Ludington Wednesday morning. She was unable, for some reason, to find that port, and passed the time in running up and down the shore. Muskegon harbor was finally sighted, but as the captain thought he could not enter safely, the schooner was run onto the beach, where she is now high and dry. She was loaded with hay, oats and corn. In both the above instances, the Muskegon Life Saving Crew did excellent work in saving the crew.[62]

Just below the "Beached" article ran another short news story about the Muskegon-based schooner *Waleska*. The vessel survived the storm, but not before she lost part of her lumber cargo. The story illustrates not only the risks taken by those sailing the schooners but also the fears nursed by the ship owners when one of their vessels was overdue and no report on her status forthcoming:

> The schooner Waleska left this port on Saturday [November 10] with a load of lumber from A. V. Mann & Co. for Sheboygan. Fears were entertained that she was lost in the terrible storm, but this morning A. V. Mann & Co. received a letter from the Captain, J. Brun, dated at Milwaukee. Capt. Brun writes that he was three days in the storm, that he lost his deck load of lumber and was forced to put into Milwaukee harbor. He intended leaving yesterday for Sheboygan.[63]

Semper Paratus: The Muskegon Lifesaving Crew and the Wreck of the *R. B. King*

The surfmen who served at the Life Saving Station in Muskegon responded time and again to ships and crews in distress. During the eight months (April through early December) when the station was open, they received a monthly salary, with additional pay for any time they were called to duty during the off-season.[64] Since most lived near the channel, at Port Sherman or Bluffton, they could quickly respond for service in the winter months. A reporter for the *Muskegon Weekly Chronicle* described these hardy men as "sturdy and strong, no more afraid of work than of the billows, men who see a livelihood

CHAPTER 2

Unidentified shipwreck on a beach north of Muskegon Channel ([P83–312] Muskegon County Museum).

rather than danger in a roaring sea and who as one of them said, 'handle a marlinspike oftener than a pen.' "[65]

One longtime head of Muskegon's Life Saving Service was Captain Henry J. Woods, who took over the duties from the station's first keeper, William Groh, in 1882. A native of New York state, Henry was just a boy when his family moved to Wisconsin. He quickly took to the waters of Horricon Lake near his new home and eventually came to handle fishing boats on Lake Erie. In 1880, he entered the U.S. Life Saving Service at St. Joseph, and two years later was posted to the Muskegon station. In addition to his maritime skills,

Woods was an inventor who developed a patent launching carriage for surfboats. He improved on it over the years, and by the late 1890s about seventy-five of these carriages were in use at lifesaving stations around the Great Lakes. Woods also invented a patent oar lock and a hawser cutter, which were produced at a metal-working shop near the station.

Late in his career Woods was interviewed by a *Chronicle* reporter. The reporter asked him which one of the many shipwrecks was the worst in his experience. He responded, "I think the worst wreck I ever had anything to do with was the wreck of the *R. B. King*."[66]

The *R. B. King* was a small lumber schooner, eighty-four feet long, which was built in St. Joseph, Michigan, in 1863. Able to carry about 85,000 feet of lumber, she made frequent trips between Muskegon and her home port of Chicago during the shipping season. The *King* was owned by her elderly captain, J. D. Dunbar.

The schooner, traveling light, had left Chicago early on November 7, 1885, on a late-season run to Muskegon. Even though a storm warning had been issued, the *King* and several other ships dared to venture out onto Lake Michigan as the wind and waves were starting to build. The vessel was virtually blown across the lake by the storm and arrived at the Muskegon piers at 8:00 that night. As she ducked into the narrow entrance, the ship was struck by a huge wave and dashed against the newly constructed north pier. She then veered across the channel and was crushed against the south pier. Her stability lost as the waters rushed into the hull, the *King* rolled onto her side, forcing Captain Dunbar and his three crewmen to seek safety by climbing into the rigging.

At the nearby station, Captain Woods and his crew heard cries for help and immediately rushed out into the blustery night. They first fired a rocket skyward to let the stranded men know help was on the way then launched the lifesaving boat. When the boat reached the wreck, Captain Dunbar, who felt his position was secure enough for the moment, told the surfmen to assist the rest of the crew first. But just then another breaker smashed into the fatally injured vessel and the captain would have been trapped underneath if not for the quick action of the rescuers, who hauled him into their boat. One other crewman, mate Charles Anderson, was also saved. Dunbar and Anderson were taken to shore before the lifesaving crew put out again to rescue the other two sailors. However, they returned too late to bring them to safety.

Once recovered from the ordeal, Dunbar described his final run and the loss of his vessel to a *Muskegon Daily Chronicle* reporter (see appendix B). He then returned to his home in Chicago.[67]

The *R. B. King* had been valued at $2,000. At the time of her loss, the *Chronicle* stated that the vessel was considered in good condition. However, later inspection of the wreckage revealed that the *King*'s timbers were rotten. Records also showed that shortly before the disaster, the ship's insurance had been cancelled.

Years later, as Captain Woods reminisced about the event, his words made it clear that he lived by the motto of the U.S. Life Saving Service—*semper paratus* (always prepared). Anything less and the *R. B. King* tragedy could have been worse. He told the reporter:

CHAPTER 2

> That vessel came along in a gale of wind on the night of November 7, 1885 . . . and struck the north pier. They couldn't handle the vessel in such a sea. That was before the old north pier was connected to the new work and the channel widened at its entrance.
>
> The King tore her side out, capsized and went all to pieces. I was on the pier and got the men and the boat out. If I had not been all ready, we would never have saved anybody. We were in a pretty delicate place, but we got the captain and mate. The other two of the crew drowned.[68]

Woods served as head of the Muskegon Life Saving Station for twenty years (1882–1902).

"So Terrible a Reality": The Wrecks of the *South Haven*, the *Helen*, and the *L. J. Conway*

The vigilance and hardiness of Muskegon's lifesaving crew were put to the test in November 1886. Hundreds of ships were making late-season runs around the Great Lakes when a vicious snow-laden gale—considered the worst to hit the lakes since the *Alpena* storm of 1880—roared across the region on November 17–19, taking down a number of vessels. Hurricane-strength winds, clocked at sixty to seventy-five miles per hour, snapped telegraph lines around the lakes, and ship owners anxiously waited for reports to come in once communication was reestablished, knowing that the casualties would be high and dreading word that one or more of their own would be noted as missing. Just before the southwester struck, a large fleet of lumber schooners, lightened of their loads, headed out from Chicago. The lucky ones eventually rolled heavily into ports, their hulls, rigging, and sails sheathed in ice. Those unable to withstand the towering seas and icy blasts came ashore in masses of splintered timbers, all hands lost.

With relief, Muskegon's maritime community saw many of its ships make it safely home: the *Rouse Simmons*, *Thomas Hume*, *Kate Lyons*, *Andrew Jackson*, *Levi Grant*, *Jessie Philips*, *Eva Fuller*, *Myrtle*, *City of Grand Rapids*, and *Jessie Boyce*. In addition, other ships found shelter at Muskegon. The *Minnie Mueller* had left Chicago on Tuesday, November 16, bound for Manistee. After being thrashed four times across the lake, the *Mueller* finally limped into Muskegon that Friday. A barge, the *Roanoke*, was caught in the storm as she headed for Chicago from the Lake Huron port of Alabaster with a crew of eighteen and nine hundred tons of plaster. Unable to endure the heavy seas, she sought the calmer waters of the Port City. The vessel safely docked, the *Roanoke*'s captain, J. W. Martin, claimed that the storm was the worst he had ever encountered on the lakes.

In addition, the fierce winds blew a number of vessels off course, taking them far from their intended ports of call. The schooner *Annie Dall* left Chicago for Grand Haven but was blown as far north as Point Betsie. Her tortuous journey was described in the *Chicago Times*:

> [The *Annie Dall*] . . . left Chicago last Tuesday evening for this port [Grand Haven], and after beating around was caught in the southwester and carried north as far as Point Betsy, whence she put about and ran south to White lake. She could not make port, but managed again to

turn about in the plunging sea, which momentarily threatened to swallow the vessel and crew. She succeeded, however, and again was flying before the wind in a northern course until she fetched up close under Point Sauble, when she was again forced to run southward.[69]

When the *Dall* finally reached Grand Haven on Friday, November 19, her sails were coated in ice a quarter-inch thick. Her captain and crew came ashore completely spent from the ordeal, having suffered from the bitter cold and lack of sleep as the vessel was tossed about the violent seas. The men's only nourishment had been hot coffee, and that was whatever didn't spill from their cups. Another schooner, the staunch *Laura Miller*, was headed for Muskegon from Chicago, but the storm pushed her another fifty miles up the shoreline to Ludington. In her effort to seek shelter in that port, she failed to make the piers and instead was driven ashore one hundred yards north of the harbor entrance. The crew survived and the *Miller*, a newly constructed vessel, sustained little damage.

Around noon on Thursday, November 18, the lookouts at the Muskegon Life Saving Station spotted a schooner beached three miles south of the channel. The blizzard conditions made it impossible for them to ascertain the name of the vessel or the status of those onboard. Still, the lifesaving crew gathered a marine gun, buoys, and other heavy equipment they might need to perform a rescue and headed down the shore. Not only were the men, burdened as they were by their weighty gear, slowed by the sand and stacks of driftwood along the route, they were also fighting the strong winds, blinding snow, and icy spray. After several hours the rescuers came upon the scow schooner *South Haven*, broached to the beach and pounded by the waves. The vessel had been sailing light from Chicago to Muskegon to take on a load of lumber when she was caught in the storm. That morning, as the four-man crew took to the rigging in a desperate struggle to reef the mainsail, the billowing canvas broke free of their grasp and the mast snapped and fell. All narrowly avoided injury or being swept overboard by the raking seas. Once the ship grounded high on the beach, Captain Fred Harris and his crew came ashore and, finding a deserted shanty nearby, took possession of it. They hauled ashore the ship's stove and some salvaged clothing, then settled into their makeshift home, warming themselves and waiting for assistance. Only one of them sustained serious injuries. The schooner's yawl was still hanging in the davits when the seas smashed it and sent the timbers flying. One piece struck Harris in the head, causing a serious wound. He was also struck in the back by the main boom, which fractured several ribs and caused some internal injuries.

The captain was transported to the channel community of Bluffton and taken in by James Edmunds, who summoned a doctor from nearby Lakeside to tend to his injured guest. The rest of the crew—Fred McDermott, John Nelson, Theo Thompson, and John Johnson, all Chicago men—soon followed and joined their captain at the Edmunds's home. The newspaper sent a reporter to check up on them: "Your reporter visited Mr. Edmunds and found the crew all comfortably cared for by Mrs. Edmunds and through her kind hospitality enjoying a good dinner after fasting 18 hours."[70] A few days later, all but the captain had returned to their homes in Chicago. Harris remained at the Edmunds's residence until he had sufficiently recovered to travel.

CHAPTER 2

As the *South Haven* lay stranded, the lifesaving crew ran a line to her and helped recover most of the valuables onboard. The vessel, however, was a total loss. For days, the heavy surf tore at her until only pieces of the wreck covered the beach where she had gone aground.

The scow schooner, 99 feet long with a beam of 22 feet, had been built in South Haven in 1866. George Hannah, who operated a lumber mill on the city's Black River, owned the vessel during her early years and used her to carry lumber products between South Haven and various ports across Lake Michigan. In addition, during the 1870s, she brought stone to South Haven to build the harbor piers. She proved to be a profitable ship during her first fourteen years. In 1880 she was sold to Fred Murger of Chicago, who put Captain Fred Harris in command of his newly acquired vessel. Prior to her final battle on Lake Michigan, the *South Haven* emerged as one of the survivors of the tremendous storm that devastated the lake in mid-October 1880 and wrecked the schooner *Granada*, the steamer *Alpena*, and numerous other ships. On that occasion, she managed to reach a safe harbor only after her rigging had been torn away. By 1886, the *South Haven* was showing her age; a reporter for the South Haven newspaper described her as looking "like a stanch relic of war times."[71] The tired ship, worn out after twenty years, was sailing uninsured at the end of her career. Still, Harris thought her to be seaworthy and sailed his vessel till the end.

The *South Haven* was wrecked, but her crew survived. However, the same late fall storm swept other ships and all aboard them to destruction in the waters off Muskegon, leaving the lifesaving crew to piece together the parts of several shipwreck puzzles in an effort to reconstruct the identities and fates of those lost. As the surfmen scanned Lake Michigan during the early morning of November 19, they spied wreckage tossing in the waves near the channel—broken masts, spars, and rigging along with part of a hull were strewn for a mile on either side of the piers. More wreckage was found three miles north of the channel and a hundred yards from shore—an overturned hull surrounded by spars and other timbers from a lost schooner. Among the pieces near the channel were a yawl with the name "*Helen* of Chicago" painted on the stern and a quarterboard from a vessel called the *G. B. Mansfield*. The Muskegon Life Saving Service sent a telegram to authorities in Chicago to inquire about the two vessels. They learned that no ship named the *G. B. Mansfield* hailed from Chicago, and it was assumed that the *Mansfield* was one of the many boats used to transport fruit from southwest Michigan to Lake Michigan ports. However, the scow schooner *Helen* was well-known in that city and the news of her loss with all hands, including her popular captain, John Von Thadden, and his wife, saddened many.

The two-masted, ninety-foot vessel was built in Milwaukee in 1874 and originally christened the *Ulster*. Later, in 1881, she was rebuilt and renamed the *Helen*. One of the many smaller sailing ships in the booming lumber business, the *Helen* worked the Lake Michigan route between Chicago and the mill towns along west Michigan, apparently making good money for Captain Von Thadden, who was her owner as well as master. Von Thadden was a jovial man, well liked by Lake Michigan sailors, who called him "Captain

The scow schooner *Helen* shown off Manitowoc's harbor (from the Great Lakes Marine Collection of the Milwaukee Public Library/Wisconsin Marine Historical Society).

John." The captain's wife was popular in her own right and active in the daily operations of the business, accompanying her husband aboard ship, managing the ship's finances, hiring the crew—and making sure her tippling husband maintained his sobriety. The couple had two children who apparently accompanied their parents on an occasional trip aboard the *Helen*.

The *Chicago Tribune* reported that the *Helen* had left Chicago for White Lake on Wednesday, November 17, headed for the Whitehall-Montague ports for a load to transport back to Chicago. Onboard for this trip were Captain Von Thadden, his wife, and five crew members, including a boy. Shortly before the ship left Chicago, Mrs. Von

CHAPTER 2

Thadden sent her children ashore. The weather looked threatening, and apparently she felt it best that they stay home. The captain of another schooner saw this and, sensing that the *Helen* might be in for a rough passage, tried to persuade Mrs. Von Thadden herself not to go. However, she laughed him off, saying that if she did not accompany her husband, there would be no cargo, money, or vessel left.

On November 20, a man's body was washed ashore three miles north of Muskegon Channel at a place known as Scotch Bonnet. A local farmer discovered the body and notified the Life Saving Service, which brought it back to Muskegon. It was believed the man had been a sailor onboard the *Helen*. Confirmation came a short time later: The body was that of Captain John Von Thadden. Upon hearing the news, his brother-in-law, F. P. Mayer, came up from Chicago to make funeral arrangements. Captain Von Thadden was buried in Muskegon's Oakwood Cemetery.

For several days following the storm, the lifesaving crew had the grim duty of patrolling the beaches along the Muskegon shoreline, looking for any remains washed from the wrecked ships. On November 24, the body of a woman approximately forty years old was found on the beach one mile north of the harbor entrance. Over her dress she wore a sailor's jacket, and in her pocket was $25.45 in gold, silver, and paper bills. The woman was later identified as Mrs. Von Thadden. The captain's body was exhumed and both were sent to Chicago for final burial.[72]

While many of the vessels that left Chicago just before the storm struck were sailing light, one schooner, the *L. J. Conway*, was returning to Muskegon with a load of grain: 3,735 bushels of corn and 1,332 bushels of oats. The two-masted *Conway* left Chicago on Tuesday, November 16, after filling her hold at the Illinois Central elevator and was not heard from after that time. Henderson and Peterson, the Muskegon lumber firm that owned her, expressed concern for the welfare of their ship, Captain Thomas Smith, and his crew of four. On Monday, November 22, the *Muskegon Daily Chronicle* was the first to get the sad news in a dispatch that arrived from Whitehall: The *L. J. Conway* had been wrecked near Flower Creek, seven miles north of that port, with all hands lost.

The *Conway*, which had been built in Manitowoc in 1873, had sailed in the lumber trade for some years, becoming a fixture in the Muskegon harbor for the last few years of her career in the service of Henderson and Peterson. On this trip, she was returning to her home port after delivering lumber to Chicago, her hold now filled with grain harvested in the Plains states.

David Smith, the captain's brother, traveled from Muskegon to the site to investigate the wreck and, if possible, recover the body of Captain Smith.[73] He found the *Conway* had grounded about one hundred feet from shore in four to six feet of water. Both of her masts had been snapped off, the upper works were nearly gone, and one side of the hull had been torn away. The cabin lay some distance from the wreck. Much of the rigging floated about the ship's remains, and the surrounding waters were thick with corn and oats. Two miles north of the wreck site, an empty sailor's bag was found with the name "E. M. Kensmann"; Edward Kensmann was one of the *Conway*'s crew. Apparently in an effort to keep the ship from being blown ashore, the crew had put out three anchors, which were still holding as the wreck lay stranded with her stern resting on the shore. David Smith's heartbreaking mission fell short on one key point—the bodies of his brother and the rest of the crew could not be found. It was believed that the men, so close to shore, had either taken to the yawl, which had been found washed up nearby, or had tried to swim the short distance to the beach. There was nothing to indicate that they ever made it to land.

Details about the *Conway*'s last hours drifted in to the *Daily Chronicle* and raised disturbing questions. The newspaper first got word about the wreck on Monday, November 22, when they learned that two farmers in the vicinity of Flower Creek came upon the wreck of the *Conway* on November 18. For some reason the farmers did not report their discovery. On November 21, several employees of a lumber mill at White Lake were strolling the beach when they discovered the schooner's yawl and further along found the wreck. They contacted the authorities in Whitehall who, in turn, notified the Muskegon newspaper.

Only on the late date of November 26 did the *Daily Chronicle* report that witnesses had seen the *L. J. Conway* and her crew shortly before the disaster: "It now comes to light that farmers and others living near the coast where the 'Conway' was wrecked, saw the distressed vessel and the four men upon her. They state that the men seemed to take turns in coming on deck, two at a time. For all this no attempt was made to help them from the shore, nor did they even kindle a fire to cheer the poor fellows through the night. Had they but done so, some of them might perhaps have been saved."[74] A reporter for the *Chicago Tribune* spoke with one of the farmers who saw the ship in distress and added the following details: "The vessel was first seen by a farm-hand last Thursday afternoon. She was then rolling heavily in the trough of the sea, and he could hear her crew shouting wildly for help. He made no effort to save them, and the vessel was soon lost sight of in the blinding snow-storm. The farm-hand says that when he last saw the schooner before she struck the beach she was heading out into the lake and the seas were sweeping over her."[75] Such news must have provided David Smith with cold comfort and added a good measure of cynicism to his sorrow.

Captain Thomas Smith had moved to Muskegon with his wife and four children only three years before. The thirty-eight-year-old Smith had been master and managing owner of the *L. J. Conway* for a brief two months but had sailed other lake boats for some years. Described as a "brave, strong, temperate and robust man," Captain Smith earned praise for a particular act of heroism.[76] In 1884, while in command of the schooner *Walter Smith*, Smith was headed to Muskegon when he encountered a waterlogged schooner, the *Brigham*, in danger of sinking. He made a daring rescue of all five of the *Brigham*'s crew, a deed for which the *Brigham*'s captain later rewarded him with an exquisite watch.

Besides Captain Smith, the *Conway*'s crew consisted of a Norwegian named Jimmy, who was first mate, John Gooten, and Edward M. Kensmann. Also aboard was twenty-five-year-old Captain Charles McGraw, the master and owner of the schooner *Eliza*. Captain Smith had approached him onboard the *Eliza* while both ships were in Chicago and requested a piece of plank. He explained his centerboard box was broken and leaking badly, and he needed the wood to patch it. The *Eliza*'s captain was glad to oblige. In addition, when Smith mentioned that he was shorthanded and asked him if he would join him on the run to Muskegon, McGraw agreed. He left his father and brother in charge of the *Eliza* and joined the *Conway*'s crew.

Captain Smith was shorthanded because his first mate had left the ship while she was docked in Chicago, the reason for his departure unknown (a possible premonition?). Whitehall happened to be the mate's hometown and he was there for the duration of the storm. When the news broke of the *Conway*'s loss so near his home, he went to the wreck site and remained there several days, keeping vigil in the hope of recovering the bodies of his former shipmates.

The list of casualties—vessel and human—grew as news came in from as far north as Marquette in Michigan's Upper Peninsula and as far east as Goderich, Ontario. On November 22, the *Chicago Tribune* printed the tally of losses from the three-day gale: thirty-six ships foundered or driven ashore, eleven gone to pieces, several still missing. Forty-seven sailors were known dead and the final number was expected to go as high as sixty. Financial losses were reported to be in the hundreds of thousands of dollars.[77]

The full extent of the storm's destructive blow had yet to be realized when a Muskegon newspaper writer, sensitive to the fears and deadly dangers faced by sailors on the lakes, was moved to express his thoughts. By painting a dramatic scenario, he reminded the people of Muskegon of the risks taken by those who sailed the treacherous waters and the great debt owed to the local seamen:

> How easy it is to sit by warm fires and, watching the storm, to give a pitying thought to vessels in distress and the drowning seamen. And yet we do this in a superficial way, which really amounts to nothing, and is but a shadowy passing thought, a dim and indistinct vision of so terrible a reality. Do we picture vividly the raging waters reaching up with powerful arms to grasp the devoted vessel; the white manes tossing as these marine war horses rear and prance in ceaseless charges; the keen wind, laden with blinding snows and icy particles beating upon the struggling mariners; the terrible doubt growing into a more terrible certainty as the fated crew approach their doom; the clinging for life, with benumbed bodies and despairing souls, to broken rigging and spars; the thoughts of home and loved ones which strike a colder chill through the heart than that of the storm; the slow hours dragging their weary length along while despair watches over its victims and desolation mocks them in the voices of the angry deep; the sinking at last into dull insensibility but to awake struggling in the grasp of giant waves, from which a few may escape, or all go down to a terrible death. Then, a few days later, disfigured and storm beaten corpses flung contemptuously upon the beach by the waves which are tired of their ghastly playthings, and a grave watered with loving tears, or sadder still, an unknown tomb in some strange and lonely land. This is what the recent storm meant to hundreds of those who make sea and lake traffic possible, and the men who dare all this are those who tread our streets daily, often unnoticed and almost unknown. Muskegon should give many a kindly thought to her mariners.[78]

Legend and Mystery: The Fate of the *Rouse Simmons* and the *Thomas Hume*

The wealth engendered by the lumber business made it possible for Muskegon's lumber barons to maintain their own small fleets of schooners and other vessels. John Torrent owned the schooner *H. B. Moore*, the steam barges *R. McDonald*, *Ida Torrent*, and *Nellie Torrent*, and the tugboat *North Muskegon*. Ryerson, Hills and Company maintained the large lumber schooner *Minerva* and the small steamer *Carrie A. Ryerson*, which was used to ferry employees and company goods between the two mills, one near Ryerson Creek on the city's east side and the other at Bay Mill at the northwestern end of Muskegon Lake. The Hackley and Hume Company's fleet included several tugs—the *McGordon* and *J. H. Hackley* among them—and a number of schooners: the *Kate Lyons*, *Andrew Jackson*, *Cape Horn*, and two others that ended their days in the realm of legend and mystery—the *Rouse Simmons* and the *Thomas Hume*.

The three-masted schooner *Rouse Simmons* was built in Milwaukee in 1868 for owners based in Kenosha. Hackley and Hume bought the 127–foot, 195–ton schooner around 1873 and for nearly twenty-five years she served the business well, carrying lumber to Lake Michigan ports, primarily Chicago. During those years, the *Simmons* experienced the usual troubles that plagued hardworking lake schooners, from collisions with other ships in the fog to battles with the late-season gales from which she emerged coated in ice. But the vessel was resilient and through her long and active career became a regular workhorse for the lumber firm. She was the last vessel owned by Hackley and Hume, sold off on December 6, 1895, to Captain Wilhelm Johnson when the company closed down its lumber mill. In making the sale, Hackley and Hume described the *Simmons* thus: "She is a 3–masted schooner, in good condition rating A2 1/2, she carries about 300,000 ft. dry lumber and is a light draft boat very still and carries most of her cargo on deck and has always been a very profitable vessel. We only sell her because we have gone out of the lumber business here. Price $3,000. She is laid up here."[79]

After the *Simmons* changed hands, she continued to ply the lakes with lumber products. Now based in Chicago, she had to roam far down Lake Michigan to pick up her loads. Muskegon's lumber era had ended, but the white pine stands further north continued to supply the raw material for Michigan's lumber trade. However, the schooner became most famous for the final cargo of the shipping season—evergreen trees that were transported from the Upper Peninsula to Chicago to be sold as Christmas trees. Other schooners also carried on this late-season trade. Captains usually would sell their cargo to shopkeepers and other middlemen. However, Chicagoans would especially anticipate the arrival of the *Simmons* and her captain, Herman Schuenemann, who gained popularity by selling his load of trees directly to them when they visited his ship at the wharf near the Clark Street bridge.

This tradition lasted for some years until late November 1912, when the *Simmons* left the Upper Peninsula port of Thompson, near Manistique, heavily laden with evergreens. The vessel never made it to Chicago; a wintry storm moved into the region just after the ship set sail, and the gale-force winds and huge seas soon overwhelmed the aged schooner. She went down with all hands off Two Rivers, Wisconsin. In the months that followed, trees from the ship were washed up on Lake Michigan shorelines, including the beaches near Pentwater and Ludington. Paul Pearson, one of the surfmen at the Pentwater U.S. Life Saving Station, took one of the small Christmas trees home for that holiday

CHAPTER 2

Hackley and Hume lumber mill with schooner (*Rouse Simmons*?) at the dock, c. 1895 ([P86–013] Muskegon County Museum).

season. Another reminder of the shipwreck came ashore fifteen years later, in 1927, when a bottle containing a note was found washed up on a Lake Michigan beach. The note, written by Captain Oscar Nelson, one of the seventeen crewmen making the final voyage on the *Rouse Simmons*, read: "These lines were written 10:30 P.M. Schooner R. S. ready to go down about 20 miles southeast of Two Rivers Point between 15 and 20 miles offshore. All hands lashed to one line. Goodbye. Nelson."[80] The poignant story of the *Rouse Simmons*—the "Christmas Tree Ship"—has held a distinctive place in Great Lakes lore, and through the years has been immortalized in art, literature, poetry, and folk songs.

The *Thomas Hume*, though less famous than the *Rouse Simmons*, ended her career under mysterious circumstances that baffled even the most experienced vesselmen. The 199-ton lumber schooner, measuring 132 feet in length with a 26-foot beam, was built in Manitowoc, Wisconsin, in 1870. Originally christened the *H. C. Albrecht*, she was renamed the *Thomas Hume* in 1883. For over twenty years and under both names, she served the Hackley and Hume Company, maintaining a regular run between the Muskegon mill and the Chicago market. On Thursday, May 21, 1891, the *Hume*, along with the *Rouse Simmons*, departed the Chicago harbor, sailing light and with all canvas up on her run back to Muskegon. That was the last time she was seen. Rough weather

The *Rouse Simmons* with a load of lumber on her deck (from the Great Lakes Marine Collection of the Milwaukee Public Library/Wisconsin Marine Historical Society).

hit the lower part of Lake Michigan.[81] After several hours, the captain of the *Simmons* decided to head back to Chicago, but the *Thomas Hume*, commanded by Captain Harry Albrightson, continued on. However, the ship never made port in Muskegon or anywhere else. As sailors would say, she simply "sailed through a crack in the lake."

As distressing as this was, the *Hume*'s disappearance grew more puzzling as efforts were made to find the schooner. At month's end, Hackley and Hume hired Captain Seth Lee, the experienced local seaman and close friend of Hackley, to go out on the tug *Sills* to scour lower Lake Michigan for any evidence of the *Hume*. The *Sills* traced the intended route of the *Hume*, but after a thorough search Lee returned with word that they could find nothing—no hatch covers, no life rings, no wreckage of any kind. He also could find no one who could give him any clues or who found pieces of wreckage on water or land—especially strange since the vessel had been in the heavily traveled shipping lanes between Muskegon and Chicago. A rumor even circulated around the Chicago dockside that the *Hume* must have sailed to an unknown location, been repainted and renamed. This odd idea was the only way the sailors could rationalize such a complete disappearance of a large schooner. One seasoned Chicago vesselman made these comments:

CHAPTER 2

> The case of the *Hume* is one of the most mysterious we have ever had on the lake. If she had been loaded and sunk, her hatches would have been forced out and floated. If she went down light, there would have been something that would have floated and been discovered. There's nothing in the story that the *Hume* has changed her colors and name. Vessels have countenances like human beings. There is something different in the build of each one, and I can stand in the window of my office and tell the name of any vessel coming up the river, even when she is a block or two away. It would be impossible for the *Hume* to pass by here without my recognizing her. At the same time there is something mysterious about her disappearance.[82]

Another even more disturbing theory voiced by some seamen was that the *Hume* had been run down and sunk by a large iron ore freighter, with the freighter's captain swearing his crew to secrecy about the incident. Lee was one of those who thought this was a possibility. When asked for his opinion on the loss, he retorted:

> Collision—run down, of course, just as the *W. C. Kimball* was run down. If she capsized she wouldn't sink, and I don't believe that staunch, stiff vessel ever capsized. Some steamer ran her down. People say no captain would be heartless enough to leave a crew after running their vessel down. Pshaw! I have sailed these lakes forty years and I know of several such cases. The fine schooner *Magellan* was one of them. If the officers of some steamers see a big loss to pay for, you bet they keep mum.[83]

Charles Hackley himself firmly believed the *Hume* was run down by another ship. In any event, he figured the loss was so sudden the captain and crew had no time to save themselves. Hackley described to a news reporter his company's policy concerning its lumber fleet:

> In the 19 years we have been running our own vessels, this is the first serious accident. We never had a schooner go on the beach. All our vessels were kept in first-class condition and the captains always had instructions to get whatever they considered necessary for the security of the vessels and crew without asking for special permission. The *Hume* had $2,000 spent on her in repairs last winter. She carried a first-class life boat and everything to insure safety for the crew in case of accident.[84]

However, this theory can be questioned since no other vessel was reported missing in that vicinity at that time or came into port with what would have been certain damage from a collision with another ship. The company placed an advertisement in the *Chicago Tribune* offering a $300 reward to anyone who could provide information that might shed some light on the possible cause of the ship's loss. Such an amount could loosen the lips of any sailor who knew of the *Hume*'s fate, but no one stepped forward with any verifiable news and the money went unclaimed.

In the news accounts of the day, with the various colorful theories offered, little attention was paid to the weather conditions on Lake Michigan at the time of the *Hume*'s disappearance. Those who do mention the rough weather also state in the same breath that it was nothing the *Hume* had not been able to handle before. However, Great Lakes shipwreck lore cites several known cases of schooners and other vessels overwhelmed by sudden, violent squalls that arise either out of calm conditions or are part of a larger system of unsettled weather. The likelihood exists that the *Hume* became one more statistic of these notorious and unpredictable lake storms.[85] Still, even if this were the case, the lack of wreckage from this ship haunts the historical investigator.

Captain Harry Albrightson, who hailed from Chicago, had served for twelve years as master of several of the Hackley and Hume lumber schooners, including the *L. E. Simmons* (one of the company's first vessels), the *Rouse Simmons,* and the *Thomas Hume*. The ship's owner and namesake, lumberman Thomas Hume, knew him well and described him as "straightforward, honest, reliable." In a letter to his wife, Margaret Anne Hume, who was traveling in Ireland with the couple's daughters at the time, Hume wrote of the ship's loss, his theories on what might have happened, and Albrightson:

> We have had a marine disaster here which has rather put a damper on us. The "Hume" left Chicago last Thursday evg. (8 days ago) for Muskegon in company with the "Simmons." They separated out in Lake Michigan, they had headwind and on Friday the Simmons ran back to Chicago. The "Hume" did not run back but stayed outside. The "Simmons" left Chicago again on Saturday and got here Monday morning. We looked for the "Hume" here same time but did not come Monday, nor Tuesday nor Wednesday and has not come yet. If she had run into any port we would have heard from her, and if she was afloat she ought to have been here Monday. It is now Friday and as nothing has been heard from her we have reluctantly concluded that she must be lost with all hands. We do not know how she could be lost except by capsizing (which is almost impossible) or collision in which both boats may have gone to the bottom. There has not been any weather stormy enough but what she could take care of herself or anything like as bad as what she has gone through a great many times before. We don't mind the loss of the boat very much, but don't like losing the seven men on board of her. Harry Albrightson was captain; you know him as the man with a deep bass voice, and he was a first-class sailor. We intend to send a tug out tonight to look for her, and can probably find her if she capsized. I was in Chicago Wednesday, but we have so far had no definite knowledge of her since she left Chicago. Harry had a wife and several children. I don't know anything about the families of the other men.[86]

Hackley echoed the sentiments of his partner with regard to the captain and crew: "We don't care for the boat; it's the loss of the captain and men that makes it sad. The captain had been in our employ for twelve years, was a reliable man and every inch a sailor."[87]

Searches and inquiries proved fruitless, and this left only rumors and speculation to bob along in the wake of the missing ship. By early June, all hope of finding the *Thomas Hume,* her captain, and crew of six had faded.

Fourteen years later, on October 9, 1905, a shipwreck was discovered at the southern end of Lake Michigan, two and one-half miles off New Buffalo, when a fisherman's net became entangled in the wreckage. George Culbert, a professional diver who was called on to investigate, found the remains of a large schooner, 175 feet long, resting on the bottom. He searched the wreck, but unfortunately found nothing on it to positively identify the ship by name. However, the tentative conclusion he gave was that this was the wreck of the *Thomas Hume*.[88] Without solid proof, however, it is best to say that the *Hume* is still missing.

CHAPTER 2

"Frenchman, he don't lak to die": The Wreck of the *Waukesha*

It is one thing to speculate on the loss of a ship in which there are no survivors. However, when one crew member is able to live through such a harrowing ordeal and tell of it, the tale of the tragedy will captivate an audience.[89] The people of Muskegon who sat down with a copy of the *Muskegon Morning News* on Tuesday, November 10, 1896, no doubt were caught up in the firsthand account of the wreck of the schooner *Waukesha* as told in a sworn statement by the ship's sole survivor, Frank Dulach.

The three-masted *Waukesha* had gone down in stormy seas on the night of Saturday, November 7, about one-and-a-quarter miles off the piers of Muskegon harbor. She was a 300–ton, 138–foot schooner, formerly known as the *Nabob*, which had been built in Manitowoc, Wisconsin, in 1864. During the 1896 season, she was used to transport salt from Manistee and Ludington to Chicago for Joy, Morton and Company, and on her final run, she had been carrying 600 tons of salt and 25 barrels of apples from Ludington to South Chicago.

When the vessel anchored off Muskegon harbor late in the afternoon of November 7, the Life Saving Station noted that she was not flying any distress signals and appeared capable of riding out the storm. Still, Captain Woods of the Life Saving Service felt uneasy and decided to take some precautions. With the wind blowing from the southwest, Woods figured that if her anchors parted, the *Waukesha* most likely would be driven onto the beach north of the harbor entrance. In preparation, he ordered a surfboat to be dragged to that site and another boat put out near the station's boathouse. The man who usually patrolled the beach for two miles south of the channel was called back to the Life Saving Station. Through his telescope, a lookout noticed that the schooner had hoisted a fly to signal for a tow. The tug *Carrie Ryerson* was summoned, but due to the rough seas and absence of the tug's captain, Bob Rice, the *Ryerson* crew hesitated to go out to the ship. Instead, they stood by in the channel.

What the lifesaving crew could not see was that the *Waukesha* was leaking badly and her crew could not pump out the water fast enough. The aged schooner was waterlogged and breaking up in the rough seas. The first indication that something was wrong was when the ship's lights went out about 9:00 P.M. Then, in the early morning hours one of the lifesaving crew, while patrolling the beach south of the channel, found apples and wreckage washing up along the shore. Later, shortly before dawn, Captain Woods and others searched the beach and discovered several bodies among the pieces of the broken ship. Daybreak came, and the men set out in a surfboat to examine the wreckage where the ship had last been seen. They did not expect to find any survivors. Only when the boat came close enough did they see a man clinging to a broken mast, feebly waving his hand to them. Frank Dulach had survived. He was immediately taken to the Life Saving Station, where he was given a brisk rubdown to restore circulation in his numbed extremities, then treated to dry clothes, a good meal, and some much-needed rest. That evening, in a sworn statement in the presence of his rescuers, reporters, and Justice of the Peace Peter W. Losby, Dulach gave his account of the loss of the *Waukesha*, her captain, and crew.[90]

Artist's depiction of the schooner *Waukesha* (from the Great Lakes Marine Collection of the Milwaukee Public Library/Wisconsin Marine Historical Society).

Frank Dulach was a thirty-five-year-old Frenchman with many years of experience sailing around the world, visiting China, Australia, and Greenland, as well as ports around the Mediterranean Sea. He had spent the last eight years working aboard ships on the Great Lakes. In all his years on water, he had been shipwrecked twelve times. In each event, however, the entire crew had survived. Just the previous fall, Dulach had survived the wreck of the *G. W. Davis* on Lake Erie. The *Waukesha* was his thirteenth—and presumably final—shipwreck. It is unknown whether he ever went to sea again.

Dulach had joined the crew of the *Waukesha* while in Chicago on October 31. He and a newfound friend—a young man of Irish descent whom he knew only by the nickname "Irish"—were broke and desperate to ship out on any vessel that needed extra hands. Though not impressed with the *Waukesha*'s worn condition, the two felt they had little choice. The ship was commanded by Captain Duncan Corbett, and the crew consisted of the first mate, John Johnson, the ship's black cook, Thomas Gayton, and two other sailors, Fred (last name unknown) and a Swede (name unknown).

The schooner left Chicago bound for Ludington to pick up a cargo of salt and apples—the latter being for the captain's personal use. After leaving Ludington in the late afternoon of Friday, November 6, the old ship, already leaking, started taking on more water. The crew had been working around the clock to keep the pumps going, but the situation worsened as they sailed along the Michigan shoreline.

Because of these conditions, Dulach and his partner tried to convince the captain that it would be best to put in at a nearby harbor. The captain refused to listen and insisted he knew what he was doing. An argument broke out, with the two sailors criticizing his decision to continue on, and Captain Corbett and Mate Johnson ordering the men to go back to pumping out the waterlogged vessel. The situation grew critical when a storm moved in Saturday afternoon. By evening, when the lights of some piers were sighted, no one—not even the captain—knew exactly where they were. Some—including Dulach and Irish—guessed Muskegon, others Grand Haven. The captain ordered the crew to drop the anchors; they would ride out the rough weather and then put in for repairs the next day. Again Dulach argued with him, insisting they head immediately for the protection of the harbor. By now, there was about four-and-a-half feet of water in the hold.

Corbett seemed confident that they did not require any assistance from the local lifesaving crew. That confidence, however, apparently came from the bottle of whiskey he shared only with the mate and Fred, whom Dulach referred to as the "old fellow." Early that evening, the captain informed the crew that the yawl had been washed off by the waves; a short time later, when the bow davit went, he said it was "too bad." Under the circumstances, that was bad enough, but Dulach also noticed the ship was down in the bows and figured she was starting to break up there. When he and his shipmates were ordered to go below to caulk the seams with oakum, they found the hold flooded, with water coming in, he said, "just as though it was being thrown in with a bucket."[91] He immediately sought out the master to alert him to the danger and request torches so they could signal for help. But Corbett refused to give him the torches, telling him that come morning, they would run up a flag for assistance. When Dulach tried to raise his lantern to signal shore, the captain abruptly stopped him.

Dulach went below as ordered and did his best to caulk the ship, but he soon realized the futility of his efforts. Convinced that the ship's master was too drunk to acknowledge, much less deal sensibly with, the impending disaster, Dulach and Irish decided to take matters into their own hands. They would cut both anchor chains and let the vessel drift in toward shore, where they figured they would have a better chance of survival. They managed to break the starboard anchor tackle, but the one on the port side would not give way.

By now the ship was in her death throes, going to pieces as the billows crashed over her deck. The captain picked up two life preservers—one for himself and the other for the first mate. The rest of the crew also grabbed life preservers and all rushed to the forward mast. But the list of the ship caused the mast to break free and the men were thrown into the icy waters. The main mast came crashing down, grazing Dulach on the shoulder and hitting the cook in the face, killing him instantly. The raging seas claimed another crewman—the "old fellow" Fred—who was swept away. Dulach made it to the fore rigging and managed to lash the foremast and foreyard together. The others struggled to the makeshift raft, which lay tangled in the shrouds, and sat astride it—the captain at one end, Irish next to him, then the mate, Dulach, and finally the Swede. The captain, who had his bottle of whiskey with him, pulled it out and took a swig, then handed it to the mate who, after indulging, passed it back to the captain. None was offered to the others. The Swede was the next to die, and Dulach, who had been helping him hold on, let him go into the water.

The four men rode out the stormy night on the wreckage, drenched by the waves and frozen by the raw wind. Whether due to the numbing cold, inebriation, or both, the captain fell off his perch on the mast. Later, the mate was washed off the wreck. Dulach and his friend managed to grab ahold of them and pull them back to the wreckage. However, when both the captain and mate lost their struggle to live, the remaining two did not have the strength to hang onto their lifeless bodies and released them to the waves.

For eleven hours, Dulach and Irish clung to their raft and barely to life. Finally, about dawn, Irish succumbed to the bitter cold and, unable to hold on any longer, slipped into the water. Dulach himself was nearing the end of his endurance, and with the loss of his friend resigned himself to the same fate. Within minutes, though, he saw the small white boat bobbing toward him and mustered enough strength to wave to the lifesaving crew.

News of the *Waukesha*'s fate spread quickly and attracted hundreds of people to the Lake Michigan shore, where they walked off with pieces of the wreckage as souvenirs. An inquest was held on the afternoon of Monday, November 9, at which Frank Dulach gave his graphic testimony of the wreck of the *Waukesha*. He wanted to set the record straight and did not hesitate to place blame on both the poor condition of the ship and the captain's drinking for the resulting disaster. He stated that the ship had been leaking all the way from Chicago, but the crew had managed to keep the hold pumped out. Only after the ship left Ludington did the leaks worsen such that the pumps could not handle the incoming water. Dulach also mentioned that this voyage was not the first he had made with Captain Corbett. He had served under him some years previously and commented that when sober, Corbett was one of the kindest men he had known; however, when drunk, he was overbearing and short-tempered.[92]

The bodies of all of the lost crew were recovered; only the captain's body remained missing. (Dulach testified that Corbett had taken a life preserver but for whatever reason failed to secure it to himself.) Later the following week, the coroner's jury rendered the verdict of accidental drowning in all five cases and attached blame to no one.

Friends and family members came to Muskegon to claim the bodies of their loved ones.[93] In the meantime, Frank Dulach's ordeal was not yet over. When his testimony reached Corbett's family and maritime colleagues in Chicago, a storm of protest arose. Shocked at the portrayal of the captain as an incompetent drunk, they insisted Dulach was lying. They argued that Corbett was not a drinking man but a skilled and sober shipmaster with many years of experience on the lakes. They further claimed that Dulach's actions in slipping the cable of the main anchor caused the disaster, that he "murdered" the captain and crew of the *Waukesha*. According to one of the captain's colleagues, Captain Dennis

CHAPTER 2

Sullivan: "The evidence against Dulach on his own statement will convict him of the murder of the captain of the Waukesha. In slipping the big anchor and thereby letting the schooner go toward the beach, Dulach and his companion committed murder on the officers and suicide for themselves."[94] Within a few days Corbett's many supporters raised the funds necessary to prosecute Dulach in the federal courts on charges of mutiny.

Dulach's reaction was unequivocal. He stood by his sworn statement that the captain's heavy drinking had rendered him unable to make critical decisions. On November 19, the *Muskegon Weekly Chronicle* published his stern response to the charges made against him (see appendix D). Since he was the sole survivor of the wreck, there were no witnesses who could refute his statement. It was this line of reasoning that Charles R. Kremer, an admiralty lawyer, upheld when he was presented with the case by Captain Sullivan and the others. With no witnesses, no successful prosecution could be made against Dulach. Reluctantly, Corbett's supporters dropped the charges.

What happened to Frank Dulach? He told the *Chronicle* reporter that he had $14 in wages coming and asked how he might collect it. Whether or not the ship's owner in Chicago eventually paid him is unknown. His only possessions were the clothes he was wearing at the time and a gold watch, for which he had paid $9 and had managed to save during his ordeal. Of family he had none, and his only friend—Irish—had died. He did stay in Muskegon long enough to visit a photographer and have his picture taken with a life ring recovered from the ill-fortuned *Waukesha*.

The Charmed Life of the *Lyman M. Davis*

> And I have loved thee, Ocean! and my joy
> Of youthful sports was on thy breast to be
> Borne, like thy bubbles, onward; from a boy
> I wanton'd with thy breakers—they to me
> Were a delight; and if the freshening sea
> Made them a terror—'twas a pleasing fear,
> For I was as it were a child of thee,
> And trusted to thy billows far and near,
> And laid my hand upon thy mane—as I do here.
>
> from *Childe Harold's Pilgrimage* by Lord Byron

In 1873, the Arnold Company built a full-sized schooner that would become one of the fastest on the Great Lakes and one that Muskegonites viewed with pride and affection—the *Lyman M. Davis*. Lyman Mason and Charles Davis, owners of the Mason Lumber Company, commissioned the ship to carry lumber to Chicago, and their own lumber, including some of the choicest white oak, went into the construction of the schooner. To

Sole survivor of the *Waukesha* wreck, Frank Dulach (Courtesy of Hackley Public Library).

build her, the Arnold Company hired experienced shipwrights of Swedish and Norwegian stock who had learned their craft in their homelands. They constructed a ship made to endure the hardships of the lumber business and the worst weather conditions on the lakes and to do so with ease. In her many years of service, the *Davis* was carefully maintained and remained staunchly seaworthy to the end of her days.

The *Lyman M. Davis* was a moderately sized schooner, 123 feet long, with a width of 27'2" and depth of 9'4." Her hull consisted of planking two inches thick, 14 inches in diameter, and 40 feet long, cut from wood that had no knots or imperfections.[95] She carried two masts that were equal in height and very high, rising 114 feet from the deck. Rigged as a typical fore-and-aft schooner, she carried a total of nine sails. Overseeing every detail during the construction of the *Davis* was Captain Frederick N. Barnes, who was given command of the ship when she was launched in spring 1873. He remained her captain for many of the years the schooner called Muskegon home.

CHAPTER 2

Schooner *Lyman M. Davis* under full sail ([P86–140] Muskegon County Museum).

The *Davis* gained a reputation around the Great Lakes as the fastest sailing vessel lake sailors had ever known. Barnes boasted that in his eleven years as the ship's master, his vessel was unbeatable: "[I]n all that time no vessel, large or small, ever sailed by her, either in head winds or fair winds, not in gale or light winds, so she sure was some sailor."[96] A sailor on the *Davis*, William Markle, attested to her speed: "The harder it blew, the faster she went!"[97] A larger lumber schooner could carry more cargo, but it might take a week to sail the round-trip from Muskegon to Chicago. The smaller *Davis* was able to compete by making two to three trips to Chicago in a week.[98] Her speed and reliability in all kinds of weather more than made up for her size. Throughout her long career on the lakes, the *Davis* was often challenged to a race. In one contest from Kewaunee, Wisconsin, to Muskegon, she beat the lumber steamer *George C. Markham*. Only once was she known to have lost a race, when in fall 1915 the three-masted schooner *Hattis Hutt* came out ahead of the *Davis* as they ploughed down Lake Huron from Silver Inlet on Georgian Bay to Port Huron. The defeated *Davis* arrived six hours behind the *Hutt*.[99]

As the lumber era ended in Muskegon, the *Lyman M. Davis* continued to work in her home port, carrying pickets from Canada and transporting lumber from the

Upper Peninsula to Muskegon's Thayer Lumber Company. In 1897 Thomas Munroe of Muskegon bought the *Davis,* and later the schooner was sold to the Brinen Lumber Company, also of Muskegon.

In winter 1912, the schooner—aging, but still in excellent shape—was sold to the Graham Brothers of Kincardine, Canada. She was refitted early in spring 1913, and on May 6, the *Davis* left Muskegon for the last time. On the trip down Lake Michigan, a storm blew up out of the southwest, and the new owners had the chance to experience firsthand the legendary speed and agility of the ship, as well as the ease of handling her even in the turbulent seas and roaring winds. Through it all they found the experience exhilarating. Once past the Straits of Mackinac, the weather moderated, but brothers Angus, Colin, and Alex Graham, along with their crew, realized the worth of their newly acquired vessel.[100] The people of Kincardine welcomed the *Davis* and grew to love her as Muskegonites had over the past forty years.

Under the Graham brothers the *Davis* was kept busy, carrying lumber, posts, and slab wood from the Georgian Bay area to the ports on the lower lakes. But her lumber days ended in 1919 when she was sold and her new owners took the ship through the Welland Canal to Lake Ontario. In her new role, she transported coal between ports on the Canadian and U.S. sides of the lake. When the *Davis* was put up for sale in 1928, she was purchased by Captain Henry Daryaw of Kingston, who continued to use her for carrying coal.

By the early 1930s, the *Lyman M. Davis* was one of several old schooners still sailing the Great Lakes. Her days may have been numbered, but her end came in a most undignified way. Captain Daryaw sold the *Davis* to the Sunnyside Amusement Association, a Toronto firm that had burned obsolete or small boats as a waterfront spectacle for the people's enjoyment. However, Sunnyside's management was looking for larger craft. In 1931 Daryaw had sold them a derelict old schooner, the *Julia B. Merrill,* which was beyond repair. Plans to burn the *Merrill* for show caused many to voice their disapproval, but Sunnyside ignored them and staged the firey demise of the aged ship off the city's shoreline.

When Sunnyside bought the *Lyman M. Davis* in 1933 for the same purpose, the cries of indignation were even louder. Unlike the *Merrill,* the *Davis* was still in good condition. To Canadians, she was a familiar and beloved sight in their ports, a dignified relic of bygone days that faithfully stayed the course even as the modern era rushed past her. The editor of the *Toronto Telegram,* C.H.J. Snider, led a crusade to save the ship, frequently writing about the *Davis* in his column "Schooner Days." In one edition he wrote: "Citizens of Toronto do not want the *Lyman M. Davis* demolished by fire to create a passing thrill for night-going sightseers, or to boost sales of hot dogs to peanuts."[101] The criticism was leveled at the park's manager, Major D. M. Goudy, who remained unmoved by the controversy. People signed petitions, wrote letters, and tried to raise funds—not easy to do during the Depression—to save the ship from the flames. When Muskegonites got word of the danger facing their old friend, they, too, expressed their outrage. Some offered suggestions on ways to save her, one of which was to bring the

CHAPTER 2

Davis back to Muskegon and turn her into a floating museum containing artifacts from the city's historic lumber era.[102] Finally, the mayor of Toronto intervened and persuaded Goudy to delay the burning, during which time Goudy offered to sell the ship for a reasonable price. But when no individual or party could raise sufficient funds by the summer, the *Davis* was readied for her final voyage.

At midnight on June 29, 1934, a huge crowd watched as the vessel—coated with tar, saturated with kerosene and oil, and loaded with dry wood—was towed by a tug from the dockside out into the lake, where she was set ablaze. As the flames climbed higher into the rigging, they lit the fireworks fastened there, which shot off into the dark sky. The *Davis* burned for more than an hour before finally, when the fire reached the dynamite stored deep in her hull, a muffled boom signaled the coup de grace. Although she burned to the waterline, a part of the *Davis* survived; the transom, consisting of four planks with the name of the ship painted on them, along with portions of the ribs, washed ashore on Hanlan's Island. (See appendix E for an eyewitness account of the *Lyman M. Davis* burning.)

Thus the amazingly long and felicitous career of the *Lyman M. Davis*—a full sixty years of dancing on the waves of the Great Lakes—came to an end as a cheap thrill show. Yet during those years she had endeared herself to many on both shores—American and Canadian—with her speed and grace and was not forgotten. Even today, to the people of Muskegon who know her story, the *Lyman M. Davis* holds a special place of honor and is remembered with pride and love.

The passing of the lumber schooners around the turn of the century marked the end of one era and the beginning of another. The number of large passenger steamships and later the freighters and car ferries crowded out the old sailing ships in Muskegon and other Great Lakes harbors. But the romance of earlier times was not forgotten, and many looked back on them with nostalgia. In 1909, author James Oliver Curwood noted this maritime "changing of the guard":

> To Lake people it is pathetic, this death of the lumber fleets of the Inland Seas. An old soldier who had sailed on a lumber hooker since the days of the Civil War once said to me, "They're the Grand Army of the Lakes—are those old barges and schooners, and they're passing away as fast as we old fellows of '61." Today no vessels are built along the Lakes for the carrying of lumber. Scores of ancient "hookers" and picturesque schooners of the romantic days of old are rotting at their moorings, and when a great steel leviathan of ten thousand tons passes one of these veterans the eyes of her crew will follow it until only her canvas remains above the horizon.[103]

CHAPTER 3

Steamships and Car Ferries of Muskegon

> The low-pressure steamer Huron would leave Muskegon for Grand Haven and Chicago on Tuesday, Thursday and Saturday at 1 P.M. during the season of 1859.
>
> *Muskegon Reporter,* May 5, 1859 (First advertisement for a steamer carrying passengers and freight from Muskegon to Chicago.)

Along the eastern shores of Lake Michigan, the dunes stretch for miles in seeming sameness. But a closer look over time reveals change—sometimes subtle, other times dramatic, but always unstoppable. As in human affairs, change is the one constant in the nature of the dunes. The grains of sand are blown into one formation or another by the winds that come howling down from an arctic air mass or tearing up from the southwest plains. They form new dunes that build up and encroach on the nearby woodlands, eventually killing stands of mature trees. In time, the tall, whitened trunks protrude through the sand as "ghost forests." Wind and water also combine forces to change the land formations. When the lake's water levels are high, pounding waves erode the shore, undermining bluffs and menacing the homes and summer cottages built atop them. Along the beaches and at the mouths of channels, the breakers and currents build up then wash out sandbars, shifting their hidden locations daily. Nothing stays the same along this lakeshore.

Most lumbermen of Muskegon did not see change coming. In the early years, those in the business were confident the stands of timber would play out after about five hundred years of constant harvesting. By the mid-1880s, this prediction was readjusted to a shorter time span, but many still thought the lumber business would continue at least for another generation.[1] But when the boom ended in the mid-1890s, the city was caught in uncertain times. Rather than risk unemployment, a number of men in the industry—mill hands, booming men, lumberjacks—left town to continue work in the trade, which still flourished in northern Michigan, Wisconsin, and out west in California and Oregon. Even some of the lumber barons left town with their fortunes. Those who remained had to ask some hard questions: What new direction should Muskegon take? What new industries could be attracted to the area? Could they create steady jobs?

Charles Hackley and his partner, Thomas Hume, were two of the prominent lumbermen who chose to stay in Muskegon and help the city make the transition to other industries. As early as 1879, they and others started investing in other manufacturing firms, predominantly wood related, such as the Temple Manufacturing Company, which made curtain rollers, and a furniture factory.[2] With the support of the local board of trade, they invested capital in more diverse firms: the Muskegon Chemical Fire Engine Company, the Chase Brothers Piano Company (which later became the Chase-Hackley Piano Company), and the Muskegon Cracker Company. Some of these survived into the early twentieth century, but others folded after a few years.[3] In addition, Hackley acted as trustee of monies that were raised and then invested on a short-term basis, with the interest and some of the principal forming the financial fund known as the "bonus plan." The bonus plan administered by Hackley, Thomas Hume, representing the city's Chamber of Commerce (the former board of trade), and John Torrent of the city's Common Council, was used to attract existing businesses to relocate their operations to Muskegon. While the city fathers primarily sought to attract existing, successful companies, they also offered bonus plan funds to promising entrepreneurs who wanted to set up new firms in Muskegon. Two men who benefited from this assistance were A. W. Shaw and Louis C. Walker. In 1899, after working in the furniture business in Grand Rapids, they decided to establish their own firm in Muskegon, manufacturing office furniture and filing systems. The Shaw Walker Company went on to become one of the major industries in the Port City. All told, the efforts of Muskegon's business leaders paid off; by the turn of the century, a number of new and diverse industries had arrived in Muskegon and offered employment to thousands.

Muskegon was not the only lumber town that had to face this drastic economic downturn. While some west Michigan boomtowns never saw the wealth and influence they enjoyed in their prime, they nevertheless found new sources of revenue. Manistee—Muskegon's only main west Michigan competitor in terms of the amount of lumber harvested and milled—developed other industries based on natural resources in the region—salt, oil, and natural gas. Further north, the area around Traverse City enjoyed a climate well suited for vineyards and orchards, and soon was producing fine wines and millions of bushels of cherries. The ports of Whitehall and Montague continue to enjoy popularity as charming resort towns, and Grand Haven, which once capitalized on its mineral springs to draw visitors from around Lake Michigan, is still popular for its shopping district, waterfront activities, and annual National Coast Guard Festival. Even before the lumber era ended, all of these towns benefited from their locations along the golden beaches of Lake Michigan and lured vacationers from Chicago and other urban areas. The dunes and sandy shoreline, once so desert-like and forbidding to settlers, now attracted many seeking lakeside recreation and natural beauty far from the crowded cities.

One dream shared by Muskegon's leaders at the turn of the century was the establishment of a large shipyard and dry-dock firm at one of the abandoned mill sites. The ideal location, the employment of hundreds of workers, and convenience for local ship owners needing repairs all played into this idea. By the turn of the century, however, major shipyards had been in operation in ports around the Great Lakes for decades and establishing a new firm of this kind was a daunting enterprise. However, in 1902, the chamber of commerce succeeded in enticing the Racine (Wisconsin) Boat Company to move its operations to Muskegon, offering the firm the lakefront property that had been the Ryerson and Hills lumber mill. The company constructed three buildings, including a foundry, on the site, and nearly three hundred men found employment there. The Racine Boat Company built a variety of small boats with both steel and wood hulls: tugs, pleasure yachts, rowboats, canoes, and lightships for government service. In 1910, the firm led a merger of seven other boat-building companies to become the National Boat and Engine Company, which sought to control the manufacture of pleasure boats in the eastern United States. Less than a year later, however, the company, having failed to finance the merger, fell into the hands of a receiver. In spite of the Racine Boat Company's efforts to reorganize with two other boat companies, further financial and legal problems brought down the troubled business in 1915.[4]

One vessel built by the Racine Boat Company for government service was a lighthouse tender, the *Milwaukee 95*. In late December 1911, just four days before she was to be turned over to the government, the boat sank at the dock in twenty-two feet of water. She was raised the following February and went on to fulfill her duties in Milwaukee's busy harbor. Strangely enough, this would not be the only incident of a government vessel sinking at a Muskegon dock (see "The Halcyon Days in Muskegon" in chapter 4 of this volume,).[5]

Well before the lumber industry shut down, changes already were taking place around Muskegon Lake. As long as the incessant whine of the sawmills filled the air, the schooners crowded the harbor, creating a forest of masts on the waterfront. By the 1890s, the demise of the state's once endless forests of pine reduced the number of sailing vessels on the lakes, with those few remaining into the 1930s symbolizing the rough but romantic era that made Muskegon a thriving city. But even from as far back as the late 1850s, other sounds competed with and eventually drowned out the familiar snap of the canvas and slap of the lumber being stacked—the splash of huge paddle wheels, the shrill blast of a steam whistle, and the laughter and chatter of excursionists out for a pleasure cruise on a stylish and comfortably furnished vessel. Whereas the lumber schooners were well suited for carrying a certain type of cargo, the steamships that plied Muskegon's waters varied in size and function. They were designed to carry passengers on business or vacation trips; transport lumber, fruit, pianos, and billiard tables to market in Chicago; and ferry railcars and automobiles across Lake Michigan to Milwaukee. The story of the steamers covers a period over a century long—a time span that saw tremendous changes in the local and national economies, transportation systems, and maritime developments.

Steamship travel began on the upper lakes in 1818 with the small side-wheeler *Walk-In-The-Water*. By the early 1850s, huge ships were being built as floating palaces, carrying hundreds of passengers in luxury between the affluent cities of Buffalo and Chicago.

CHAPTER 3

Such vessels naturally bypassed the small rough-hewn town of Muskegon. In contrast, the early Muskegon steamers were used mainly to transport various cargoes, especially produce grown locally, such as celery and fruit, delivering them to Milwaukee and Chicago. Lumber also was increasingly shipped on steam barges. While most lumbermen employed schooners to ship their products to market, some preferred steam to sails for several reasons. With these hardworking vessels, there was no need to rely on the harbor tugs or favorable winds. In addition, these ships could tow one or more lumber-laden schooners or barges, thus at least doubling the shipment at little extra cost. Muskegon lumberman John Torrent especially favored the steam barge and had two constructed at the Wyandotte, Michigan, shipyards. These he named the *Nellie Torrent* and the *Ida Torrent* after his two daughters. Early Muskegon newspaper editor and historian James L. Smith recalled the days when the lumber barges worked their way into the Muskegon harbor scene:

> The steambarges began to capture the lumber carrying trade in a limited way in the later years of the seventies. I recall regular visits of two rather small steam lumber carriers, [one of which was] the George Dunbar. They were gradually followed by quite a fleet of steambarges. Adverse winds seldom interfered seriously with the round trips to lumber distribution centers by the steam barges and the "White Wing" fleet gradually was displaced by crafts propelled by steam and in a few years the Lyman Davis and the little Arendall were the only wind power vessels hailing from Muskegon.
> ... In the last years of the lumber carrying era, a syndicate composed of Mathew and William H. Wilson, Donald and Dennis McMillan, and Captain James Sanford, operated a fleet of steambarges composed of the John Otis, the Mathew Wilson, and the S. M. Stephenson. For several years the Brinen Lumber Co. used their steamer, the [George] Markham, in bringing lumber from the northern ports to Muskegon.[6]

Steamers also handled heavy freight, such as the machinery needed to build the lumber mills. One of the early Muskegon-owned propeller steamboats was the *Foss*. John Torrent described his move from Grand Haven to Muskegon, starting his trip on the *Foss* as she carried circular machinery for the L. G. Mason sawmill, then under construction, in fall 1857:

> I lived in Grand Haven two years, moving to Muskegon in November, 1857. At Grand Haven I had been in the employ of the Ferrys. "Mont" Ferry had built a machine shop and was engaged in the manufacture of circular machinery for sawmills. L. G. Mason was building a new mill in Muskegon and when it came time to put in the machinery I was sent over to do it.
> There were no piers at Muskegon harbor at that time and if it was kind of rough the boats couldn't get in. When it came time to put in the machinery I came over on the boat—the propeller *Foss*—with it but when we got to this port there was so much sea on we couldn't get in, so we went back to Grand Haven. I didn't want any more of the boat and so I abandoned it, preferring to come overland through the woods alone from Ferrysburg.[7]

During the 1850s, the *Foss* made regular trips between Muskegon and Chicago, transporting lumber, supplies, and a small number of passengers.

Unlike the schooners, which offered cramped quarters to the few passengers who traversed the lakes, the steamers could provide roomier private cabins and this attracted more and more people who enjoyed the pleasures of lake travel. By the late 1800s, large passenger steamers with the finest accommodations were built to serve the growing number of west Michigan travelers. They provided fast and often elegant means of travel for those going to the big cities on business or shopping trips, or to smaller towns and resorts. Captain Albert E. Goodrich, who founded the Goodrich Transportation Company in 1856, was a pioneer in the Great Lakes steamship business. For seventy-six years the Goodrich line carried passengers and freight to ports around Lake Michigan. The competing Crosby line, founded by Captain Edward G. Crosby of Milwaukee, maintained a fleet of ships that regularly visited Muskegon and provided cross-lake service over a number of years. In addition, the Chicago-based Graham and Morton line also figured prominently in the Lake Michigan steamship business. While other smaller companies set up their own lines, they often met with limited success against the Goodrich, Crosby, and Graham and Morton fleets.

Albert Goodrich's father, Russel Goodrich, operated the Goodrich Hotel in New Buffalo, Michigan, a town that became a hub for shipping and railroad lines. Young Albert, fascinated by lake travel at a very early age, gained experience under the guidance of an uncle who captained a side-wheel steamboat on Lake Erie. After his apprenticeship on his uncle's vessel, Goodrich succeeded in earning his master's license. His dream of operating his own steamship line came to fruition in 1856 when he and a partner, George C. Drew, founded the Goodrich Steamboat Line, which later became the Goodrich Transportation Company.[8] The Goodrich line flourished and at its height either owned or leased more than fifty steamships.

Captain Goodrich established his main office in Chicago. From that harbor, his ships ranged the length of Lake Michigan, following either the west or east shoreline. The course of the west shoreline had Milwaukee as its main port of call but also included stops at Racine, Green Bay, Sturgeon Bay, Escanaba, and Manistique. The Goodrich steamers of the east shoreline made stops at Grand Haven, Muskegon, and, later, White Lake. As the line developed, Goodrich provided cross-lake service from Milwaukee to Manistee and Ludington.

The earliest Goodrich steamers that visited Muskegon included the *Huron*, a 348-ton side-wheel steamer built in 1839, which Captain Goodrich bought from the well-established Ward Line, and the *Comet*, also a side-wheeler, built in 1859 specifically for the new company. When first leased from the Ward Line, the staunch 165-foot *Huron*, with Goodrich in command, sailed the west-shore route, but for the 1859 season, starting in May, she carried passengers and freight between Chicago, Grand Haven, and Muskegon. The following year she served the Wisconsin side until August and then returned to the west Michigan ports. The *Huron* became popular around the lake and provided Goodrich with an auspicious beginning to his enterprise. Accommodations aboard the *Huron* and other small steamers would be considered primitive by later standards. Any food on the vessel was whatever the passengers brought aboard with them. The cabins provided shelter

CHAPTER 3

from the elements and little else. Passengers often would sleep either in deck chairs or on the open deck.[9]

The 158-foot *Comet* proved to be as popular as the *Huron* and offered a more luxurious means of travel. In the May 4, 1860 edition of the *Muskegon Reporter*, a correspondent gave the new vessel high marks:

> THE STEAMER COMET—This fine steamer is now making regular trips between Chicago and Muskegon, touching at Kenosha, Racine and Grand Haven. She was built at Newport, on the Saint Clair River, by Captain Ward, of Detroit, for Messrs. Drew & Goodrich, of Chicago. She is a staunch, fast, and splendid looking steamer, and is, in every particular, well adapted for this route. Her cabins, or saloons, are large and elegantly furnished and all her accommodations for passengers are excellent. She has already proved herself a good sea boat and has, we believe, shown an average speed of 15 miles per hour.[10]

One of the captains hired by Goodrich was Fred Pabst, who later presided over the famous brewery in Milwaukee. At different times Captain Pabst commanded both the *Huron* and the *Comet*.[11]

Just when the steamship business from Goodrich and others was starting to broaden Muskegon's economic horizons, the Port City suffered a major setback. In April 1863, Goodrich bought the wooden side-wheel steamer *Seabird* from the Ward Line, and set her on the Chicago-Grand Haven-Muskegon route. The *Seabird*, at 638 tons burden, was larger than the other vessels in the Goodrich fleet. After only a month on the new schedule, Goodrich notified Muskegon's city officials that he was discontinuing service to the port because of the shallow and unpredictable channel entrance. His larger ships could not safely navigate the waters into the harbor. He also pointed out that since they ran on a tight schedule, his steamers needed access to their ports of call at all times. Steamships from other lines followed suit and avoided calling on Muskegon. It was then that the city's business leaders took action and, with the help of the steamer *Caldwell*, deepened the channel to allow safer passage for both steamers and schooners. But even after improvements were made, Goodrich kept the *Seabird* on the west-shore route and did not include Muskegon on his schedule for several years.[12]

By the late 1860s Goodrich could foresee the time when steamers with side-wheel propulsion would become outmoded. The latest trend in ship design was the wooden-hulled propeller steamships, which were equipped with a screw drive. In 1867, he bought two propellers—the 158-foot *G. J. Truesdell* and the slightly larger *Ottawa*—from Martin Ryerson, who had been using them to carry lumber and passengers between Muskegon and Chicago. Ryerson, an early settler who arrived in Muskegon in 1836, was not only a lumberman but also one of the first in the area to operate a passenger steamboat line. Both vessels were in excellent condition—the *Truesdell* only four years old—but Goodrich wanted to use them for overnight service, and so they were taken to the shipyards at Manitowoc to be remodeled and fitted out with finer accommodations for passengers. Once relaunched, however, they did not return to Muskegon but instead served the ports along Lake Michigan's western shore.[13]

Early Goodrich side-wheel steamer *Huron* ([66–115] Muskegon County Museum).

The popularity of traveling by steamship grew to such an extent that Goodrich had difficulty keeping up with the demand. He realized his line needed a more formal business structure, and in 1868 he reorganized the Goodrich Steamship Line as the Goodrich Transportation Company. It was at this time the company's vessels took on their distinctive styling that made them instantly recognizable. The hulls were painted black up to the main deck, with the cabins and upper works in white. Most Goodrich ships had a single stack, which was painted bright red with a wide black band at the top. From a tall mast flew a white dovetail pennant with the initials "G. T. Co." in red. During the 1870s, Goodrich added more ships to his line—side-wheelers *Orion* (185 feet) and *Muskegon* (193 feet), and the propellers *Navarino* (184 feet) and *Menominee* (184 feet)—which became familiar sights in the Muskegon harbor.

By the 1890s, large steamships built specifically to carry passengers were plying the waters of Lake Michigan. The Goodrich Transportation Company owned a number of these popular ships that made Muskegon a customary port of call: the *Atlanta, Indiana, Iowa, Georgia,* and *City of Racine* (later remodeled and renamed the *Arizona*).

One of the first of these vessels was the *Virginia*. The early passenger steamers were made of wood over an iron framework. However, Goodrich commissioned Globe Iron Works of Cleveland to construct a fast, elegant passenger ship made of steel. Built in

CHAPTER 3

Early Muskegon-based steamers *G. J. Truesdell* (left) and *Laketon* ([P86–159] Muskegon County Museum).

1891, the *Virginia* was 285 feet long and 38 feet wide, and at 1,985 tons she drew 14 feet of water. Her two triple-expansion steam engines provided enough horsepower to maintain a speed of 18–20 miles per hour. At first, the *Virginia* was placed on a route between Milwaukee and Chicago, and during that time she gained a reputation as one of the fastest steamers on the lake. But by July 1908, the Goodrich Company responded to the demand for better passenger service on Lake Michigan's eastern shore and set the *Virginia* on a new run from Chicago to Grand Haven and Muskegon. For the next ten years, the ship regularly visited the Port City.

A description of the *Virginia*'s special features will give a clearer picture of the comforts she offered her passengers. Older ships still used oil lamps, but the *Virginia*'s polished mahogany paneling, trimmed with gold and ivory, gleamed under electric lights. The decks were covered with thick carpeting, and passengers could relax in the main cabin, or "saloon," in comfortable easy chairs, entertained by music from a grand piano. The state rooms, each with four berths, surrounded the outside of the main cabin, providing accommodations for three hundred passengers. She could easily hold her own with any luxury hotel of the day.

Bird's-eye view of the lake harbor of Muskegon ([PD229] Muskegon County Museum).

On November 4, 1909, while making one of her last runs of the season, the *Virginia* set a record in Muskegon for carrying the greatest load of cargo ever handled by a local passenger steamer. Early that day, extra men were hired to help the regular deckhands load the vessel with an astonishing variety of goods produced by Muskegon-area farms and factories. These products included: three carloads of apples, several hundred boxes of celery, seven pianos built by the Chase-Hackley Piano Company, twelve Continental Motors, furniture built by local furniture companies, and several slate billiard and pool tables made by the Brunswick-Balke-Collender Company. The load filled the hold so completely that excess freight had to be left behind at the dock. The *Virginia* bypassed Grand Haven on this trip and sailed directly to Chicago. Goodrich enlisted another steamer, the *Georgia*, to transport freight and passengers from Grand Haven to Chicago.[14]

America entered World War I in 1917, and the following year the U.S. Navy took over the *Virginia*, refitting her at Manitowoc for war service. After the war, the ship was renamed the *Avalon* and provided passenger service off the California coast for another thirty years.

Milwaukee entrepreneur Captain Edward G. Crosby formed the Crosby Transportation Company in 1893, acquiring a fleet of passenger steamers that soon rivaled the Goodrich line in service and style. An energetic man with keen business savvy, Crosby had worked in several trades, including construction, railroad, and lumber, before he was drawn to the lakes. In 1881, he founded the E. G. Crosby Company, which constructed

CHAPTER 3

The Goodrich dock in Muskegon, with the *Alabama* (foreground) and the *Virginia* ([P83-369] Muskegon County Museum).

piers and dry docks in ports along Lake Michigan's shores. In addition to his construction company, Crosby maintained a fleet of tugboats and scows. The business grew, and by 1893 he was financially secure enough to start up his own steamship line. The following year Crosby established direct service between Milwaukee and Muskegon, later including Grand Haven on the schedule.

One of the first Crosby ships, the steamer *Nyack,* entered Muskegon on April 20, 1894. That day, hundreds of people came to the dock to tour the ship of the new line. Among them was a reporter from the *Muskegon Chronicle,* who had an eye for color and style: "The cabins are roomy and inviting, the ceiling colored blue and white, the sides white relieved with buff. Brussels carpets adorn the floor and the prevailing shade in the upholstering is a dark, rich red. The staterooms are unusually roomy, and contain all the equipments and conveniences of modern make. The dome lights over the cabin are of stained glass in arabesque designs of pleasing color."[15] Clearly the *Nyack* was on par with the ships of the Goodrich line. Built in 1878, the *Nyack*'s early career was in the passenger and freight business on Lake Erie, sailing between Buffalo and Detroit. The wooden-hull vessel with steel arches measured 253 feet in length and had a 39-foot beam. She could accommodate 250 passengers, and her hold could contain up to 1,400 tons of freight. Her master was Charles A. Lyman of Grand Haven (formerly of Muskegon), who had served for a number of years as mate on one of the Goodrich ships and had also been commander of the small Muskegon steamer *Carrie A. Ryerson*. At first, the *Nyack* docked at the terminal at the foot of Division Street on property owned by the Muskegon, Grand Rapids and Indiana Railroad, but in 1895 the Crosby Company moved to the Grand Trunk terminal at the end of Eighth Street.[16]

The Crosby Transportation Company's first season was rough, and it ran at a loss. However, business quickly picked up and the line prospered. A second steamship, the *Wisconsin*, was added to the line in the mid-1890s, and the two vessels provided daily service from Muskegon to Grand Haven and Milwaukee. The *Wisconsin*, an iron-constructed vessel built in 1881 in Wyandotte with a length of 204 feet, a 35-foot beam, and a 12-foot draft, was originally commissioned by Goodrich. The Goodrich line used her to carry cargo from Ludington to Manitowoc for the Flint and Pere Marquette Railroad Company. But when the railroad started its own fleet of vessels for this purpose, Goodrich lost a lucrative business and was forced to sell the *Wisconsin* and two other ships. The Detroit, Grand Haven and Milwaukee Railroad took her over and she worked briefly for the railroad line, sailing between Grand Haven and Milwaukee.

Under Crosby's ownership she was renamed the *Naomi* in honor of Captain Crosby's daughter. During her career, the steamer was overhauled several times. Around 1898, she was sheathed in steel at considerable expense. In 1906, in order to accommodate the growing number of passengers, the *Naomi* was remodeled and given a new deck allowing space for additional state rooms. The business proved to be a financial success, and in 1916 the Crosby Company added to the line, purchasing the side-wheel steamship *City of Holland* from the Graham and Morton Company of Benton Harbor and placing her on the cross-lake route, alternating with the *Naomi*. Four years later, the *City of Holland* was renamed the *Muskegon*.

On the night of April 15, 1912, Captain Edward G. Crosby, his wife, Catherine, and daughter, Harriette, were onboard the *Titanic* returning to the States from a vacation and business trip in Europe. As the doomed vessel sank, Captain Crosby remained on deck, calming and reassuring other passengers, while his wife and daughter escaped in one of the lifeboats.

In his book *Titanic: The Great Lakes Connections*, Cris Kohl describes the tributes accorded to Captain Crosby when word of his death reached the Great Lakes:

> Out of respect for the late Captain Crosby, all operations in the Crosby transportation offices ceased for five minutes on Thursday morning April 25, 1912, from 10:30 to 10:35. Even the Crosby ships steaming across the lake stopped their engines for five minutes. Memorial services were held all around Lake Michigan: at the Grand Army Posts in Milwaukee, in Grand Haven and in Muskegon, and on board the company's flagship, the *Nyack*, at Grand Haven, as well as aboard his namesake, the passenger steamer, *E. G. Crosby*, on April 28.[17]

The Crosby Transportation Company continued operations with Captain Crosby's son, Frederick G. Crosby, as president and general manager.

Besides the large steamships that frequented Muskegon's harbor, there were some small wooden steamers that carried on a vital service on Muskegon Lake and along the

CHAPTER 3

Crosby's steamer *Nyack* ([P83–393]Muskegon County Museum).

Lake Michigan shore to nearby resorts and communities. Two of the most popular coastal steamers/ferries were the *Carrie A. Ryerson* and *Erie L. Hackley*.

The *Carrie A. Ryerson* was built in Grand Haven in 1883 at the Duncan Robertson shipyards and launched in July that year. The *Ryerson*, only 66 feet long, 17.5 feet wide, and 7.8 feet in depth, was powered by a steam engine, the steam being produced by a steel boiler. In addition, she was fitted out with a Worthington fire engine and over six hundred feet of hose—a great reassurance along the docks stacked with lumber and covered in sawdust. The little steamer's career of thirty-eight years saw her take on several roles. Her first owners, Henry Jacobs and Henry H. Getty of Muskegon, used the *Ryerson* for towing logs between the two Ryerson and Hills sawmills, one located at the eastern end of the city's main street, Western Avenue, and the other, known as the Bay Mill, situated at the western shore of Muskegon Lake, north of the channel. The vessel also provided ferry service for passengers between the mills. Traveling on a regular schedule and making five round-trips a day, the *Ryerson* would stop at docks along the waterfront, picking up and discharging people and cargo. Through special arrangements the *Ryerson* could be booked for summer excursions to the Bay Mill site with its picnic facilities.

In 1892 the *Ryerson* was acquired by the Crosby Company and started passenger service along the Lake Michigan shore, with stops at Grand Haven, Muskegon, and Whitehall. Crosby later sold the *Ryerson,* and between 1901 and 1921 she worked for

Coastal steamer *Carrie A. Ryerson* ([P86–148] Muskegon County Museum).

several owners and served other ports, from Montague to Chicago. Her end came on April 23, 1921, when she burned offshore of Willow Springs, Illinois. All five people onboard at the time survived, but the little steamer was a total loss.[18]

The screw-steamer *Erie L. Hackley,* named for the foster daughter of Charles Hackley, was built in Muskegon by the Arnold Company in 1882. She was similar to the *Ryerson*, although longer at 79 feet, with a beam of 17 feet and depth of 5 feet. Like the *Ryerson*, she served the area well. Owned—and possibly captained—by Hackley's friend, Seth Lee, the *Erie L. Hackley* cruised Muskegon Lake as a ferry, with stops at the Central Wharf in downtown Muskegon, at Bluffton and Bay Mill on the west side, and North Muskegon across the lake. She was one of four ferries Captain Lee operated, the others being the *Centennial, Mary Minter,* and *Mayflower*.

Today, the residential city of North Muskegon covers the peninsula bounded by Bear Lake, Muskegon Lake, and the channel connecting the two. But in the mid-1800s, those living there occupied just the strip of the south shoreline and, like Muskegon across the lake, the settlement consisted of little more than sawmills along with the usual complement of boardinghouses, company stores, and saloons. Until 1867, when lumberman George Arms constructed the "crooked bridge" across the marshlands at the head of Muskegon Lake, ferryboats served as necessary connections between Muskegon and Reedsville, as North Muskegon was known before 1881. The first ferries were sailboats, but April 1863 saw the launching of the *Mayflower,* a paddle-wheel steamboat built by

CHAPTER 3

The small steamer *Erie L. Hackley* at Captain Seth Lee's ferry dock in Muskegon ([P86–129] Muskegon County Museum).

O. W. Califf and George L. Christie. Other small steamers, including the *Hackley*, followed, providing regular transportation between the two towns.

In 1903 the *Hackley* was sold for $3,000 to Captain Joseph Verous and his partners, who had just established the Fish Creek Transportation Company, a passenger and package service in the Green Bay area of Lake Michigan. Early on the evening of Saturday, October 3, only a few months into her new schedule, the *Hackley* was on a run from Menominee to Egg Harbor on the Door Peninsula when she was overwhelmed by a violent squall or, according to some reports, a tornado.[19] She sank within minutes, taking with her eleven people, including Captain Verous. Eight others survived, clinging to pieces of wreckage until picked up the next morning by the steamer *Sheboygan* (see appendix F for one survivor's account of the wreck). It wasn't until 1980 that the wreck of the *Hackley* was located.

Starting in the 1860s, the demand for railway service grew among the towns of western Michigan. Until then, land travel was slow and uncomfortable. The elegant passenger ships became increasingly popular, and as long as there was open water, the Goodrich line provided a valuable service for lake travelers. But when winter sheathed the lakes in thick ice, the people of Muskegon either had to wait until the spring thaw or endure a rough journey overland by stagecoach. Trains proved to be reliable, running year-round and able to carry both freight and passengers quickly and comfortably. In short order, local businessmen formed an association to build a railroad between Muskegon and Ferrysburg, and the first train arrived at the depot—a temporary one located at the Hackley office on Eighth Street—late in December 1869.[20]

However, the early railroad lines along the Lake Michigan shore proved to be too limited and unable to meet Muskegon's needs, and the city fathers began to court larger lines that could connect Muskegon with Grand Rapids and cities further east. A major requirement for extending an existing railroad line to Muskegon was that the city had to provide terminal facilities. The necessary funds were raised, and in the late 1880s the Grand Rapids and Indiana (later the Muskegon, Grand Rapids and Indiana) Railroad began local service, operating out of a terminal at the foot of Division Street. Another line—the Toledo, Saginaw and Muskegon—was formed about the same time. It was later taken over by the Grand Trunk Railroad.

By the mid-1890s, when the lumber boom ended, business leaders of Muskegon looked to invest in other moneymaking ventures. One by one the lumbermen closed their mills, and as a result some of the mill sites on Muskegon Lake were bought by the railroad companies to serve as terminals for the trains and docks for the passenger steamers, some of which were owned or chartered by the railroad lines. The Detroit, Grand Haven and Milwaukee Railroad operated two steamers—the *City of Milwaukee* and the *Wisconsin*—between Muskegon and Milwaukee by way of Grand Haven.[21] In other instances, space was leased or sold to the popular shipping lines. The Hackley and Hume Company closed their lumber mill in 1894 and subsequently provided docking space, a freight warehouse, and an office for the Barry Brothers line and later for their own Hackley Transportation Company. In 1861, the lumber mill that had originally belonged to lumbermen Lyman G. Mason and C. H. Goodman, and later Blodgett and Byrne, closed down its operation. Three years later the Goodrich Company bought the dock and mill site. Goodrich developed the property, building a new warehouse and office and dredging the docking spaces for their big ships. The company also acquired the former Thayer Lumber Company Mill No. 2 dock to the east of this property where more Goodrich steamers could be berthed.

The railroad companies saw the immense benefits of establishing direct cross-lake service between Muskegon and Milwaukee. Such a route would save time by avoiding the long way around Lake Michigan and through Chicago, which had its own congestion of railroad tracks. The Muskegon, Grand Rapids and Indiana railroad line was the first to start regular transportation across Lake Michigan, carrying passengers and freight on the steamer *Favorite*. Pillow and Cleghorn (a small outfit run by the boat's engineer, P. Pillow, and captain, Alex Cleghorn) bought the staunch steamer, rated A2, from the Kirby & Carpenter Company at Menominee for the sum of $16,000. With the railroad's backing, the steamer went into business.

The *Favorite* met with misfortune on her first trip to Muskegon on June 17, 1888. About 8:00 that evening, a small double-deck excursion steamer, the *A. C. Van Raalte*, left Muskegon harbor on a moonlight cruise. The sixty-five passengers onboard were enjoying the cool lake breezes and the music of the popular City Band as they steamed through the

CHAPTER 3

The *Favorite*—first Muskegon steamer to serve the railroads in cross-lake service ([P86–158] Muskegon County Museum).

channel on their way to Grand Haven. Near the mouth of the harbor, Captain A. C. Majo of the *Van Raalte* watched the *Favorite* as she entered the channel. Captain Cleghorn saw the excursion boat, and both masters blew their whistles as they passed. Suddenly, the *Favorite* veered from her course and struck the *Van Raalte* near her port bow. With water pouring in, Captain Majo ordered the engines put into reverse and quickly swung the vessel around so her stern rested against the south bank. The collision knocked the *Van Raalte* excursionists off their feet. Shaken, they made their way to the upper deck as the vessel settled and, with assistance from the lifesaving crew and tugman Captain Miles Barry, were helped to shore. A *Muskegon Weekly Chronicle* reporter described a nearly comic scenario unfolding aboard the *Van Raalte:*

> The usual amusing incidents inseparable from such affairs were also to be seen, one man insisting upon putting a life preserver upon his baby and pitching the little creature overboard, while another maintained his position upon a coil of rope, trying in clumsy fashion to adjust a life preserver, though the rope was wanted to make the boat fast until a courageous woman pushed him off, and threw the rope to Captain Barry, who was calling for it from the shore. Others were so excited that they did not know how to adjust a life preserver at all, making futile and laughable attempts until compelled to desist.[22]

No one was injured in the incident and all made it back to town, many on the undamaged *Favorite*, the steamer *Savage*, or one of the tugs, while others refused to travel by water and opted for some form of land transportation.

The *Van Raalte* was soon raised, repaired, and put back into service. In a goodwill gesture, the *Favorite*'s owners agreed to pay for the raising and repairs of the excursion boat. Several theories on the cause of the accident were put forward. One was that the big steamship with its deep draft struck a glancing blow on the channel bottom and swung into the *Van Raalte*. Another claimed that the *Favorite* was going too fast and the currents pushed her bow off course. Captain Majo and Engineer Brown received widespread praise for their composure and skill in handling the smaller vessel in the little time they had to make it to land and safety.

The *Favorite* enjoyed a short career of cross-lake runs. In 1890, she was sold to the Swain Wrecking Company of Cheboygan and modified to become a wrecking tug. Fire destroyed the vessel at St. Ignace in January 1907.

The eventful career of the *Van Raalte*'s captain, A. C. Majo—a well-seasoned mariner and long-time Muskegon resident—deserves a closer look. He began his sailing career on the lakes in 1863, but when he settled in Muskegon five years later, he intended to put his seafaring days behind him and take a landsman's job. However, he was hired by the Muskegon Booming Company and set to work on one of the tugs. Within three years, he was made captain of the *Miranda*—a Grand Haven tug temporarily chartered by the booming company—then the *Ezra Stevens*, and, finally, together with Jack Barry, the *Ira O. Smith*. When Majo left the booming company, he continued to work the Muskegon waterways for the next six years as master of the harbor tug *Newell Avery*. It was in this capacity that on that stormy October day in 1880 Captain Majo found himself heading up the rescue team for the stranded crewmen of the wrecked schooner *Granada* (See "A Tragic Homecoming: The Wreck of the *Granada*," in chapter 2 in this volume). In the years that followed, he spoke modestly of his heroic effort to save the ship's men. Later, Majo went into the excursion boat business, owning a share of the *Van Raalte* and another steamer, the *George P. Savage*. Although the *Van Raalte* was put back into service after the collision with the *Favorite*, the incident soured many on traveling aboard local excursion boats, and the business suffered. Majo sold his interest in the vessel, bought out his partners on the ownership of the *Savage*, and sailed his vessel to Duluth, then at the height of its lumber and mining boom, where he continued his maritime career.[23]

Sailing Blind: The Wreck of the *Wabash Valley*

Just as the schooners often faced disaster on stormy Lake Michigan waters, a number of steamships also fell victim to nature's wrath. One of the early steamers owned by Goodrich, the *Wabash Valley*, met her end along Muskegon's shoreline on November 22,

CHAPTER 3

1860. The wooden propeller was only four years old when Goodrich purchased her in May of that year for $19,000. Built in Buffalo, the 592 tons burden vessel was set on a route between Manitowoc and ports around Green Bay.

Late in fall 1860, Goodrich leased the *Wabash Valley* to the Detroit, Grand Haven and Milwaukee Railroad as a temporary replacement for one of the railroad's steamships. Under the command of Captain Sanford "Shanty" Morgan, the *Wabash Valley* left Milwaukee for Grand Haven on the night of November 21—her first trip for the DGH&M line. While the cross-lake trip was made in good weather, an early-winter storm moved in as the lights on the west Michigan shore appeared. But something was not quite right. The lighthouse beacon the captain saw did not flash like the Grand Haven light, but shone a steady beam. The *Wabash Valley* was off Muskegon harbor, not Grand Haven. The placement of the range lights on the Muskegon shore added to the confusion since the pattern was very similar to that at the Grand Haven channel. About 3:00 A.M., as the vessel approached the harbor, the snow-laden storm swept the eastern shore, bringing zero visibility and heavy seas. In the whiteout, the channel was lost to view and the pounding surf drove the ship onto the beach, where she broke in two. All onboard disembarked safely—including Captain Albert E. Goodrich himself, who was one of the thirty-six passengers. While the *Wabash Valley* lay broken and beyond repair, her furniture and cargo were salvaged, and later the boilers and other machinery were removed from the wreck and installed on a new Goodrich vessel, *Sunbeam*. In spite of the loss of his ship, Captain Morgan remained in favor with his employer. He commanded other Goodrich steamers and served for many years with distinction.[24]

Lost to the Depths: The Wreck of the *Alpena*

While the wreck of the *Wabash Valley* was unfortunate, a far worse catastrophe would befall Goodrich twenty years later. The loss of the big side-wheel steamer *Alpena* in October 1880 proved to be one of the profound tragedies of Great Lakes history and hit the people of Muskegon, Grand Haven, and Chicago especially hard.

The 197-foot *Alpena*, built in 1856, was a 653 gross-ton vessel. She was a classic side-wheel steamer, with a single-cylinder vertical-beam engine that powered her immense 24-foot diameter paddle wheels. Bought by Goodrich for $80,000, the ship was put into service to replace the *Seabird*, which had been destroyed by fire off Waukegan in April 1868.[25] From 1870 on, the *Alpena* carried passengers and freight on a route from Chicago to Grand Haven and Muskegon. The ship had been rebuilt in 1876 and was considered in excellent condition.

In the late afternoon of Friday, October 15, 1880, an estimated seventy passengers boarded the *Alpena* at the Central Wharf in Muskegon. The weather was sunny and mild and the lake calm as the steamer, commanded by the highly respected Captain Nelson W. Napier, left the Port City and plied the twelve miles along the shore to Grand Haven. There she picked up a few more passengers and cargo, and at about 10:00 P.M. she

The side-wheel steamer *Alpena* at the Goodrich dock in Chicago ([P86–162] Muskegon County Museum).

sailed out into Lake Michigan, bound for Chicago. Three hours later, the *Alpena* passed another Goodrich steamer, the *Muskegon,* and the ships blew their whistles in greeting. The *Muskegon* arrived in Grand Haven on schedule; however, the *Alpena* never made it to Chicago harbor.

During the night a tremendous storm blew up over Lake Michigan, with blasts of freezing cold whipping the lake into a fury and creating havoc for the many vessels caught unprepared for violent wintery weather. The unrelenting winds, clocked in Grand Haven at 40–48 miles per hour but no doubt much higher on the open water, hammered the lake for several days—an intensity that, to many, was unprecedented. A telegram from Grand Haven reached Chicago with the following report on the severe weather:

> The sea was the roughest that the oldest inhabitant has ever seen here, and the wind has been of terrible force. At 3:30 P.M. Saturday the wind's velocity was forty-eight miles per hour from the southwest, and at no time during the day or night did it fall below thirty-five miles per hour. The average velocity from noon Saturday to noon Sunday was thirty-nine miles per hour. This is something never known here before. The wind has frequently reached higher velocities for a short time, but the average for twenty-four hours is frightful when it's known that the velocity on the lake is always greater than on land.[26]

The steamer *Muskegon* reached Grand Haven just before the gale hit. However, concern grew for the safety of the *Alpena* and two other Goodrich ships headed for Chicago— the *De Pere,* which had left Grand Haven, and the *Menominee,* en route from Milwaukee. Some relief came with the news that the *Menominee* had run before the storm and reached safety in Manitowoc. Later, on October 18, a telegram from an S. C. Glover, one of the *De Pere*'s passengers, reported that vessel had made it to Manistee.[27] But no good news arrived concerning the *Alpena.*

CHAPTER 3

One of the last people to see the *Alpena* as she labored in the huge seas was the captain of the schooner *S. A. Irish*. After weathering the storm at anchor outside the Chicago harbor, he brought his ship in, with her main sail and stay sail lost and part of her load of shingles washed into the lake. The captain gave the following account:

> The Alpena was bound from Grand Haven to Chicago. We (the *S. A. Irish*) were out from Grand Haven also. About 9 o'clock yesterday morning [October 16] we sighted the Alpena ten or eleven miles off Kenosha. The wind was blowing the worst gale I ever saw. A man couldn't stand up on deck a minute. The Alpena was tacking about some, but finally headed nearly in shore. We were within sight of her more than two hours. While we could see her she seemed to be doing as well as we were, and to be trying to get in under the shore. Since I have heard that she did not reach Chicago I don't know what to think of her chances.[28]

While some ships, like the *S. A. Irish,* were ravaged by the storm, they eventually made it to a safe port. A number of others, including the ill-fortuned schooner *Granada*, were broken up and wrecked along the shoreline, with the raging seas and bitter cold claiming the lives of many seamen.[29] The *Alpena*, however, was lost somewhere in the middle of Lake Michigan, with no survivors from among her seventy-three passengers and crew.[30]

Several days after the disaster, pieces of the lost steamer washed ashore between Holland and Grand Haven. Items with the *Alpena*'s name on them also were found on the beach, giving hard evidence of her fate. A few days after the ship went down, the bottom of a grape box was found floating along the shore just south of St. Joseph. Written on it were these sad and telling lines: "Whoever picks this up, remember the writer is only an orphan. I am happy and perfectly willing to die, for I have no one to care for me now, or cherish any memory when I am gone. At this time we all know our doom. The Alpena is very fast going to pieces. We know we can never reach land or ever see it again. Boat going to pieces. 11:20 (Signed) D. Caddie."[31] On the beach a short distance away, a shingle, rudely cut in the shape of a boat, was inscribed with these few words: "The Alpena is going to pieces. We will all be lost. Capt. Napier."[32] The handwriting was identified as that of the *Alpena*'s captain.

Captain Goodrich, his Chicago office besieged by grieving relatives, gave a Chicago reporter his thoughts on what might have happened to the steamer:

> We can theorize as much as we like and we may be very far from the facts. My idea is this: Capt. Napier has been on the lake a great many years. He was known as a man of great courage. He would never allow himself to be beaten—would never turn back in a gale. I think on the night of the storm his courage ran away with his judgment. He kept on his course too long, and when he did turn back, absolutely compelled by the fury of the storm, the steamer dropped into the trough of the sea. Her cargo shifted to leeward. One of her wheels got out of the water. Capt. Napier couldn't right her, and she hammered along until she went down. In such circumstances nothing could have withstood such a storm. She had about ten car loads of freight on board—eight of apples and two of shavings for stuffing mattresses. With so light a freight she was naturally high out of the water, and exposed to the force of the wind.[33]

Painting of the *Alpena* based on eyewitness description of the ship in the October 1880 storm ([P86–161] Muskegon County Museum).

Of all the passengers and crew, only six bodies were recovered. The exact location of the wreck, thought to lie about thirty miles off of Holland, has never been found.[34]

To those in the maritime community who knew him, Captain Nelson Napier was considered very lucky. He had taken to the life of a seaman at the young age of fifteen and had spent forty-five years as captain on lake boats. In all that time, he never lost one. For the ten years prior to the *Alpena* disaster Napier commanded vessels of the Goodrich line and had served as harbormaster in Chicago. The captain, sixty-seven years old when lost on the *Alpena,* left a wife and two young children at his home in St. Joseph. He was also father to three grown sons and a daughter from a previous marriage.

A coroner's jury held session early the next year. The verdict rendered on the loss of the *Alpena* stated that the ship was not seaworthy (this in light of her recent improvements), and the life preservers onboard were rotten and useless in an emergency. While Napier and the ship's engineer were well seasoned, the rest of her crew were new and inexperienced. Goodrich received strong criticism—even blame—for allowing the *Alpena* to sail under such conditions. Thus, when the jury concluded that the Goodrich Transportation Company was fully liable, the company halted its Muskegon-Chicago route for the 1881 season. That year, Muskegon merchants struggled with this inconvenience, relying on lumber schooners to transport their goods to market. However, much to the merchants' relief, Goodrich restored service the following spring with the *Menominee* and *De Pere*.

A Steamer for All Seasons: The *Alabama*

The success of the steel steamship *Virginia* encouraged Albert W. Goodrich, son of Captain Albert E. Goodrich and then president of the Goodrich Transportation Company, to build another passenger steamer that would join the *Virginia* on the same route, further capitalizing on the growing popularity of steamship travel to the cities and resorts around Lake Michigan.[35] However, while the *Virginia* and most other ships were laid up in port during the brutal winter months, the new ship would be built with ice-breaking capabilities so she could sail the lake year-round.

This new ship was the *Alabama*, built by the Manitowoc Shipbuilding Company and launched in December 1909. Like the *Virginia*, the ship was constructed of steel, but it featured a heavy hull, up to an inch thick at the bow and along the keel so that she could withstand possible damage from ice. The bow was filled with concrete, the weight of which increased her ice-crushing ability. In addition, she was given a double bottom and six watertight compartments. Safety was a priority, and Goodrich claimed the vessel was equipped with the best fire protection system of any steamer on the lakes. At 272 feet in length with a 45-foot beam and 14-foot draft, the *Alabama* boasted a triple-expansion steam engine and with 2,500 horsepower could maintain a cruising speed of 15 miles per hour.

The Goodrich Company spent $400,000 on the new steamer. Such expense was reflected not only in her extra strength but also in the luxurious furnishings expected on any ship of the Goodrich line. The main dining room, which could accommodate 125 persons per sitting, was enriched with mahogany and other inlaid woods. Numerous windows gave the passengers broad views of Lake Michigan, the passing shoreline, and ports of call. Passengers who booked some of the large, higher-priced cabins, called parlor rooms, enjoyed accommodations that featured a double bed, lounge chairs, a built-in sofa, and their own private bath.

When the *Alabama* first entered Muskegon harbor on June 30, 1910, crowds gathered at the dockside to view the elegant and powerful new steamer. That evening, the *Alabama* left on a run to Chicago. Between 1910 and 1917, the *Alabama* and *Virginia* jointly worked the Chicago-Grand Haven-Muskegon route during the regular season, with the *Alabama* continuing the schedule throughout the winter months. Not only did the western Michigan communities rely on her service for transporting passengers and freight, but the car ferries and other vessels also came to depend on her to help free them when they became trapped in the ice.

The *Alabama* faced her worst test in winter 1918, when frigid temperatures and strong winds created high windrows of ice along the Michigan shoreline. The ship, commanded by Captain Gerald Stufflebeam, left Chicago on January 12. The next day,

The *Alabama* leaving Muskegon Channel ([P83–490] Muskegon County Museum).

just off of Grand Haven, a raging blizzard blasted the lakeshore and a huge ice floe, driven in by the northwest winds, choked the entrance to the Grand Haven channel. The *Alabama* and Grand Trunk car ferries *Milwaukee* and *Grand Haven* were unable to make it to the safety of the harbor and became icebound in the field that formed offshore. The three vessels waited two weeks for a shift in the wind, which eased the ice and allowed them to enter Grand Haven. During the wait, some of the cargo destined for Grand Haven was unloaded and hauled to shore. The few passengers on the *Alabama* decided early on to jump ship. They struggled through blinding snow and high ridges of ice and, once ashore, took the Inter-Urban train to Muskegon. When the ship was finally free, Captain Stufflebeam briefly docked her in the nearby port but decided to continue on to Muskegon, thinking the ice conditions there would be less severe than those in Grand Haven.

He soon regretted his decision. Muskegon Lake was frozen over with ice fourteen inches thick—so thick that the staunch *Alabama* became trapped at the western end, five miles from the Goodrich dock. In her struggle through the frozen lake the vessel broke a propeller blade; then when trying to back up she damaged her rudder and steering engine. The Goodrich office in Grand Haven was called and a tug was sent up to try to free the steamer. But the tug's attempts to reach the ship were thwarted by the ice. The decision was made to let the *Alabama* lay up as she was in Muskegon's harbor until spring.

In the meantime, the ship's cargo, which consisted of hundreds of tons of groceries and other goods, including three tons of sugar, could not wait several months to get to market. It was winter, but it was also wartime and such necessities were needed by the people of Muskegon and Grand Rapids. As in Grand Haven, arrangements were made to offload the cargo from the ship and transport it by two-horse sleighs to the shore. From

CHAPTER 3

Main cabin of the *Alabama,* looking toward the dining room ([P83–381] Muskegon County Museum).

there, the goods were loaded onto a train of the Inter-Urban Line and delivered to stores in Muskegon and the other communities.

Another commodity the *Alabama* carried was coal for her steam engines. However, it did no good on the ship immobilized by the ice. Enough coal was kept onboard to maintain her boilers, but the bulk of it was given over to the people of Muskegon, who were suffering from a severe coal shortage in those winter months.

By mid-February Lake Michigan was frozen all the way across, and all shipping came to a standstill. The *Alabama*'s crew was paid off for the rest of the winter. Finally, on March 17, conditions improved enough for the Goodrich steamship *Georgia* to enter Muskegon with a load of coal for the *Alabama*. While the trapped vessel built up steam, her reassembled crew chopped through the ice and managed to free her, their efforts witnessed by about four hundred locals who ventured out onto the frozen lake. She finally headed out of Muskegon and made her way to Manitowoc for repairs. It wasn't long before she was back on her regular Lake Michigan run.

The *Georgia* works to free the *Alabama*, icebound on Muskegon Lake ([PD231] Muskegon County Museum).

The *Alabama*'s battles with severe ice pack picked up again during winter 1924, which brought blizzards and sub-zero temperatures to the Great Lakes. Another steamship, the *Sheboygan*, also suffered troubles in the frozen waters around Muskegon on her first visit to the port, filling in for the steamer *Georgia*. The *Georgia*, owned by Goodrich, had been chartered by the Crosby Transportation Company to provide service between Muskegon and Milwaukee. However, an accident laid her up and Crosby then enlisted the Hill Transportation Company's *Sheboygan* to replace her.

On January 19, the *Alabama* headed out of Muskegon harbor for Chicago. A short distance from the mouth of the channel, her passage was blocked by floes and huge icebergs nearly as high as the south pier's lighthouse. The ship waited sixteen hours before managing to proceed up the lake, only to be caught in ice off Grand Haven as a blizzard struck the region. The weather created misery for other vessels: the steamer *Missouri* was trapped near Holland, and the *Sheboygan* spent twelve hours struggling through ice-covered Lake Michigan from Milwaukee. The *Sheboygan* entered the harbor only to be held fast in Muskegon Lake's thick ice, still a good distance from the Crosby dock. Her cargo was offloaded and transported to shore by truck. By the night of January 23, the winds shifted and loosened the ice, freeing all three vessels to continue to their destinations.

A second blizzard struck Lake Michigan on January 25, paralyzing Muskegon and other shoreline communities. When the storm abated on the twenty-eighth, rail and shipping traffic resumed. The *Sheboygan*, with a crew of thirty-seven, left the Crosby dock about noon and set out for Milwaukee. But as she cracked a path through the ice, her rudder broke, leaving the vessel stranded in the frozen wilderness two miles from the channel, a potential victim of the drifting ice field. Her distress signal—four long blasts of her whistle—was heard by Captain Stufflebeam while aboard the *Alabama* on Muskegon Lake as his ship headed for the Goodrich dock. He immediately ordered his vessel turned around and set out to the rescue, unaware of the exact danger faced by the crippled ship (the *Sheboygan* did not have a wireless). When the *Alabama* reached her, Stufflebeam ordered his vessel about, the crew threw several lines to the *Sheboygan,* and as hundreds of people onshore braved the cold to watch, the Goodrich ship towed the disabled steamer back to the channel. The *Sheboygan* was temporarily handed over to the Coast Guard until the Crosby Company could decide how to handle the situation.

Winter 1925 also proved to be a brutal one for the *Alabama* and other vessels. On January 18 the steamer, two car ferries, and a fishing tug were held fast off the entrance to Muskegon harbor in exceptionally thick ice. (See appendix G for one passenger's story of a late winter voyage on the *Alabama.*)

Despite these icebound trials, between 1910 and 1932 the *Alabama* enjoyed a successful career under Goodrich ownership as the flagship of the line. Her reliable service was a boon to Muskegon shipping interests. In addition, a favorite summer excursion for Muskegonites was the "loop the loop"—cruising down to Grand Haven on the *Alabama,* then returning to Muskegon on the Inter-Urban rail line. But when the Depression hit, the Goodrich Transit Company[36] went bankrupt and was forced to sell off its fleet of passenger steamers to other operators. The Gartland and Sullivan Steamship Company acquired the *Alabama,* and during summer 1933 the ship was back on her traditional Chicago-Grand Haven-Muskegon route. However, in the following year she was transferred to Lake Superior. As time went on, the aging steamer passed through a number of owners on the Great Lakes until she was finally laid up in Holland, Michigan—virtually abandoned for thirteen years. The late 1960s found her converted to a tow barge for a Bay City construction company.

While the *Alabama* was being stripped of all the elegant interior furnishings in preparation for her new, less prestigious job, an admirer of her fine woodwork salvaged the lovely inlaid-wood mural in the ship's "social hall" depicting an Alabama cotton field. This piece is now on permanent display at the Holland Museum.

The story of the *Alabama* cannot be fully told without further mention of her captain of eleven years, Gerald Stufflebeam. "Jerry" Stufflebeam's destined career was almost a given; he was brought up on Lake Michigan, with his father, an uncle, and other family members serving as lake captains. At age eighteen, he took a job as cabin watch on the *Pere Marquette No. 4* car ferry at Ludington. When only twenty-four, he became the master of the steamer *City of Kalamazoo,* distinguishing himself as the youngest captain on the Great Lakes at the time.[37] But within a year he had moved on, going back to the Pere Marquette car ferry line, this time as captain of several of the ferries. Later, he took command of several Goodrich steamers: the *Iowa, Indiana, Nevada,* and *Alabama.*

The *Alabama*'s captain, Gerald Stufflebeam ([66–102B] Muskegon County Museum).

The *Iowa* had an interesting history. When the old Goodrich steamer *Menominee* was about to be scrapped, her hull was found to be in excellent condition and Goodrich decided to use it in the construction of a new ship. She would not be able to compete in strength with the steel-hull steamers like the *Virginia* and *Alabama,* but the wooden vessel was given a reinforced bow and was fitted with sheet iron, which covered her hull up to six feet above the waterline. These improvements would help her handle the winter ice. Built in 1896, the *Iowa* had a number of troubles plague her over the years— including groundings and collisions—and she gained a reputation as a jinxed ship. The many captains who served on her testified to her difficult temperament. However, she was a popular ship among lake travelers and made good money for the Goodrich line during her nineteen-year career.

One major incident in Captain Stufflebeam's career occurred during the severe winter of 1914–15, while he was master of the *Iowa*. The *Iowa* had left Racine late in the evening of February 3, 1915, en route to Chicago. Although conditions were hazy, the vessel steamed through open water, only to encounter a thick field of ice that extended far off of Chicago's harbor. Stufflebeam kept his ship in the open water until daybreak. Another steamer, the steel-hulled *Racine* of the Chicago, Racine and Milwaukee Line, came by and the two ships looked for the best passage through the ice pack. Earlier the

CHAPTER 3

Alabama had cut a path through the ice, and although the water had frozen over since, the way seemed navigable. With the *Racine* in the lead, the two vessels ploughed through the ice toward the harbor.

Progress was slow but steady. However, at about 10:00, the wind increased and the ice started to "run," trapping both ships. The pressure from tons of ice slowly crushed the wooden *Iowa*, prying her pilothouse and hurricane deck two feet from the hull. At 10:10, Stufflebeam sent an urgent last message on the *Iowa*'s wireless: "Send tug at once. Fast in ice. Ice running. Starboard forward gangway planking struck loose. Leaking badly. *Racine* stuck ahead."[38] When he stepped onto the ice to inspect the damage, he could see the steamer was mortally wounded and ordered all onboard to abandon ship. By 11:00, all had gathered on the ice to watch as the *Iowa*'s hull heeled over and sank, leaving parts of her hurricane deck and pilothouse strewn on the frozen lake surface. Stufflebeam led the solo passenger and crew of seventy safely to shore four miles away. As they trekked across the ice, they occasionally had to jump over open water between ice floes.[39]

In 1917 Stufflebeam took command of the *Alabama* and, over the next eleven years, became closely identified with his ship. He later estimated that he made 2,400 round-trips from Muskegon to Chicago. For many years he called Muskegon home, but in 1928, as the new superintendent of the state car ferry fleet up at the Straits of Mackinac, he resettled in St. Ignace. Still, with this and other career moves that kept him up north, he stayed in contact with a number of friends in Muskegon.

Captain Stufflebeam was only fifty-two when he died on September 17, 1938, at Sault Ste. Marie while he was on a brief salvage assignment. His body was found in the St. Mary's River. An inquest ruled his death accidental.[40]

The sudden death of the popular lake captain came as a blow to the people of Muskegon. Many remembered him as an amiable man who stood on the dock, greeting passengers as they boarded his ship. Once the steamer was en route, he would stroll the deck and stop to talk with some of the regular passengers with whom he was acquainted. The captain was known as an excellent conversationalist and storyteller. The *Chronicle* described Stufflebeam's influential and popular career and his warm relationship with Muskegon lake travelers:

> There was no more able seaman on the Great Lakes and yet Jerry was more than the captain of the ship. Almost every passenger who made the trip across the lake came to know Jerry personally. He always had a smile and a word of greeting, and he contributed much to the success of the Goodrich line.
>
> Daily hundreds went to the Goodrich dock to await the arrival of friends or relatives or just to see the boat dock. The figure of Jerry standing on the bridge became a familiar figure through the years.[41]

Up Against the Big Guns: The *Charles H. Hackley*

It was tough for smaller steamship lines to compete with the powerful Goodrich fleet and its only other major rival, the Crosby Line. Goodrich eliminated one such contender when it purchased the steamer *Charles H. Hackley* from the Hackley Transportation Company in 1906 and renamed her the *Carolina* in keeping with the tradition of naming the fleet's ships for various southern states. The story of the *Charles H. Hackley/Carolina* illustrates the tooth-and-nail competition facing ship owners, especially those of the less prestigious lines.

The *Hackley* was built in Philadelphia in 1892 for the Hartford and New York Transportation Company and christened the *Hartford*. She was 220 feet long with a beam of 34 feet, and depth of 11 feet. Powered by twin compound engines, the steel ship of 1,304 tons had a cruising speed of nearly 15 miles per hour. Her early years were spent on the East Coast, carrying passengers and freight between Hartford, Connecticut, and New York City. But in 1898, during the Spanish-American War, the *Hartford* was taken over by the Quartermaster's Department of the United States and renamed the USQMD *Terry*.

After the war, the *Terry* was decommissioned and laid up in a southern port. Captain Miles E. Barry of Chicago found her thus and, along with lumberman Charles Hackley and another Muskegon businessman, purchased her at auction for $19,600 for service on the Great Lakes. The ship was given back her original name *Hartford* for the voyage north and, under the command of Captain Barry, headed up the coast. The trip was an eventful one. At Montreal, the ship suffered a boiler failure. Then, while en route through the St. Lawrence River, the *Hartford* struck a Grand Trunk Railroad bridge in the Welland Canal. The mishap caused considerable damage to the bridge, and Canadian authorities demanded that Barry pay a heavy fine to cover repair costs. The feisty captain, however, refused to pay up and quickly headed for American waters with the Canadian revenue cutter *Petrel* on his tail. He managed to elude the cutter and continued on to Muskegon, arriving on September 14, 1901.

That day, hundreds of Muskegonites gathered at the dock site by the old Hackley and Hume mill and were given a chance to tour the newcomer. They approved of the spacious accommodations—44 state rooms with 160 berths. A *Chronicle* reporter praised the ship's streamlined looks: "In exterior appearance the boat is trim and sharp and seems capable of speed so far as one may judge from the hull. Her nose is long and the boat sets with birdlike lightness on the water. Her lines are graceful."[42] While in Muskegon the steamship was renamed the *Charles H. Hackley*, with Miss Kate B. Lee, daughter of Captain Seth Lee, having the honor of christening the steamer with the new name. The following day the *Hackley* made her first trip to Chicago, where she came under the ownership of the Chicago and Muskegon Transportation Company, of which Barry was president.

A brief background needs to be given on Miles E. Barry and his two brothers. The Barry brothers had strong ties to Muskegon. After working in the lumber trade in northern Michigan, they built up a fleet of three or four tugs and established themselves in Chicago's busy harbor. Later, the brothers relocated to Muskegon and set up their business near the channel. For a number of years their tugs *Getty* and *Commodore Jack Barry* (reportedly the fastest tug on Muskegon Lake) towed the lumber schooners to and from the local mills. In 1900, as the schooner heyday was ending, the Barry brothers set

CHAPTER 3

The steamer *Charles H. Hackley* flying pennants with her new name and her former name, *Hartford* (Courtesy of Hackley Public Library).

their sights on larger vessels when local merchants protested the freight rates imposed by the Goodrich Company and offered to provide the brothers financial backing if they could start a competing line of steamships. They started with two small steamers—the *Pere Marquette No. 1* and *Mabel Bradshaw*—but soon acquired larger vessels.

Along with another Barry-owned steamer, the *Alice Stafford*, the *Charles H. Hackley* maintained a regular schedule of passenger and freight service to the ports of Chicago, Grand Haven, and Muskegon from 1902 to 1904. Competition between the Barry and Goodrich lines was lively at best, fierce at worst. Time and again, Goodrich lowered its rates until Barry could no longer compete. In addition, the Pere Marquette Railroad line was contracted to service the Goodrich fleet but refused to deliver freight to the Barry ships. The pressure finally forced Captain Barry to sell both vessels. The *Stafford* was taken over by the J. O. Nessen Company of Manistee, and the *Hackley* was bought by Thomas Hume of Muskegon's Hackley and Hume firm on April 21, 1905. Hackley and Hume were simply protecting their interests since the company had heavily invested in the Barry Line. With the one ship, the Hackley and Hume Company formed the Hackley Transportation Company, setting themselves up in direct competition with Goodrich. Like the Barry line, the Hackley Transportation Company found it was a poor match for its well-established shipping rival.

On March 18, 1906, the Goodrich steamer *Atlanta* caught fire and was burned beyond repair off Port Washington, Wisconsin. Goodrich needed to find another ship immediately to replace the *Atlanta* and approached Hackley, offering to buy the *Charles H.*

Hackley. A deal was quickly struck, and by the end of March the *Hackley* was added to the Goodrich fleet and given the name *Carolina*. Her route remained the same, with Whitehall added to the summer itinerary. Thus ended Charles Hackley's venture in the passenger steamship business. The *Carolina* remained in the Goodrich fleet until the company closed during the Depression years. In 1938, the vessel was cut down to a barge.

Interestingly, the *Charles H. Hackley* and the *Atlanta* had developed a sporting rivalry, the captains and crews engaging the boats in races between Grand Haven and Muskegon. The two ships would usually meet in Grand Haven and the men would make bets on which one would first reach Muskegon. The competition grew so intense that finally government inspectors stepped in to end it.

"Carelessness Becomes a Mortgage to Danger": The Wreck of the Steam Barge *Milwaukee*

At 8:00 on the morning of July 9, 1886, the propeller *Michael Groh* arrived in Muskegon with disturbing news. On the run from Chicago, the *Groh* encountered a field of debris—two water tanks, a ship's hurricane deck painted a rust red, a stove pipe, a small ventilator, and a flagpole—floating in the heavily traveled shipping lane. The *Groh's* captain identified the wreckage as belonging to the steam barge *Milwaukee,* a vessel engaged in the lumber trade and a familiar sight along the docks of Muskegon. A short time later that morning, another vessel, the propeller *Berrien,* came into port with a ladder picked up at the same wreck site. A number of vesselmen who were well acquainted with the *Milwaukee* positively identified the ladder as belonging to that ship.

The *Milwaukee's* owner, Muskegon's mayor Lyman G. Mason, had received a telegram from the ship's captain, William Armstrong, at 3:56 P.M. just the previous day, reading, "Milwaukee will be there tomorrow." However, as other steam barges that had left Chicago at the same time as the *Milwaukee* came into port on time, it became clear the missing ship had gone down. Two local tugs—the *North Muskegon* and *Commodore Jack Barry*—steamed out onto Lake Michigan to search for more evidence and possibly some survivors. They later returned, their mission unsuccessful.

The news quickly circulated, becoming the main topic of discussion on the dusty street corners around the city. Theories were bandied about as to what might have happened on the calm Lake Michigan waters. Perhaps a boiler on the ship had exploded, or she had sunk in a collision with another vessel. Sailors who had just returned from a Chicago-Muskegon run reported smoky and foggy conditions on the lake. Michigan had been plagued by drought that summer and forest fires had blackened large tracts of land along the western side of the state. The smoke from these fires drifted across Lake Michigan and made sailing hazardous due to low visibility. For vessels caught in dense smoke or fog, the best recourse was to either drop anchor and wait for conditions to clear or proceed with caution, with their whistles constantly sounding their presence to other ships.

CHAPTER 3

The *Charles H. Hackley* in the lead, racing the *Atlanta* from Grand Haven to Muskegon ([P86–164] Muskegon County Museum).

However, any theory that was suggested held no comfort for the relatives of the missing crewmen. Families and friends of the *Milwaukee*'s engineer, Alfred Green, her cook, Samuel Mullen, and a number of others whose homes were in Muskegon anxiously waited for further word of the ship's fate and especially the fate of their loved ones. Finally, a telegram reached Mayor Mason about 3:00 that afternoon:

Chicago, July 9
   The steam barge "Milwaukee" sunk by a collision with the steam barge "Hickox" last night when about thirty miles off the vicinity of Saugatuck. One man was lost but the balance of the crew was saved and brought here on the propeller "Hickox," signed, William Armstrong, Capt.[43]

The details could wait. Knowing that the captain and most of the crew of fourteen were safe brought relief to the city.

The *Milwaukee* had started her career as a freight and passenger steamer. Built in Ogdensburg, New York, in 1868 and measuring 135.5 feet in length with a 26-foot beam, the vessel was part of a sizable fleet of thirty-two steamers and three tow barges belonging to the Northern Transportation Company. The *Milwaukee*, along with her fleet mates, sailed a lengthy route, connecting Ogdensburg with the cities of Chicago and Milwaukee as well as other ports along the way. When the shipping firm went out of business in 1881, the vessels of the line—at the time numbering fourteen steamers and three barges—were dispersed to various owners. All but two of the remaining steamers,

The steam barge *Milwaukee* (from the Great Lakes Marine Collection of the Milwaukee Public Library/Wisconsin Marine Historical Society).

including the *Milwaukee*, were cut down to steam barges.[44] The *Milwaukee* was acquired by Lyman Mason, one of Muskegon's early lumber barons and then mayor (for the year 1886). The winter before she was lost, the steam barge had been taken to Grand Haven to be completely overhauled and refitted. She was considered "in first class trim and condition throughout" and was valued at $10,000.[45] However, the vessel was sailing under the shadow of a lawsuit. Several years before her loss, the *Milwaukee* had struck the new breakwater as she left Chicago's harbor, causing some damage to the breakwater. The government was seeking compensation for the repair work and had brought a lawsuit against the ship's owners.

Along with the *Milwaukee*, the other steam barge involved in the accident, the *C. Hickox*, called Muskegon home. She was jointly owned by the lumber firm of A. V. Mann and her captain, Simon O'Day. Built in 1873 at Black River (Lorain), Ohio, the wooden-hulled *Hickox* measured 130.5 feet long, with a beam of 24.6 feet. Cleveland was her original home port, but she relocated to Muskegon in 1884 to work as a lumber hooker at the height of the boom years.

CHAPTER 3

On July 6, the *Milwaukee* was loaded with lumber at the Petries and Company's dock in North Muskegon and steamed out on a run to Chicago. With the cargo unloaded, Captain Armstrong sent word to Mayor Mason on July 8 that he was heading back to Muskegon. If all went well, he would enter the port the following day, his vessel light and ready for another load.

About 7:00 P.M. on the eighth, the *C. Hickox*, under the command of Captain O'Day, left Muskegon fully loaded with 250,000 feet of lumber for a trip to Chicago. In tow behind the steam barge was the schooner *Apprentice Boy*, also lumber laden, which had sprung a minor leak just as the ships were leaving port. The *Hickox* maintained a moderate speed to accommodate the schooner. The paths of the two lumber steamers were set to cross somewhere in mid-lake late that evening.

As the midnight hour approached, the lookout on the *Milwaukee* sighted the masthead light of a steamship directly in line with their path. He alerted Captain Armstrong, who immediately ordered the wheel turned hard to starboard. At about the same time onboard the *Hickox*, Captain O'Day sighted the other ship's light and issued the order to turn to port. As the ships took measures to avoid a collision, a bank of fog or smoke drifted across the lake's surface, enshrouding both ships and obscuring them from each other. Armstrong stood in the pilothouse, his watchman, Dennis Harrington, near at hand, both trying to discern the other ship's position. Suddenly, out of the haze immediately off the starboard bow, the *Hickox*'s masthead light broke through. At that very moment, the green light from the *Milwaukee*'s starboard side was sighted by O'Day. Both captains shouted orders: "Hard a'starboard!" cried Armstrong to his wheelsman while he yanked the whistle cord twice to warn the other ship of the direction he was taking. O'Day shouted, "Hard a'port!" to the *Hickox*'s wheelsman. His effort to sound the ship's whistle failed when the cord snapped as he tugged it. Their desperate actions came too late, as the *Hickox* ploughed into the side of the *Milwaukee*, striking her just abaft of the forerigging, rolling her far onto her port side. Moments later, she disengaged herself and disappeared into the murky atmosphere.

Near panic gripped the crew onboard the stricken *Milwaukee*. The ship's engineer, Alfred Green, ran to the after hatch and, seeing water pouring into the hold, alerted the captain. One of the firemen emerged from the hold with word that the rush of water had already extinguished the fires. Fearing their vessel would capsize at any moment, a number of crewmen made a run for the lifeboats. The thick haze intensified their fears; when they could not see the other ship, they thought she had left the scene and would not return to rescue them. Armstrong acted quickly to rally his men and immediately set them to pump out the hold while he examined the damage. The collision had smashed a large hole in the side of the ship and it was clear that she would go down in very short time. With all hands working to stave off the inevitable sinking, he hurried to the pilothouse and desperately blew the whistle, sending a distress call into the darkness.

After the *Hickox* disengaged and drifted away, O'Day had her checked for damage. With relief, he learned that although her stem was damaged, she was still seaworthy—no leaks or damage to her hull were found. The towline to the *Apprentice Boy* had parted during the accident, but the *Hickox* located the schooner and again took her in tow. As he ordered the wheelsman to continue on course to Chicago, he heard the *Milwaukee*'s distress signals:

> When I found out that we were not leaking, I turned to the wheelman and ordered him to square the vessel away for Chicago. Hardly had the order left my lips when four long whistles, the lake signal of distress, came from the direction of the Milwaukee. I strained my eyes to catch a glimpse of her lights, but the fog was so dense that it was impossible to see anything more than a few yards distant. Then I checked the Hickox's speed and answered the distress whistles. They were repeated again and again, and answered by me each time. I worked the boat carefully in the direction from which they seemed to come, but, strange to say, fully three-quarters of an hour elapsed before I sighted her masthead light. Then I saw a boat lowered from her side, and it bore down on me. There were four men in it, and they notified me of the Milwaukee's predicament. I ran the Hickox alongside of the sinking steamer, but not without considerable trouble, and in a short time all of her crew, with the exception of Harrington, were standing safely upon the deck-load of my vessel.[46]

Dennis Harrington, the *Milwaukee*'s watchman, had left the pilothouse just before the ship was struck and had rushed to the leeward side. It was believed that he was knocked overboard by the shock of the collision and lost in the dark water. However, the *Chicago Times* reported that Harrington was seen on the deck talking with the captain some time after the collision. Yet, when the *Milwaukee*'s men had assembled onboard the *Hickox*, Harrington was not among them.[47] His loss remained a mystery.

The crews of both vessels worked hard to save the *Milwaukee*. They cut a sail from her mast, hung it over the hole and fastened it securely under the hull to make what sailors call a "canvas jacket." This had little effect in maintaining the ship's stability. They also stuffed mattresses and bedding from the *Hickox* into the hold, but the water continued to flow in unabated.

Another vessel, the steam barge *City of New York*, had also heard the *Milwaukee*'s distress signals and responded. It was believed that the sinking steamer could still be saved if she could be towed to a port. Before abandoning their ship, the *Milwaukee*'s crew had attached a line thrown from the *Hickox* to a tow post forward. A second line was run to the *City of New York*. But the water-filled hull, slowing rolling from side to side, started to settle. As soon as the would-be rescuers realized it was too late to save her, the lines were cut and the *Milwaukee* allowed to sink stern first into the depths of Lake Michigan. The other two vessels, with the schooner in tow, continued on their way to Chicago. As soon as the *Hickox* docked, Captains Armstrong and O'Day headed for the office of the government steamboat inspectors to report the loss of the *Milwaukee*.

Testimony was provided by the captains and crews of the vessels in an effort to determine who, if anyone, was to blame. O'Day and crewmen from both ships considered the incident an accident: It was "one of those accidents that the best seamen are liable to meet with at any time, and which the most careful attention to the laws of navigation is unable to obviate."⁴⁸ While O'Day believed no one was to blame, he admitted there must have been a misunderstanding on the part of the *Milwaukee*'s helmsman on the proper way to pass another vessel:

> As we drew near, the Milwaukee put her wheel to starboard, and the Hickox ported hers, my intention being to pass to the right or port side as is customary in such cases. Then I heard the whistle of the Milwaukee sound twice, the signal that she intended to pass to starboard, and I jumped to blow my whistle in answer, but the rope parted and I was unable to warn the Milwaukee that I was porting my wheel, and immediately afterward the collision came, the Hickox striking the Milwaukee on her starboard side, just aft of her forward hatch.⁴⁹

For his part, Captain Armstrong stated that he originally turned his ship to port, but when he lost sight of the other ship's red (port) light, he put his wheel hard to starboard and blew his whistle twice. It was reported, too, that he had told O'Day he had turned the rudder to starboard "because she steered better under a starboard pressure than she did under port."⁵⁰

A reporter for the *Chicago Tribune* had harsh words for the masters of the two steam barges. In "Sunk in Midlake," he blames both captains, especially Armstrong, for the accident: "From their own statements it is plain that the disaster was the result of carelessness on the part of both Captains and the unskillful handling of his boat by the Captain of the Milwaukee."⁵¹ In his opinion, both skippers, upon sighting the lights of the oncoming ship, should have ordered their engines reversed. They could have avoided a collision, or if they had hit, the blow would not have caused such great damage.

A writer for the *Muskegon Daily Chronicle* also weighed in with a commentary that was critical of what he believed was a lack of caution exercised by those onboard the ships, especially with all the safeguards they had available to them:

> The loss of the Milwaukee, as usual carries its lesson, and one too apt to be forgotten. Without at present blaming the officers of either of these boats which collided in mid lake, it is evident that somebody blundered or that greater care is necessary. Though the smoke lay heavily upon the waters, these barges have steam whistles, bells, and other appliances for guarding against collisions, and a proper and careful use of the same should be sufficient. On the route to Chicago are always a large number coming and going, and carelessness becomes a mortgage to danger which may be foreclosed at any time. Even when seas run high a steam whistle can be heard and its guarantee of safety should not be overlooked or neglected. In this case valuable human lives were saved, and that is well, but the next time it may be that human beings, as well as wood and iron may go down into the deep waters.⁵²

The *C. Hickox* sailed for the next twenty years. Details on her career are not well-known, although it is recorded that she was sold to Canadian interests in June 1906. On December 4, 1906, while bound from Oswego, New York, to Belleville, Ontario, with a load of coal, she caught fire and burned. Although the vessel was a total loss, all onboard were saved.

Trials by Fire: The *Naomi* and the *Nyack*

Like the Goodrich fleet, the popular ships of the Crosby line provided the people of Muskegon with fast transport and comfortable accommodations on their trips across Lake Michigan. However, as with Goodrich, Crosby had its share of troubles and losses.

On May 21, 1907, the *Naomi*, commanded by Captain Thomas Trail, was steaming for Milwaukee with fifty-six passengers onboard. At 1:10 A.M., about thirty miles out from Grand Haven, a blaze broke out belowdecks near the bow. Highly flammable freight, including cartons of matches, caused the fire to spread quickly and black smoke billowed throughout the ship. When the fire alarm rang out the crewmen responded within minutes, but they soon realized the intense blaze could not be fully contained; instead, they did what they could to slow the spread of the flames. The passengers were awakened at once and escorted to the upper deck, where they were helped into the ship's lifeboats. The operation ran fairly smoothly, the captain and crew working with coolheaded efficiency and the passengers, although frightened, showing little panic.

The flames from the *Naomi* lit the sky and attracted a number of vessels in the vicinity. The bulk freighters *C. B. Kerr* and *Saxona,* as well as another Crosby steamer, *Kansas,* quickly reached the stricken vessel and picked up the passengers in the lifeboats. All were transferred to the *Kansas.* The *Kerr*'s captain then directed his vessel to approach the stern of the *Naomi,* where some the crew and passengers had crowded, awaiting rescue from the encroaching flames and suffocating smoke. The two ships made contact, and with the intense heat scorching the freighter's bow, those on the *Naomi* jumped to the *Kerr.* Only minutes later, the *Naomi* was completely ablaze.

Not all onboard the doomed steamer made it to safety. Four crewmen who were belowdecks became trapped and died in the flames. Three perished while fighting the blaze; one, apparently overcome by smoke and fumes while he slept, was found in his bunk. One of the passengers, James M. Rhoades of Detroit, delayed leaving his cabin and found himself trapped. The ship's purser sought him out and dragged him from the burning room. Suffering from severe burns, Rhoades was later taken to Butterworth Hospital in Grand Rapids where he died. Witnesses concurred that the calm waters of the lake and the crew's effective handling of the crisis kept the number of casualties low. (See appendix H for the account of *Naomi* survivor Guy E. Jones.)

Captain Trail was the last to leave his steamer, taken off by the *Kerr* in the daring bow-to-stern rescue. While the passengers and crew boarded the *Kansas,* Trail, along with Chief Engineer Barney Hopkins, stayed aboard the *Kerr* and directed the efforts of salvaging the vessel.

The *Kansas* arrived in Grand Haven about 6:15 A.M. Later that morning, the charred hull of the *Naomi,* still wreathed in smoke, was towed into port. Once the fire was out the bodies of the four deckhands were recovered. The ship was soon taken to Manitowoc,

CHAPTER 3

Crosby steamer *Naomi* ([66–157] Muskegon County Museum).

where she was completely rebuilt and fitted out with elegant furnishings at the cost of $200,000. Several years later, she was renamed the *E. G. Crosby*.

When the United States entered World War I, the *E. G. Crosby* was enlisted for war duty by the United States Shipping Board. After the war, she returned to the lakes under a different name and with new ownership. In 1922 the Crosby Line bought an oceangoing excursion steamer, the *City of Miami*, renamed her the *E. G. Crosby*, and set her on the Muskegon-Milwaukee route. Eight years later, the second *E. G. Crosby* was taken out of service to be replaced by the *Illinois*.

Fire also claimed another popular Crosby ship. On December 30, 1915, while tied up for the winter at her dock in Muskegon, the *Nyack* caught fire. The blaze broke out amidships about 4:00 A.M. shortly after the night watchman had gone off duty. Coal in the bunkers and hold fed the flames and a strong wind fanned them into an inferno. Firefighters on the scene had to direct their hoses not only to the burning vessel but also to the dock, which was threatened by the windblown sparks and intense heat. Only late in the day did they get the blaze under control, but by then the wooden-hulled boat was a smoldering shell. While no one was injured, the *Nyack* was a total loss.

The burning of the *Naomi*, sketched by artist C. T. Fairbanks from aboard the *Kansas* (courtesy of *Muskegon Chronicle*).

"They Will Probably Send Me to Hell": The Wreck of the *Muskegon*

In purchasing the side-wheel steamer *City of Holland* in 1916, the Crosby line took ownership of one of the most elegant passenger vessels on the lakes. Designed by famed ship architect Frank E. Kirby, she was built in 1881 in Wyandotte by the Detroit Dry Dock Company and christened the *City of Milwaukee*. A wooden-hulled ship of 1148 gross tons, she measured 230 feet in length with a beam of 33 feet and depth of 12 feet. Passengers were treated to a luxurious saloon, the floor covered with thick carpeting, and furniture fashioned of black walnut and cushioned with deep red, plush upholstery. A floor-to-ceiling mirror hung at one end of the room, and the other end opened up to form a rotunda with a grand piano. Fanciful painted designs adorned the doors and

CHAPTER 3

The burned-out *Nyack* at the Crosby dock in Muskegon ([P83–390] Muskegon County Museum).

paneling throughout the ship. Goodrich originally owned the ship, but after only two years he chartered then sold her to the Detroit, Grand Haven and Milwaukee Railroad Company. In 1906, the Graham and Morton Line took ownership and changed her name to the *City of Holland*.

However, by the time the Crosby line added the vessel to its popular fleet and later gave her the name *Muskegon*,[53] the ship had gained a reputation not only for elegance but also misfortune. A number of troubles plagued her over the years, from mechanical problems to damaged paddle wheels, that would delay her arrival into port. The ongoing list of problems convinced many that the ship was jinxed. One of the worst incidents happened on June 27, 1919, when the ship, still under the name *City of Holland*, encountered a strong gale on her Milwaukee-Muskegon run. Her engine broke down, and for over twenty-four hours the vessel drifted off course. She had no wireless and so could not send out a call for help. In light of this latest mishap, the Crosby Company made substantial repairs to the otherwise staunch ship, giving her a new engine, propeller wheels, and a stem. She was also given a complete inspection. The company did what it could to keep the *Muskegon* in seaworthy condition and running smoothly. But the fates were to overrule such attempts and instead set the ship on course to its final voyage and violent destruction.

That same year, early on the evening of October 27, the *Muskegon*, under the command of forty-six-year-old Captain Edward Miller, prepared to depart Milwaukee. Miller was well-known on the lakes and highly regarded during the twenty years he served as the vessel's master. The day had been fair with cool temperatures. Still, as was his custom, the captain checked the weather forecast. Moderate winds were predicted—nothing to indicate a difficult crossing. At about 9:00 P.M., with thirty-nine passengers and a crew of fifty-two onboard for the overnight trip to Muskegon, the ship left Milwaukee and steamed out onto the calm waters of Lake Michigan.

By midnight the weather had changed. The wind from the northwest picked up and quickly intensified until it reached gale force, clocked at sixty to seventy miles per hour. The steamer, halfway across the lake, handled the storm well and buffeted her way through the huge waves, resolutely ploughing on to the safety of Muskegon's harbor. However, when the channel lights came into view, Captain Miller had to make a hard decision: Should he let the vessel ride out the storm offshore, or take the risk of guiding her between the piers—a space of two hundred feet—as the breakers slammed against her?

From experience, often hard-won, Muskegon had witnessed the dangers facing ships as they made their way into the harbor, especially in rough seas, and since the 1860s had made many improvements. The lighthouse, foghorn, and extended piers made navigation between the big lake and Muskegon Lake safer for the many vessels that came to call. But these navigational aids still were not enough. In foul weather, vesselmen entering the port feared not only the striking breakers that could push a ship off course and onto the piers but also the treacherous undertows and the hidden sandbars created by the pounding surf at the channel's mouth.

Captain Miller was aware of these dangers as he considered which course of action he should take. He decided to make a run for it. While the wheelsman Ted Mique struggled to line up the ship between the piers, the captain ordered the oil tanks on both the port and starboard sides be opened in hopes that the oil would calm the waves enough to ease the ship's passage. However, the oil had no effect on the raging waters. The ship had just passed the end of the south pier and was nearly abreast of the foghorn house when a bump was felt and the vessel lost its forward momentum. Powerless, the steamer fell into a trough and, seconds later, was hurled violently against the pier where she stuck fast.

The survivors of the wreck gave nightmarish accounts of those final minutes before the *Muskegon* was battered to pieces by the relentless waves. The disaster occurred at 4:20 A.M. when most of the passengers were asleep in their berths. Just after the ship struck the pier, the lights went out. Cabin boys ran down the dark corridors pounding on doors to awaken those still unaware of the crisis. Those who woke in time and managed to escape struggled through the blackness in their nightclothes, surrounded by the cacophony of snapping wood, howling winds, and crashing waves—and the cries of those trapped in

CHAPTER 3

The Crosby steamer *Muskegon,* 1919 (Dossin Great Lakes Museum, Detroit, Michigan).

their cabins as the water rushed in. The collision had punctured a hole into the engine room and crewmen there, blinded by the clouds of escaping steam, could barely find their way out. Numbed by shock and the cold rain and waves drenching them, passengers and crew scrambled onto the pier to escape the stricken vessel. Captain Miller, first mate Albert Hoffman, and second mate Fred Steffens made every effort to assist them to safety. The ship hung onto the pier for several crucial minutes before the swells pulled her off. After that it took only ten to fifteen minutes for the pounding breakers to reduce the once proud steamship to broken iron framework surrounded by splinters of wood which clogged the channel and littered the nearby shoreline. Shortly after she went down, the distraught captain exclaimed, "They will probably send me to hell, but I did all that I could."

Onshore, the only witness to the disaster was Assistant Light Keeper Ransom Jakubovsky, who was on lookout duty at the fog signal house. He immediately gave the alarm, then rushed down the catwalk. With the beam from his flashlight, he helped guide the rescue efforts for those who had fallen into the water. He later lamented that his beam of light could not focus more widely on the scene and that people were lost because he failed to locate them in time.

The Coast Guard, under the command of Captain William Gatfield, responded to the alarm, rescuing a number of crew and passengers and assisting the injured who made it to the pier. One Coast Guard officer found two women, wearing only their nightgowns, huddled together in the cold, both suffering from broken ankles. With only a wheelbarrow for transport, he placed them in it and carted them to the station for treatment. Steffens clung to the pilothouse when it was washed off the wreck. As he floated down the channel toward the wild lake, the head light keeper, Captain Thomas Robinson, and several of the Coast Guard spotted him. They managed to throw Steffens a line and pull him to safety.

Most of the passengers and crew, including Captain Miller, survived the disaster. Their rescuers assisted them along the length of the pier to the shelter of the Coast Guard station and the nearby home of Captain Gatfield. As soon as word reached town, a number of local doctors rushed to the scene to treat the injured. Ambulances and other vehicles transported many to the city's hospitals. With daybreak, the Coast Guard assumed the task of recovering the bodies of those who had perished. The final count revealed thirty-one casualties, making the *Muskegon* shipwreck the worst maritime tragedy in Muskegon's history.

That day, hundreds of locals gathered along the shores of Lake Michigan to gawk at the tons of wreckage strewn over two miles of shoreline south of the channel. Many seized the opportunity to carry off some of the portable cargo along with ship items, everything from blankets and furniture to soap, candles, and candy. The personal effects of the passengers—luggage, clothes, jewelry—were also taken. Within a few days, a huge crowd estimated at 25,000 mobbed the beach. Police, along with armed guards and Crosby representatives, managed to restore some order to the free-for-all and piled the salvaged items in one place to be sorted and, if possible, returned to their rightful owners—not an easy task.

On October 29, the Grand Haven Coast Guard District Headquarters held a federal inquiry to determine the cause of the disaster. When called on the stand, Captain Miller, who had stayed on the bridge the entire voyage, gave his testimony. (See appendix I for his full statement.) In describing his actions following the ship's collision with the pier, he stated:

> There isn't much to tell. I was on the upper deck, and the boat swung around as we were about a third in the piers. She struck the south pier with great force and then, caught in the undertow, swung around. I at once gave the signal to the cabin officer to sound the alarm. I know he did, and I stuck to my post. The lights went out and the sea tossed the boat, and it began to give away. I do not know what went on below deck, as the boat was being torn to pieces under me, and I saw figures in the darkness jumping onto the pier. I kept giving orders. Then I jumped for my life, and here I am.[54]

In an intriguing sidelight, on the first day of the hearing the *Muskegon Chronicle* related an account of one of the survivors, who suggested that something might have gone wrong with the *Muskegon*'s engines. Harry B. Robinson, who was the chief engineer on the Goodrich steamer *Arizona*, told the reporter, "I do not wish to say anything about the engines now, but if called on the stand I will give my opinion of them."[55]

CHAPTER 3

People viewing the wreckage of the passenger steamer *Muskegon* ([P83–314] Muskegon County Museum).

Robinson and his assistant, Clyde Boyle, were going to their hometown of Muskegon while the *Arizona* was in dry dock in Manitowoc. "We had intended taking a car ferry to Grand Haven, but Clyde and I decided to take a chance on the Crosby boat." The feeling that something was wrong came just after the ship left Milwaukee:

> About 9:30 Monday night when we were just out of Milwaukee, I said to Boyle, "Clyde, I don't just like the looks of things. Let's take a look around the boat." So we went out into the cabin and took note of the doorways. Our stateroom was up on the hurricane deck forward. The boat was making all kinds of noises, so we went down to the crank room and opened the hatch door that looks in on this part of the machinery. Shortly after that, we went to bed.

Robinson was up early as the ship was approaching the harbor. Just after the collision he awakened Boyle, but the ship's lights went out before they could fully dress. He felt that the darkness contributed to the loss of life. "The lights hadn't gone, I don't think there would have been many drowned. But the people on the weather side of the boat had no way to get up out of their staterooms, and I think they were all drowned." (Other witnesses and survivors concurred that the darkness contributed to the confusion and resulting number of casualties.)

After struggling to escape their cabin, the two men made the risky jump to the pier with only minutes to spare. "Boyle and I had a hard time crawling along the upper side of the cabin, and could hardly get the door open. We slid down the side of the boat and had to take a jump from the bottom over to the pier. We were on the pier about five minutes before the ship sank."

Not only did Robinson suggest that the ship's engine was not working right; he also claimed the alarm was not sounded and the battery-powered emergency lights were not switched on: "I see that the papers claim the alarm whistles were sounded. I didn't hear any. The law requires that there be a gong or bell in every stateroom. They are all controlled by a switch from the pilot room and are not connected with the engine room. Batteries furnish the power for the alarms and also for the emergency lights, which the law requires. The emergency lights were not on."[56]

Robinson later talked with one of the surviving crewmen, William Calkin. Calkin was a first-class oiler on the *Muskegon*, but on the final run temporarily took on the job of coal passer. Robinson related that Calkin had a foreboding about the trip: "He told me he was scared all the way over." The crewman escaped from the steam-clouded engine room as the water rushed in through the hole punctured in the ship's hull.

The fears felt by Robinson, Boyle, and Calkin may have been shared by Captain Miller and another crew member. The ship's steward, E. O. Jones, talked with Muskegon's Chief of Police Peter Hansen concerning premonitions that he and the captain mutually expressed early that evening. Chief Hansen told the *Chronicle:* "I talked with Jones after the accident and he told me that he saw the skipper after leaving Milwaukee and that the skipper told him he didn't like the look of things. Jones told him that he, too, had fears. Jones said the captain spoke about turning back and that he advised him to do it before they got out too far."[57] Jones's uneasiness kept him up most of the night, and he was awake and dressed when the ship hit the piers.

The implication that something was wrong with the *Muskegon*'s engines was dismissed by F. A. Pixley, a general freight agent for the Crosby Company. He had been sent immediately to Muskegon to assist survivors, enlist guards to watch over the salvaged belongings of the passengers, and handle a number of other details. Pixley stated that the machinery on the boat was not at fault: "It was all inspected when we had her overhauled a few months ago, and pronounced in first-class condition."[58]

Officials at the inquiry focused on three major factors: the conduct of the *Muskegon*'s crew, the assistance provided by the Coast Guard, and the seaworthiness of the steamer. All three were found to have performed to high standards. Captain Miller was absolved from any blame for the wreck. In addition, the Coast Guard received praise for their quick action. The *Muskegon,* despite her history of misfortune, was deemed a seaworthy vessel, especially in light of the extensive—and expensive—repairs made several months earlier. The inquiry concluded that no one was to blame for the loss of the *Muskegon* and thirty-one lives.

As to the charges made by Robinson, it will never be known if there was a problem with the vessel's machinery. Was something actually wrong, or were his accusations those of a company man out to discredit the rival line? It is clear that the engines powered the steamship across Lake Michigan and only at the end of the crossing did the forces of nature wreak destruction. Whatever battered remains of the steamer's engines and other working parts that could be found were too damaged to give any conclusive answers.

Possibly as a result of the *Muskegon* tragedy, Captain Miller ended his career on the lakes only a few years later. He died at his Milwaukee home following a heart attack in January 1951.[59]

Adrift in Changing Times: The Story of the *Illinois* and the *Missouri*

By the 1920s, a number of changes brought about the demise of the Crosby and Goodrich lines. The number of passenger ships in operation dwindled as travelers opted to take passenger trains and increasingly the automobile. The cargo that the steamers had transported to markets around the Great Lakes could be more efficiently handled by rail or trucks. To stay solvent, the steamer lines were forced to sell off the many vessels they had in their fleets. A few boats sailed on for a while longer, either on the Great Lakes or on saltwater. Others were cut down and made into barges. In some cases, these once elegant ships were shunted around from one port to another, their destiny held by the dictate of economics and the whims of the changing times, and no one seemed quite sure what to do with them. The steamers *Illinois* and *Missouri* suffered this last ignoble fate.

The schedule held by the *Illinois* and her sister ship *Missouri* encompassed the length of Lake Michigan. Although the *Illinois* was the older of the two—built in Chicago in 1899—the vessels were identical in size (240 feet long, with a 40-foot beam and 26-foot depth) and similarly powered by a single triple-expansion type engine. From the start, the ships, under Northern Michigan Transportation Company ownership, carried passengers and freight from Chicago to the northern resort towns of Charlevoix, Petoskey, Harbor Springs, and Mackinac Island. Those traveling on these stylish steamers were either vacationers at the exclusive resorts or owners of summer homes. It should be noted that before the advent of cars and trucks, the *Illinois* and *Missouri* and other vessels of the line provided the primary means of transportation for tourists and freight available to the small towns along the shores of northern Lake Michigan. Residents there deemed it a major event when one of the Chicago boats steamed into their port, and many would turn out to welcome it.[60]

Due to tough economic times in the early 1920s, Northern Michigan sold the *Illinois* to Goodrich, and the vessel served ports along Lake Michigan's western shore for several years before the Depression hit in 1929. The next three years found the vessel tied up and idle in Milwaukee's harbor.

In 1925, the Crosby line was reorganized and became the Wisconsin and Michigan Transportation Company. The Goodrich Company, however, did not survive the Depression. When Goodrich went bankrupt, Wisconsin and Michigan bought the *Illinois* and brought her to Muskegon to be cleaned up and refitted for service. For several years the *Illinois*, along with the *Missouri*, carried passengers, freight, and automobiles to ports that included Muskegon, Chicago, and Milwaukee.

The *Muskegon*'s pilothouse is washed ashore ([P83–315] Muskegon County Museum).

By the mid-1930s, the government started imposing new regulations on the operation of equipment on steamships. These requirements, plus the heavy costs of operating the vessels and the dwindling number of passengers, forced the Wisconsin and Michigan Steamship Company[61] to suspend service from 1935 to 1937. In spring 1938, the *Illinois* was given a new lease on life when she was commissioned for summer sailings between Muskegon and Milwaukee.

While the *Illinois* continued sailing, the *Missouri* was laid up for several years at Muskegon's Mart dock. About 1:40 P.M. on May 11, 1939, fire was discovered belowdecks, apparently having broken out in the engine room. The interior of the 225-foot steamship quickly became a roaring inferno, the blaze fed by coal in the bunkers and mattresses stored on the main deck. Muskegon firefighters battled intense heat and dense smoke in an effort to save the ship's superstructure. But by the time they extinguished the fire, the *Missouri*'s upper decks were a total loss.

In 1942, the aging *Illinois* (her sailing days over) and the *Missouri* (a burned-out hulk) were towed from Muskegon to Chicago to be dismantled and fitted out as barges.

CHAPTER 3

The engine from the *Muskegon* lies in the channel (Dossin Great Lakes Museum, Detroit).

However, for some reason the changeover was not completed, and the vessels, partly dismantled, were towed back to Muskegon and again tied up at the Mart.

In the early evening of March 16, 1945, a fire broke out in the afterhold of the *Illinois*. The fire department responded to the call and quickly extinguished the small blaze. Once the flames were doused, Lt. Jay Sietsema went below to inspect the damage. When he came partway up the ladder, he reported the fire out, then fell back into the hold, overcome by gases created by the fire. Three other firefighters, unaware of the danger, immediately went down to assist him and also were stricken. All four, along with a civilian on deck, died of asphyxiation. During the attempts to rescue the victims, six more firefighters were overcome, even though they were wearing gas masks. Two policemen present and the Coast Guard Chief Ernest E. Ward also were felled by the noxious fumes. The nine men were taken to Hackley and Mercy Hospitals, where they recovered.

For the two years following this tragedy, the *Illinois* lay idle at the dock. The final blow came in May 1947 when the Fisher Steel and Scrap Company bought and reduced to scrap the hulls of both the *Illinois* and the *Missouri* for the foundries of Muskegon.

The "Queen of the Great Lakes": The *Milwaukee Clipper*

The *Milwaukee Clipper*, with her sleek lines and distinctive green hull familiar to many in Muskegon, hardly bore any resemblance to her original incarnation as the passenger steamer *Juniata*. Built in 1905 in Cleveland by the American Shipbuilding Company, the *Juniata* and her sister ships, the *Tionesta* and *Octorara*, served the Anchor Line, which was owned by the Pennsylvania Railroad. Compared to most passenger steamers of the time, she was considerably larger—346 feet long, 45 feet wide, and 25.3 feet deep—and was powered by a 3,000-horsepower quadruple-expansion steam engine, the steam provided by four coal-fired Scotch-type boilers. She featured many of the luxuries offered on the other ships, but the *Juniata*'s special feature was running water provided in many of the state rooms. Cabins occupied three decks, with freight stowed on the main deck. During her service with the Anchor Line, she carried passengers from Buffalo to Duluth.

In 1916, the Anchor Line was forced to shut down. New regulations issued by the Interstate Commerce Commission prevented railroad lines from operating steamboats. The Great Lakes Transit Corporation took over the *Juniata* and her sister ships but maintained their established routes, with an exception made in 1933 and 1934, when the *Juniata* visited Chicago during the World's Fair.

The *Juniata* underwent several rebuildings on her way to becoming the *Milwaukee Clipper*. One was a major reconstruction job, which added a number of passenger cabins, created an enclosed observation deck at her bow where a library and music room had been, and gave her a new pilothouse.

In 1937, the *Juniata* lay idle in Buffalo. The *Morro Castle* disaster in 1934[62] led the Bureau of Marine Inspection and Navigation to require that ships comply with strict safety regulations. The *Juniata*'s wooden superstructure was deemed a liability and potential fire hazard. However, due to budget constraints, the owners of the *Juniata* and her sister ships could not make the necessary changes and reluctantly laid up their vessels. For the record, all three ships had demonstrated excellent service over the years, unmarred by safety problems.

Several years later, the *Juniata* and *Octorara* were sold to the Wisconsin and Michigan Steamship Company. The new owners planned to set the *Juniata* on the route between Milwaukee and Muskegon, transporting passengers and cars across the lake, but as a ship reborn for a new era. In October 1940, the old steamer was delivered to the Manitowoc Shipbuilding Company, where she was placed in dry dock to undergo a major conversion into a modern passenger and car ferry.

Before 1940, no Great Lakes ship had undergone so complete a transformation as the *Juniata*. This rebuilding changed the vessel's entire profile, with a completely new superstructure made of steel giving her a smart, contemporary look. The stern was extended until she reached the length of 361 feet. To create space for over 100 autos she could ferry each trip, the main deck was virtually gutted. The ship could accommodate as many as 900 passengers, who enjoyed comfortable, air-conditioned state rooms and open-deck lounging, along with many progressive features, including a sports deck for

CHAPTER 3

The steamer *Juniata* (Historical Collections of the Great Lakes, Bowling Green State University).

recreational activities, a 144–seat movie theater, dance floor, children's playroom, and souvenir shop. For the captain and crew, the latest navigational aids were installed on the top deck. Safety features were built into the new design to meet or exceed those required; the ship's construction made her virtually fireproof, yet an automatic sprinkler system was installed throughout the vessel.

The transformation was complete the following spring. On June 2, 1941, the *Juniata* sailed to Milwaukee where she was christened the *Milwaukee Clipper*. The following morning she arrived in Muskegon and moored at the Mart dock, her arrival greeted with a festive community-wide celebration. Following the music and speeches, people were allowed to tour the ship. The *Clipper* departed later that morning for Milwaukee and then left on a cruise to Chicago and other Lake Michigan ports, showing off her new streamlined profile.

For nearly thirty years, the *Milwaukee Clipper* maintained a favored relationship with the city of Muskegon. Thousands enjoyed summer excursions aboard her, trading the hot, congested highways around Chicago for the refreshing lake breezes on their summer vacations in Michigan and Wisconsin. Between 1946 and 1963, the *Clipper*

The *Milwaukee Clipper*, c. 1941 ([P83-399] Muskegon County Museum).

sailed year-round. This schedule was cut back between 1964 and 1970, when she operated only during the summer season.

The *Clipper*'s happy career was marred by several incidents. In January 1949, a sudden swell of water knocked her against the concrete dock in Milwaukee, resulting in a broken rudder. She was towed to Manitowoc for repairs, returning to service the following May. Later that same month, rudder problems caused the ship to lie crosswise in the Muskegon Channel, but this mishap caused no damage to the vessel. Worse was to come in 1960 when, while sailing in dense fog, the *Clipper* hit Milwaukee's outer breakwater. Fourteen passengers suffered minor injuries, and damage to the ship was estimated at $7,000. She was laid up for two weeks while undergoing repairs. Winter travel also presented problems. During the particularly severe winter of 1962, the *Clipper* became trapped in a thick ice pack that extended fifteen miles from Muskegon's shoreline. She was about three miles out, Milwaukee-bound, when the ice caught her. For three days (January 22-24) the *Clipper* drifted north in the ice floe, finally breaking free and heading across the lake.

To the dismay of the people in Milwaukee and Muskegon, the *Milwaukee Clipper* faced retirement in September 1970. Although she had been carefully maintained over the years, her age was starting to show. In addition, she was hamstrung by new Coast Guard regulations. This combination of factors resulted in her being laid up in Muskegon until 1977, when she was bought by a Chicago businessman. The ship was towed to Sturgeon

CHAPTER 3

Bay for repairs and refurbishment, then sailed to Chicago to be docked at Navy Pier as a floating restaurant and banquet center. The business was less than successful, and subsequent years saw the *Clipper* shuttled around to various locations in the Chicago area. In May 1990, she was acquired by the Hammond (Indiana) Port Authority and towed to their waterfront, where she was used as a convention center. Various regulations doomed this venture, and the ship was again towed off, at one time sitting idle on the Detroit River at Windsor, Ontario. In late 1996, she could be found languishing once more in the Chicago area, where she was subjected to vandalism and looting.

Hope for the aging vessel came the following year. A group from Muskegon sought to bring her back to the Port City. Great Lakes Clipper Preservation—which later changed its name to S.S. Milwaukee Clipper Preservation—succeeded in acquiring the ship and on December 2, 1997, brought her back to Muskegon for restoration and conversion. In her new role, she will serve as a floating museum and learning center for the history of the passenger ships on the Great Lakes and will feature bed-and-breakfast accommodations and banquet facilities. To this end, monies from fund-raisers and tours of the vessel, income from a store selling *Clipper*-related items, and individual donations are contributing to the effort. Since returning to Muskegon, the *Clipper* has found a temporary home at the old Grand Trunk Railroad dock. One major concern is finding a permanent berth for the ship along the Muskegon lakefront.

The *Milwaukee Clipper* made news in 1999 when a video crew received permission to use the ship's interior in recreating scenes for a documentary on the wreck of the ocean liner *Andrea Doria*. Actors from Grand Haven's Central Park Players filled in to play passengers onboard the ill-fated ship, which sank in the Atlantic after colliding with the Swedish ship *Stockholm* on July 25, 1956. The footage was used in the History Channel series *Wrath of God*.[63]

All Dressed Up and Nowhere to Go: The *Aquarama*

Though not playing much of an active role in the life of the Port City, one luckless ship should be included here simply for the long years she lay idle in Muskegon Lake. Christened the *Marine Star* when first launched by the Sun Shipbuildng and Drydock Company at Chester, Pennsylvania, in 1945, the C4-S-B5 Cargo/Transport measured 520 feet long with a beam of 71 feet and depth of 26 feet. She was bought in the early 1950s by Sand Products Corporation of Detroit to provide passenger and car service between Detroit and Cleveland. However, the vessel was too large to navigate the seaway, and thus with the upper decks removed and her hull buoyed by pontoons, she was towed up the Mississippi to Chicago, arriving there September 13, 1953. From there the ship—newly renamed the *Aquarama*—was taken to Muskegon to undergo an extensive conversion, which took two years and cost a whopping $7,500,000. The *Aquarama*'s makeover was stunning. Passengers—up to 2,500—could enjoy a movie theater, two dance floors, and five bars and restaurants. For the kids, there was a playroom and nursery. The ship's nine decks, which included a sports deck, a sun deck, and a club deck, were connected by escalators—the first escalators on a Great Lakes ship. She could also transport 160 vehicles.

At first the *Aquarama* was considered a model for future Great Lakes passenger ships. But for all her size and luxury, it was her overall design that tarnished her reputation and caused numerous problems for others on the lakes. Her high profile would catch the wind, making her hard to handle, and collisions resulted, usually with docks. The first such incident occurred when she departed Muskegon for the first time amid grand fanfare: "When her mighty bronze wheel began thrashing the water, a dock facing got in the way. And as *Aquarama* sailed [the] first yards of her maiden voyage, she carved her initials along the steel sheet-piling of the Mart's outer sea wall."[64] In a more embarrassing accident, the *Aquarama* bumped into a large warship, the USS *Macon*, which was docked in Cleveland for an open house. Both ships suffered minor damage, but the incident served to put another notch in the *Aquarama*'s record of troubles.

The *Aquarama*'s speed was amazing; she could easily reach twenty-two miles per hour. But small craft learned to stay clear, as her wake was known to have swamped a number of them. These accidents usually occurred when the ship cruised the narrow confines of the Detroit and St. Clair Rivers.

Between 1957 and 1962, the *Aquarama* maintained a regular schedule between Detroit and Cleveland, with occasional trips up the St. Clair River to Port Huron. But a new home had to be found for the ship when the docking agreement with the City of Detroit expired and the city would not renew it. Plans were floated to bring the ship back to Lake Michigan and, under the ownership of the *Milwaukee Clipper*'s company, sail the Milwaukee-Muskegon route. However, the dock in Milwaukee was not deep enough to accommodate a ship that big. In addition, resulting costs for the dredging and fees levied for the ship's use of the dockside proved prohibitive. The *Aquarama* returned to the Port City and sat out the next twenty-five years at the eastern end of Muskegon Lake.

In 1987 the ship was towed from Muskegon to Sarnia, Ontario. Some investors planned to use her as a floating hotel and convention center in Port Stanley. But as in Milwaukee, the water at the Port Stanley dock was too shallow for a ship with such a deep draft, and the investors did not have the funds to dredge the site. From Sarnia, the *Aquarama* was again towed off, this time to Windsor, and tied up in the Detroit River just below the Ambassador Bridge.

New owners with big plans bought her, and in August 1995 the *Aquarama*—under her old name *Marine Star*—was towed to Buffalo, this time to be redesigned as a casino ship in some undetermined city. Since then the vessel, now owned by Empire Cruise Lines of Delaware, has been tied up at Buffalo. She is structurally sound, although outwardly she is starting to look somewhat derelict, with her four upper decks rusting out. However, the owners plan to replace the decks with three new ones, complete with twelve-foot ceilings and a number of windows. The estimated cost of the renovations is $32–35 million. They envision the *Marine Star* cruising to ports on Lake Erie, offering both accommodations for overnight travel as well as short dinner-and-entertainment excursions. The obstacles

CHAPTER 3

The *Aquarama* (Historical Collections of the Great Lakes, Bowling Green State University).

will be difficult to clear, but with renewed interest in cruising on the Great Lakes, there may be hope for the troubled ship.

"A Monster of Its Kind": Muskegon's First Car Ferry

By the late 1800s, railroad companies had established terminals in cities along Michigan's western shore—Muskegon, Grand Haven, and Ludington—and depended on the steamships to carry their freight across Lake Michigan to the Wisconsin ports of Milwaukee and Manitowoc. However, this meant hard work on the docks. Laborers would transfer the tons of freight from the trains, loading it onto the vessels. Once across the lake, the reverse occurred—the ships were unloaded and the trains took on the freight for transport to market. Not only was valuable time spent performing the work, but the labor costs of loading and unloading the cargo were a heavy burden for businesses. When a special vessel was built—the car ferry—these problems were virtually solved. Slips were built with aprons that had tracks running down to the edge. Tracks ran the length of the car ferry hull so that the railroad cars, with their burden of freight, could roll right onto the vessel, then roll off at the destined port. The new system proved both fast and cost efficient, and for nearly the next hundred years, Muskegon and other Lake Michigan ports were served by these hulking, hardworking vessels.

Steamships and Car Ferries

On October 7, 1897, an advertisement appeared in the *Muskegon Weekly Chronicle* announcing that a giant car ferry would begin service between Muskegon and Milwaukee on December 1. The Detroit, Grand Rapids and Western Railway bought the old Nelson and Tillotson mill sites and some surrounding property at Port Sherman, the small community bordering the south side of the channel and the very western part of Muskegon Lake. There they would construct a special car ferry slip sixty feet wide and three hundred feet long, with an apron to accommodate the vessel. In addition, plans to dredge the waterfront and build sidetracks and a roundhouse were laid out.

Local shipping interests predicted the car ferry would dramatically boost Muskegon's economy and prove the city's importance as a major Great Lakes port. One of the men involved in the enterprise expressed their high hopes thus:

> When we have demonstrated to the entire country that Muskegon is the best port on the east shore of Lake Michigan, and that we have the railroads here for handling all the freight that can be offered and sending it in any direction wanted, and over almost any system of railroads, there will be a wonderful increase in shipments by this route....
>
> The effect on Muskegon will be to elevate this city and harbor to the prominence they deserve, as a great natural shipping point. The great grain, flour and other shipments from the northwest en route to seaboard points or for export will come largely by way of Milwaukee and Muskegon. The westbound shipments to be drawn this way will consist largely of high grades of coal and coke and high class freights that are sent in car loads not to be broken until they reach their destination.[65]

Muskegon's first car ferry, *Shenango No. 2*, first entered the harbor on the snowy morning of December 2, 1897. The huge steamer, described as "a monster of its kind,"[66] was escorted across Muskegon Lake by the Crosby tug *O. M. Field* and eased into the east slip of the Goodrich dock, where she was to stay until she started service on December 15. (At that time, workers were hurrying to complete the apron at the car ferry's dock site at Port Sherman.) Once she was secured, a party of railroad officials, a *Chronicle* reporter, and a few others accompanied Captain George Thompson on a tour of the ship.

Built just two years earlier, the *Shenango No. 2* measured 300 feet in length, with a 54-foot beam. Unloaded, she drew 11 feet of water, but when loaded with freight cars she had a draft of 13 feet, 6 inches. The wooden car ferry was powered by two fore-and-aft compound engines, with two Scotch boilers 12 feet in diameter and 14 feet in length providing the steam. Constructed for year-round service, her heavy hull was reinforced to give her ice-breaking capabilities. She carried a crew of twenty-six and could accommodate sixty-three passengers, offering them a dining room, large state rooms, and other amenities. However, the ship's most impressive feature was the car deck, which could handle up to twenty-six 30-ton, 38-foot freight cars or thirty shorter, 20–25 ton cars. These could be loaded on the boat in a mere 30–35 minutes. The reporter noted, "The interior of the steamer on this deck looks more like a street car barn than anything else. Four tracks, two on each side, extend almost the whole length of the steamer. 'It is a floating railroad,' remarked Captain Thompson with a smile."[67]

During her first two seasons the *Shenango No. 2* had served Port Dover and Port Stanley in Ontario and Conneaut, Ohio. On her new Muskegon-Milwaukee run she was expected to make the eighty-mile crossing in seven hours or less. Along with the new schedule came a change in her name. Within a short time of her arrival in the Port City, she was renamed the *Muskegon*.

The *Muskegon* could handle her tough assignment but endured several battles with Lake Michigan's heavy seas. On December 19, 1899, on her way to Muskegon, the vessel was caught in a storm that rocked her badly, and she struggled back to Milwaukee's harbor. In another fierce winter gale on February 23, 1900, the car ferry's rudder quadrant was broken, and as the vessel wallowed in the huge swells, the railcars were thrown about her hold, causing damage to the hull, the cargo, and the cars. The crew managed to make temporary repairs to the rudder and the *Muskegon* finally reached safe harbor at Racine.

Misfortune dogged the *Muskegon* even in calm seas. On May 28, 1900, the car ferry was steaming across the fog-covered lake near Manitowoc when she ran down the 96-foot scow schooner *Silver Lake*. The smaller, lumber-laden vessel sank, losing one of her crew.

The *Muskegon* served her namesake port for only four years. The company that owned her—Chicago and Western Michigan Railroad—merged with the Ludington-based Pere Marquette car ferry line. The *Muskegon*'s name was changed to the *Pere Marquette 16* and she continued her runs across Lake Michigan from her new home port fifty miles away. In the end, all the lofty plans for making Muskegon a major car ferry port were scuttled. It would be another thirty years before the city would compete again in this capacity.

The *Shenango* Legacy: The Grand Trunk Car Ferries

In the first decades of the twentieth century, the car ferries that plied Lake Michigan originated from the ports of Grand Haven and Ludington along the Michigan shore. While Muskegon's first car ferry, the *Muskegon*, served the Port City for only four years before a business merger forced her departure, the idea of restoring the service was often discussed in local business circles. Finally, Muskegon's potential as a major car ferry terminal was recognized by the Grand Trunk (GT) Railroad when GT took controlling interest of the Muskegon Railway and Navigation Company on Belt Line in 1927. The Belt Line, with its terminal at the foot of McCracken Street, the site of the former Stimson, Fay and Company lumber mill on Muskegon Lake, had planned as early as 1919 to reestablish car ferry service to Milwaukee. Over the next few years, GT brought the idea to fruition. Among other factors prompting this move was the size of Muskegon Lake; the big ships of the GT line had found it difficult to maneuver in the limited space of Grand Haven's harbor.[68] The construction of a slip for the car ferries and a fifty-ton loading apron was completed in 1933.

Muskegon's first car ferry, the *Muskegon* (formerly the *Shenango No. 2*) passing the fog signal house as she enters the channel in winter ([P83–469] Muskegon County Museum).

In July that year, GT moved its fleet of three car ferries from Grand Haven to Muskegon. Escorted by hundreds of smaller craft, the flagship of the fleet, the *City of Milwaukee*, steamed through the channel and into Muskegon Lake on July 17. At the McCracken Street dock, hundreds of well-wishers welcomed Captain John Cavanaugh and the ship's crew in a colorful opening-day ceremony attended by a number of dignitaries. Thus began a highly successful shipping era for the city that lasted for the next forty-five years.

All three car ferries—*City of Milwaukee, Grand Rapids,* and *Madison*—made three round-trips across Lake Michigan each day, seven days a week, year-round, transporting 22–26 freight cars in their holds. Even though they were not primarily passenger ships, they featured fine accommodations for lake travelers. The vessels were all quite new; the *City of Milwaukee*—360 feet long with a 56-foot beam—was the newest, constructed in 1931 by the Manitowoc Shipbuilding Company. The older *Grand Rapids,* built in 1926, was of the same dimensions, while the *Madison,* launched the following year, measured a slightly smaller 348 feet in length. To maintain their arduous year-round schedules the steel ships were constructed with hulls tough enough to crack their way through the frozen lakes, and their work often provided passage through open water for other ships. Once they had the momentum, their reinforced bows could crush through the ice. However, if forced to slow down, the vessels sometimes found themselves trapped in the thick ice off Muskegon harbor.

Changes came over the years. In the mid-1940s, in order to cut down on labor costs, the car ferries began using fuel oil instead of coal. Many years later, in 1971, passenger service was eliminated to save money at a time when the operation was struggling to maintain its existence. Improvements in the rail system, including more powerful diesel locomotives and Chicago's network of railroad lines equipped with electronic switching, made the car ferry system increasingly outdated and ultimately obsolete. Finally, in 1978, after seventy-five years in the car ferry business, Grand Trunk discontinued its cross-lake service.

The *Grand Rapids* and *Madison* remained at the Lakeshore Contractors dock for the next ten years. While mothballed there, the *Madison* fell victim to arsonists. In the early evening of October 12, 1987, three separate fires blazed up simultaneously, one in the crew's quarters belowdecks and two on the main deck. Firefighters struggled in close quarters to put out the fires. Muskegon Fire Chief Autry Goodman blamed youthful arsonists: "We've been plagued with these fires off and on for three years now, kids starting them either for heat or light." The previous April, a fire onboard the *Grand Rapids* caused $100,000 in damage. It was apparently sparked by looters using a cutting torch to make off with some nautical equipment. While no firefighters were injured on these occasions, the risks were well-known. Chief Goodman no doubt had in mind the fire on the *Illinois* that killed five men when he said, "It's terrible. There's no way to release the smoke or gases. It's a shame the beating the guys have to take for a senseless fire like this."[69]

The two vessels were towed away in 1989, the *Grand Rapids* to be scrapped in Port Maitland, Ontario, while the *Madison* was converted into a barge. The *City of Milwaukee* fared better. Bought by the Ann Arbor Railroad, she worked out of the port of Elberta/Frankfort, a hundred miles north of Muskegon, from 1978 until 1981, when she was laid up in Elberta following the demise of the Ann Arbor Railroad. Friends of the old car ferry formed the Society for the Preservation of the City of Milwaukee (SPCM) and with the support of city officials in Frankfort and Elberta have worked hard to have her fitted out as a museum ship. In 1991, the *City of Milwaukee* was honored as a National Historic Landmark.

As in such cases, the preservation group has struggled to raise the funds needed to maintain and restore the *City of Milwaukee*. In addition, finding a permanent dock site has been an ongoing problem. In the early 1990s, plans to move her from Elberta across Betsie Bay to Frankfort were defeated by voters in Frankfort. However, in 1999, with the vessel facing eviction from its site in Elberta, the people of Frankfort voted approval to

Grand Trunk car ferry *Madison* leaves the dock at the foot of McCracken Street ([P83–484B] Muskegon County Museum).

becoming her new home. Until a special dock can be made to berth the car ferry, she is finding temporary quarters at the Seng Excavating dock on Lake Manistee.

In summer 2001, the *City of Milwaukee* was opened up to overnight visitors as a floating bed-and-breakfast. Enough renovating had been done to the quarters formerly used by the crew and passengers to provide accommodations for guests interested in spending time aboard the historic ship and getting a taste of a sailor's life. Jed Jaworski, the ship's former wheelsman and present-day curator, recalled his sailing career: "The ship was your lifeline: It provided shelter, warmth and light when you were in the middle of this windswept abyss, these immense seas and a pitch-black night. When you're onboard a ship like this at night, you get a sense of how it was for sailors."[70] The funds raised will help with further renovations. At the present location, the vessel is an added attraction in

CHAPTER 3

Manistee—the former lumber town that today highlights its extraordinary collection of ornate Victorian houses that date from the boom years. In addition, within a few years the *City of Milwaukee* could be sailing the Great Lakes again, bringing to the public a renewed interest in the distinctive role car ferries played in both maritime and railroad history. According to Jaworski, "We want this to be a vital community resource, not a lifeless museum."[71]

CHAPTER 4
Maritime Muskegon in the Twentieth Century

Only a few centuries have passed since Europeans first explored the region, but in that time the people of the Great Lakes have seen tremendous changes in the style and size of the boats and ships that sail these waters, from birchbark canoes to car ferries and thousand-foot freighters. These changes took shape as the Industrial Revolution brought a number of technical inventions and, once armed with the technology, ship architects and builders designed and launched innovative craft. Changes in ship design also developed in response to the types of cargo transported by water, from furs and trinkets to lumber, from grain to pianos, and from iron ore to railroad cars as dictated by the political, social, economic, and industrial needs and capabilities of a particular era or region. In addition, over the past few centuries the pursuits of the people who travel the Inland Seas have changed as well. Those sailing on the ships are no longer British troops on an armed sloop or Dutch immigrants aboard a passenger steamer, but vacationers on the small ferry boats and deckhands working aboard the lakers.

Lake Michigan, Muskegon Lake, and the rolling dunes have witnessed these changes. The twentieth century in particular brought about increasing diversity in the roles ships played, with a wide range of industries and developments creating employment for a variety of vessels. These ranged from elegant passenger steamers to whalebacks, from stone-hauling barges to "salties," from auto ferries to car ferries, and from small research vessels to large iron-ore freighters.

While the lumber era saw some ups and downs, with Muskegon enjoying rollicking boom years and then suffering through several bouts of economic depression, the century that followed was filled with greater uncertainties for the port's economy. Certain events occurred that damaged the local maritime business, such as the Depression years, which forced the Goodrich line to close down. Other times, doors opened that raised expectations of a lake-borne renaissance, such as the relocation of the Grand Trunk car ferries to Muskegon and the opening of the St. Lawrence Seaway. The successful enterprises have boosted confidence in Muskegon's role as a leading port on Lake Michigan, but any loss of business has left a void—sometimes personally felt by Muskegonites—and called for a reassessment of the port's strengths, deficiencies, and possible future options. The city rode the peaks and hit the troughs of the past hundred years. It remains to be seen if there is smooth sailing ahead for the Port City.

The advent of the automobile age brought on unprecedented change in Western society, and the impact was keenly felt by all other systems of transportation. With the coming of the auto, the popularity of passenger steamers dropped off significantly. Travelers relished the freedom of having their own mode of transportation as they drove to the resorts and cities around Lake Michigan—as well as to towns farther away from the shore. In the 1920s, some of the steamships, including the *Illinois* and *Missouri,* tried to accommodate by offering to transport their passengers' cars in the cargo hold, but this met with limited success. Later, the *Milwaukee Clipper* performed the service with ease, her size and design well suited for the purpose.

The Great Depression signaled the end of the halcyon days of the passenger steamship lines. After a highly successful seventy-five-year run, the Goodrich Company went bankrupt and was forced to sell off its remaining vessels to other shipping firms, which in turn struggled to keep going. The Crosby Line was reorganized and, as the Wisconsin and Michigan Steamship Company, managed to survive in spite of the severe decline in the number of passengers and the uncertainties of the times. Adding to these woes, new safety measures for passenger ships were signed into law requiring ship companies to install sprinkler systems and make other costly renovations to their vessels. Most agreed to these changes in principle, but the regulations further hampered those ship owners unable to comply due to lack of funds. As a result, a number of passenger steamers were laid up during the 1930s, some temporarily, others permanently.

After the lumber boom, Muskegon's established business leaders, along with young, ambitious entrepreneurs, turned to other industries to keep the city moving forward. Some businesses were still tied to the lumber industry, such as the Central Paper Company and Kelley Brothers Manufacturing Company, which made interior woodwork and related products, but heavy industries also sprang up. The Shaw-Walker Company, formed in 1899, made office furniture and equipment. With opportunities opening up in the automotive field, the Piston Ring Company, which later became Sealed Power Corporation, was established by Charles E. Johnson and Paul R. Beardsley in 1911. The old Racine Boat Company building at the foot of Pine Street saw the beginnings of the Campbell, Wyant and Cannon foundry in 1908, which started by manufacturing marine engine castings, but soon moved to a larger building in Muskegon Heights and turned out parts for the auto industry.[1] With these changes, the ships that visited Muskegon in the decades following 1890 carried cargoes as diverse as pulpwood, sand, and scrap iron. They did not have the elegant lines of the passenger ships. Many, their decks cluttered with heavy equipment and hulls coated in industrial grime, were a far cry from the graceful schooners. But they got the job done and kept Muskegon's economy running.

During the lumber years, ships docked at the numerous piers adjoining the lumber mills that crowded the lakefront. Later, when the mills shut down, some of the docks were taken over by railroad firms and passenger ship lines while others, through age and neglect, fell into disrepair. One site that maintained its importance in Muskegon was the property of the old Blodgett and Byrne lumber mill at the foot of Fifth Street. The Goodrich Company bought it in 1894 and made a number of improvements to accommodate its line of passenger and freight steamers. When Goodrich went bankrupt in the early 1930s, Muskegon saw the opportunity to develop the site into a modern shipping terminal that would attract business to the Port City. The project was approved in April 1933, and the West Michigan Dock and Market Corporation immediately went ahead to build the Mart. Included in the $1,250,000 construction job was docking space for up to ten large vessels, storage space for over 100,000 bushels of fruit and farm products, a warehouse, and transit facilities. While a number of ships have docked at the Mart, two called it home for many years: the *Milwaukee Clipper* and *Highway 16*.

From Muskegon's earliest days, a favorite topographical landmark was Pigeon Hill. The huge sand dune, three hundred feet high, rose above the western end of Muskegon Lake just south of the channel and overlooked the fishing village of Port Sherman. The passenger pigeons inhabiting the dune were hunted to extinction, but the name stuck. In 1926, the Nugent Sand Company realized the worth of the location and took charge of the property. With the auto industry moving into high gear, sand was needed in the foundries of Detroit and Cleveland to make castings for molten metal products, primarily car and airplane engines, and the Nugent Company intended to provide the raw materials. The following year, the Sand Products Corporation acquired the site from Nugent and soon began to dig out the sand.

In 1936, the steamer *W. E. Fitzgerald* came into the port and docked at the foot of the dune. Conveyer belts poured the sand into her hold, and the first shipment left Pigeon Hill downbound for the steel mills. Other lakers continually cleared the port loaded with tons of sand, among them the *Sultana, Ben Calvin, United States Gypsum*, and *Diamond Alkali*. The earliest years, which included World War II with its heavy demands on the steel industry, were the busiest; between 1936 and 1948, a total of 533 boatloads of sand left Muskegon harbor.[2] The business finally ended in 1967 when Pigeon Hill bottomed out. Harbor Town Marina was built in the newly leveled area. The story of Pigeon Hill is akin to that of the virgin pine forests along the Muskegon River—a natural resource that brought a booming business to the city, but through relentless harvesting was completely depleted.

The Sand Products Corporation, founded in 1924 by Detroit industrialist Max B. McKee, played a major role in Muskegon's shipping history in the twentieth century. In addition to the sand-mining operations on Pigeon Hill, the corporation developed the West Michigan Dock and Market Corporation (the Mart). Max McKee was instrumental in arranging the merger of the Wisconsin and Michigan Transportation Company and the Pere Marquette Steamer Line into the Wisconsin and Michigan Steamship Company, which came under the Sand Products Corporation aegis. Although the tenor of the times and the onslaught of the Depression brought on a severe decline in the number of active passenger steamships, McKee kept his organization going not only by diversifying but also by focusing on providing efficient, modern cross-lake service, eventually redesigning

CHAPTER 4

Aerial view of the Mart dock with (left to right) the *Milwaukee Clipper, Highway 16,* and *Aquarama* (Courtesy of Hackley Public Library).

the old steamer *Juniata* into one of Muskegon's most popular ships, the *Milwaukee Clipper.*

With the opening of the St. Lawrence Seaway in June 1959, foreign vessels in record numbers joined the car ferries and lakers in Muskegon's harbor. The first saltwater ship ("salty") to transit the seaway and enter Muskegon Channel was Denmark's *Christel Heering,* actually coming through earlier, on April 30, 1958. Thousands gathered along the breakwaters and channel to welcome the bright red vessel, and small boats escorted her into the harbor. Her entry marked what was expected to be a record season of foreign trade in the port. The ship's owner, Peter F. Heering, executive of the Cherry Heering Company of Copenhagen, had flown in to be at the dock to welcome the captain, Axel Kirkeby, his officers, and crew. To mark the occasion, the Muskegon Yacht Club threw a celebration, at which Heering sang the praises of the Port City:

> This has been a very significant event both for my family and the company. The crest on the bow of the *Christel Heering* once was known from Alexandria to Pehang and from Dakar to

Port Sweitenham. Now, over 125 years later, it is known in your beautiful harbor and in ports in the heartland of America.

My maritime experience has been limited until now to service in the Danish Navy, but I am sure this is one of the most beautiful sheltered harbors in the world. My captain and his officers tell me it is one of the finest in their experience.[3]

The St. Lawrence Seaway gave a tremendous boost to commercial shipping in Muskegon. Throughout the 1960s and early 1970s, foreign vessels were frequent visitors. The amount of foreign tonnage jumped 194 percent between 1958 and 1959 and remained high for the next decade. The years 1964 and 1965 saw the highest number of foreign ships enter the harbor—72 and 95 respectively.[4] The *Chronicle* regularly reported their arrivals, noting the cargoes they carried to western Michigan and the local products they transported to foreign ports. Everything from petroleum and glass products to foreign cars, olives, and British china clay came into the Port City, and exports included fruit (apples and cherries), grains, cement, hides, and foundry castings. However, foreign shipping dropped from about 1970 on due to, among other reasons, the limited number of berths at the Mart dock, inadequate shipping technology, and labor disputes.[5] Foreign companies also sought to keep expenses down by limiting the number of ports of call. As a result, Muskegon was passed over in favor of Chicago and other larger cities on the Great Lakes.

Muskegon went through hard economic times in the last third of the twentieth century, which impacted the maritime businesses. The depletion of the sand at Pigeon Hill, the loss of car ferry service, the severe cutbacks in foreign shipping, and the retirement of two aging ladies—the *Milwaukee Clipper* and the *Highway 16*—all occurring in the late 1960s and through the 1970s, gave people reason to believe the city with such a large harbor would become just a backwater town, her glory days of shipping long past and her future survival based on businesses located farther back from the shore. However, some promising developments have appeared on the horizon. But whether they can substantially revitalize the Port City's waterfront will only be clear as the new century progresses.

Bad Luck Comes in Threes: The Wreck of the *Salvor*

The wreck of the passenger steamer *Muskegon* in 1919 demonstrated the need for major improvements to the harbor entrance that would ensure safe passage for ships in all types of weather. The channel piers—only two hundred feet wide—provided too narrow a passage and added to the dangers faced by vessels trying to make the harbor when the seas ran rough. In 1925, the city obtained government funding for the construction of a modern, arrowhead-shaped breakwater. When finished, the new entrance to the harbor would be wider—a distance of 555 feet between the breakwater heads—and the protected inner basin would give ships a safer approach to the channel.

CHAPTER 4

Aerial view of Muskegon Channel and the arrowhead breakwater. Outbound ship is the *Aquarama* ([P83–752] Muskegon County Museum).

A contract was made with the Love Construction and Engineering Company, and work began in July 1927. The long arm of the south breakwater came first, and with it a shore connection made of wooden pilings with a concrete superstructure. When completed in 1930, it reached 3,021 feet into the lake. The north arm—a craggy mound of riprap 3,064 feet long—was finished in December 1931. In addition, the wooden south pier was shortened and the catwalk and fog signal house removed. The remaining pier was rebuilt in concrete and the channel was further deepened to 21 feet. At the end of each breakwater arm, beacons were constructed to mark the new harbor entrance. In 1929, the harbor's second lighthouse—a red, pyramidal tower of steel, 53 feet high—was erected on the end of the south breakwater. After the north breakwater was completed in 1931, a white skeleton tower was built at the tip.

Maritime Muskegon in the Twentieth Century

To construct the breakwaters, barges equipped with derricks and cranes brought large stone boulders from northern Michigan and Wisconsin. Love Construction Company had contracted with the T. L. Durocher Company of De Tour, Michigan, for use of their barges. One of the steel barges, the *Salvor,* while working to make the harbor safer, was herself lost in a huge storm that hit Lake Michigan on Friday, September 26, 1930.

During her thirty-four years the *Salvor,* under different names, suffered several disasters, only to be resurrected and refitted for more years of service. The vessel, originally christened the *Turret Chief,* was built in Sunderland, England, in 1896 as a bulk freight turret steamer of 1,800 tons and measuring 253 feet in length with a 44-foot beam. Supposedly intended for trade on the Suez Canal, she somehow ended up plying Great Lakes waters for a Canadian firm. While sailing Lake Superior, the *Turret Chief* was caught in the Big Storm of November 1913 and became one of the relatively minor casualties when the hurricane-force winds and mountainous waves drove her onto the Keweenaw Peninsula. Her crew survived, making it to shore and trekking some miles to find shelter and assistance.[6] Although badly damaged, the vessel was virtually reconstructed. Renamed the *Vickerstown,* the ship saw service on the ocean during World War I. The early 1920s found her back on the lakes, sailing under Canadian registry and under yet another name, the *Jolly Inez.* Misfortune struck a second time on November 16, 1927, when the steamer was again stranded, this time in northern Lake Huron on a reef near Saddle Bag Island, seven miles west of De Tour. The damage to the vessel was extensive, but she was again salvaged and restored to service, but with drastic changes. Her engines removed, a tall A-frame that operated two 90-foot booms, one fore and one aft, was constructed amidships. She was thus fitted out as a bulk freight barge with the name *Salvor.*

The *Salvor* had left Gill's Rock, Wisconsin, at the tip of the Door Peninsula, on the morning of September 25 with a load of stone for the Muskegon breakwater. Towing the barge was the tug *Fitzgerald,* under the command of Captain Thomas Houle. A crew of twelve was onboard the *Salvor.* Joining them on this trip was Mrs. Ida Olmstead, sister of the cook, Miss Alice LaPlaunt, and Mrs. Olmstead's nine-year-old son, Lornie. A fourth member of the family, the women's brother Onney LaPlaunt, was a member of the crew.

Rain fell overnight, but otherwise the weather was calm, and Captain Houle expected to make good time on the trip down to Muskegon. The tug and her tow had crossed Lake Michigan at the start of the trip, reaching the Michigan shoreline near Manistee. The following day, they sailed past Pentwater and were just south of Little Sable Point lighthouse by late morning when a terrific gale tore up the lake from the southwest. The vessels struggled to make headway as they plunged through the waves, the line to the barge taut under the severe strain. The *Fitzgerald* pulled hard to keep the *Salvor* out of the shallows, but it was no match for the powerful storm. At the last minute, with the entrance to Muskegon harbor only two miles away, the towline broke. The barge had been headed into the waves but, suddenly left helpless, was pushed broadside by the huge breakers, the bow pointing north. The crew immediately dropped the anchors, but the hooks dragged, unable to hold the vessel as the surging waves carried her north and

CHAPTER 4

The stone barge *Salvor,* formerly the turret steamer *Turret Chief* (Historical Collections of the Great Lakes, Bowling Green State University).

closer to land. About 3:00 P.M. the *Salvor,* driven to a spot two miles from the channel and about half a mile from shore, hit bottom.

It was only with extreme difficulty and expert seamanship that the *Fitzgerald* fought her way to safety inside the harbor. Violent waves tipped her over so far that water ran down her stack, extinguishing the fires. The tug barely made it into the protected waters before her steam died out completely. The men of the Coast Guard had been watching the drama, but (they later claimed) because neither the tug nor the barge had signaled for assistance, they had not set out to aid either vessel. They also argued that it would have been suicidal to have sent out a lifeboat in such tremendous seas.

As soon as the towline snapped, Coast Guard commander Captain George Gatfield sent some of his men in cars and a truck loaded with their equipment to rescue the *Salvor*'s crew. To reach the barge they had to drive all the way around Muskegon Lake to Scenic Drive, which borders the Lake Michigan shoreline north of Muskegon. When they arrived on the beach below a hill locally known as Hack's Shack, they found the barge grounded, the deck awash, and only the A-frame derrick visible above the raging seas. Training their field glasses on the wreck, they could see some survivors huddled high up on the framework.

Once the *Fitzgerald* and those aboard her were safe in the harbor, Captain Gatfield joined his men at the site where the *Salvor* had foundered. The would-be rescuers considered launching a boat to reach the barge's stranded crew, but the storm's intensity increased and forced them to abandon the idea. Instead, throughout the evening, the Coast Guard tried to shoot a line to the wreck, hoping to take the men off in a breeches buoy. Three attempts were made, but each one ended in failure. Twice the lines broke, and on all three tries the strong winds forced the lines to fall far short of their mark.

In the late afternoon and early evening, some of the *Salvor*'s crew were found washed up on the shore off Pioneer Park. The men on the vessel, following the rule of the sea which calls for "Women and children first," had lashed the cook, her sister, and the boy to a life raft. One of the men, Floyd O'Connor, also got onto the raft, which was then pushed off for shore. Young Lornie Olmstead drowned when the raft broke apart in the crashing surf, but the others managed to reach the shore alive, pulled to safety by several local men. O'Connor, a Muskegon native, suffered a broken leg when the raft hit the barge just after it was launched. Still, he found the strength to save Alice LaPlaunt as they were hurled by the waves, then dragged in the undertow, until finally they were cast onto the beach. O'Connor and the two women were taken to the hospital by ambulance.

Other crewmen took their chances and, wearing life preservers, jumped into the water and struck out for shore. Twenty-two-year-old Elmer Lytle lost his struggle with the raging lake, but George Secord, Onney LaPlaunt, and the barge's foreman, Edward Winserowski, survived and were treated at local hospitals. One crew member, Clement Shurage, also survived but, unnoticed by those onshore, made his way back to the *Fitzgerald*. Until he was found there, he had been listed as missing. (Of all the survivors, he was the only one who did not require hospitalization.) Two other men—Tony Winserowski, brother of Edward, and Clarence Brunett—were lost and presumed drowned.

Of the fourteen who had been on the *Salvor*, only three remained on the wreck. Clifford Lane, Harry Smith, and eighteen-year-old Lyman Nedeau had climbed up the fifty-foot A-frame and clung to it while awaiting rescue. Even from their high perch they could not escape the waves, which continually drenched them with torrents of spray. The Coast Guard could see them but, frustrated by the failed rescue attempts, could only hope the men would hang on until the storm abated.

The storm gods had other plans. At 9:00 that night, the winds shifted from the southwest and began blasting down from the northwest. The temperature dropped and the three survivors, already wet and exhausted, now were numbed by the cold. Their chances for survival dwindled as the night wore on. Lane succumbed to the bitter weather, and his body remained on the wreck until retrieved after the storm had passed.

Word of the *Salvor* disaster reached the Coast Guard station in Grand Haven. At 4:30 A.M., Captain William E. Preston and four Coast Guardsmen set out in a new powerboat to reach the wreck site fifteen miles away and assist with the rescue. Fighting their way through the heavy seas, they reached the *Salvor* by 6:00 A.M. At first, Preston positioned the boat on the windward side of the barge and tried to throw a line to the two survivors, but the effort failed. Unable to be heard above the raging wind and breakers, Harry Smith gestured for the boat's crew to come around on the leeward side to pick them up when they jumped off the derrick. Preston positioned the boat as directed, and Smith and Nedeau plunged into the water. The two caught the lines on the side of the boat

CHAPTER 4

The A-frame of the shipwrecked *Salvor* (© *Muskegon Chronicle*).

and were hauled aboard. An attempt to enter the Muskegon harbor would have been too dangerous, so the lifeboat took the men back to the Coast Guard station in Grand Haven. From there, they were transported to Muskegon's Mercy Hospital for treatment. A short time later the courageous Captain Preston set out again in search of the *North Shore,* a sixty-foot passenger and package steamer with a crew of six. Sailing from St. Joseph to Milwaukee with a cargo of grapes, she got caught in the storm and was reported missing. The vessel was last seen near Racine, Wisconsin, and a short time later sank offshore of Milwaukee, all hands lost.

While recuperating at the hospital, Harry Smith, a thirty-five-year-old Newark, New Jersey, native, told of the desperate situation the three men had faced during those fifteen hours while atop the derrick. While the others had left the vessel or were washed off, Smith, Nedeau, and Lane climbed up the A-frame to escape the waves. Another crewman, Clarence Brunett, also sought safety on the structure, but was unable to make it. According to Smith: "Brunett wanted to climb up where we were, but every time he attempted it a big wave came along and washed him to the other side of the ship. Then he would pull himself back again along a cable only to be washed back. About 6 o'clock Friday night he went in the water. By then his strength was gone and he had little chance to make the shore."[7] At first the three tried to keep moving around to stay warm, but with nightfall they settled in, wedging themselves into the framework. Lane had climbed several feet above the beam that held Smith and Nedeau. Smith said, "Clifford kept talking to us all the time until about two hours after midnight. About the last thing I remember hearing him say was that he wanted to come down where we were to get warm."[8] Smith and Nedeau had huddled together for warmth, Smith positioning himself so that he covered the younger man, protecting him the best he could from the waves and the frigid wind. This gesture no doubt saved both their lives.

Smith spoke highly of the efforts of the Muskegon Coast Guard, countering the criticism made by the barge's foreman, Edward Winserowski, who felt they should have come out to assist the tug and barge as they struggled for the harbor. Smith stated: "It would have been suicide for them to have tried to come out in their boat Friday night as many people who do not know the power of the sea suggested.... We know the Muskegon coast guards, too, and there isn't a yellow man in the crew. They would have come out in a boat if they possibly could and if there had been anything they might have done for us."[9] Smith also expressed deep gratitude for Captain Preston and the Grand Haven Coast Guard, recognizing the risks they took to rescue him and Nedeau: "We certainly are thankful for what Capt. Preston and the Grand Haven guards did for us. When I get out of here the first thing I'm going to do is to go down to Grand Haven and thank the men for coming out to get us. They came in over the top of the hatches risking their lives to get us. They were in danger all the time of getting caught in the cables of the *Salvor*."[10] Both Smith and Nedeau praised the character and courage of the other *Salvor* crew members, especially singling out the two women. The loss of nine-year-old Lornie Olmstead deeply saddened them. Nedeau said, "He was a bright boy and never in the way aboard ship. He often ran errands for us and was as much help as a man at times."[11] (See appendix J for Lyman Nedeau's memories of the *Salvor* disaster.)

Smith's defense of the Muskegon Coast Guard's actions was echoed by T. L. Durocher, owner of the *Salvor*, who said, "I have no criticism to offer against Capt. Gatfield and his men. He had to stay with his men until the Fitzgerald got in." Durocher was convinced a worse disaster would have occurred if both tug and barge had tried to make it into the harbor: "They never could have made the harbor safely in that sea. Both boats would have been piled on the end of the Muskegon piers and probably all of the men and women would have been lost."[12] Gatfield himself defended his actions: "People who have criticized our actions do not know the power of the sea."[13]

When the weather calmed, divers hired by the Durocher company examined the wrecked barge. They found that the hull had broken in two, the result of the combined heavy weight of the cargo (2,800 tons of stone) and the violence of the waves. The *Salvor* had been valued at $300,000, but was insured for only half that amount. The Durocher company wrote off the vessel as a total loss. Today, the hull of the *Salvor* still lies where she came to rest in about twenty to twenty-five feet of water—an easy-to-reach site for scuba

CHAPTER 4

divers. It had taken three groundings on three of the Great Lakes before the luckless *Turret Chief / Jolly Inez / Salvor* reached the beach for the final time, hurled onto the sandbars of Lake Michigan near Muskegon.

Psychic Intervention: The Wreck of *Our Son*

The storm that claimed the *Salvor* and *North Shore* sent to the depths another ship, the schooner *Our Son*. The story of *Our Son* is well-known on the lakes for the strange chain of events that led to the discovery of the sinking ship by Captain Charles Mohr, skipper of the steamer *William Nelson,* and his daring rescue of the schooner's crew.

By the late 1920s, the number of schooners actively plying the Great Lakes could be counted on one hand. The *Lyman M. Davis* was still sailing over on Lake Ontario. On Lake Michigan, the *City of Grand Haven, Lucia A. Simpson,* and *Our Son* continued to work in the lumber trade. The *Our Son,* a large three-masted schooner 182 feet long, with a 35-foot beam and a hold 13 feet deep, was built in Lorain, Ohio, in 1875. During the construction of the ship, the young son of the shipbuilder, Captain Henry Kelley, was playing near the dock when he fell into the water and drowned. The grief-stricken father named the vessel in tribute to him.

It wasn't until November 7, 1921, that the *Our Son* made her first visit to Muskegon, laden with pulpwood for the Central Paper Company. She became a regular visitor for the next eight years, making about ten trips to the Port City each season. The shipping season of 1930 marked the last time a lumber schooner would enter Muskegon harbor, for it was on one of her regular runs to Muskegon—and intended to be her last trip of the season—on September 26, 1930, that the *Our Son* was caught twenty miles off Ludington by the fierce gale which swept Lake Michigan.

In the midst of the maelstrom, the schooner's captain, Fred Nelson, a veteran of the lakes, realized that the aged schooner would not survive. Huge waves scoured the deck, and although the hatches were securely battened down, water started to fill her hold through loosened seams. Vicious winds had torn her sails to shreds, leaving the ship to roll helplessly. As the waterlogged vessel wallowed in the seas, Captain Nelson ordered the flag flown upside down—the traditional signal of distress—but would anyone see it? The schooner was in the middle of Lake Michigan, blown out of the regular shipping lanes, and the likelihood of another vessel finding them in time was slim to none. Unlike the modern ships of the day, the schooner carried no wireless or radio. Hope and prayer appeared to be the only possible signals that could be sent out with any chance of being received and answered in time.

Captain Charles Mohr of the steamer *William Nelson* encountered the storm when he came through the Straits of Mackinac, bound for South Chicago with a load of sand. His plan to follow a route along the lee shore to avoid the worst conditions was inexplicably changed when he ordered the ship steered eastward and down the treacherous Manitou Passage. The steamer sustained considerable damage as she struggled through

The last schooner to work in Muskegon's waters, the *Our Son*, being towed out of the harbor ([P86–128] Muskegon County Museum).

the open lake and then down the eastern shore. Just south of Ludington, Mohr changed course again, heading westward and putting his vessel through more punishment from the pounding waves. What drove him to place his ship and crew in such danger was a strong feeling that he was needed at a certain location in the middle of the stormy lake. When he caught sight of the *Our Son* in her dying moments, the purpose of his hunch became clear.

Mohr sent an SOS and the car ferry *Pere Marquette No. 22* responded. With the *Nelson* damaged and the *Our Son* sinking, he was unsure if the rescue he was about to attempt was going to work and wanted another ship to stand by, ready to assist. The *Nelson* circled the schooner, pouring oil on the water to calm the waves enough to allow

CHAPTER 4

the steamer to approach with less risk of collision. Nelson and the six crewmen on the *Our Son* had gathered on the port side and, as the ships made brief contact, leaped to the steamer's deck. Only about a half hour later, the ancient schooner disappeared beneath the waves.

The *William Nelson*, with her grateful and relieved passengers, continued westward and then followed the Wisconsin shoreline to Chicago. Word of the exciting rescue had been wired in by the car ferry and the press was out in force to interview the key players in this drama when they made port on September 27. The story the reporters got, however, was not as strange and fascinating as what came to light some time later.

Visiting some friends in Montague, Michigan, was Joseph A. Sadony. While he and the others stood looking out on the raging lake, someone wondered if there were any ships out there. Sadony, known to have a proven talent in extrasensory perception, responded that there was a sailing ship that was off course and in danger of sinking. He detailed the appearance of the helpless schooner, adding that there was another, larger vessel which, if the captain followed his intuition, would come upon her. The people in Sadony's group doubted the veracity of his "mental vision," reasoning that no schooners were still sailing on the lakes.

Sadony and Mohr were old friends and had been aware of the psychic attunement they shared. When Mohr found out what Sadony had "seen" on September 26 as he stood near storm-swept Lake Michigan, he concluded that there must have been a three-way telepathic message sent that day—Captain Nelson of the *Our Son* sending out his desperate hope, Joseph Sadony picking up on this message and relaying it to Captain Mohr, who followed his hunch and effected the dramatic rescue.

Breakwater Blues: The Wreck of the *Henry W. Cort*

On four occasions in 1934, an aging whaleback boat, the *Henry W. Cort*, entered Muskegon harbor with a load of pig iron for the Campbell, Wyant and Cannon foundry. The *Cort* had seen better days. The 316-foot vessel with the distinctive snub-nose profile characteristic of the pigboat had been launched at the McDougall Shipyard up in Superior, Wisconsin, in 1892 and christened the *Pillsbury*. Originally, the *Pillsbury*'s typical cargo was grain for the Pillsbury Flour Mills Company. Three years into her career, the ship was sold to the Bessemer Steamship Company, which renamed her the *Henry W. Cort*. The Pittsburgh Steamship Company, in turn, bought her in 1901. Under her new ownership, the *Cort*'s main cargo consisted of iron ore transported from Lake Superior's ports to the industrial cities on Lake Erie. Upbound, she carried coal. Occasionally, late in the shipping season, grain from the fall harvest filled her hold.

Outside of the Big Storm of 1913, during which she sustained relatively minor damage, the *Cort*'s years of service were uneventful. However, this changed in December 1917. Winter came early to the lakes that year, and the cold temperatures froze the waterways, trapping a number of ships. The *Cort* and another vessel that could handle ice-breaking duties were summoned to break the ice on the Detroit River and free about a dozen vessels. While maneuvering in the river's close and crowded quarters, the *Cort* hit the large ore carrier *Midvale* and quickly sank in thirty-five feet of water, her crew taken off the vessel just before she went down. Salvage efforts had to wait till the following spring, and the effort was hampered by a number of difficulties. Finally, the whaleback was raised and towed to Toledo for extensive repairs.

In 1927, the *Cort* was sold to the Lake Ports Shipping and Navigation Company of Detroit. She was first taken to Lorain, Ohio, for major changes; in addition to a larger deck house, she had two large whirly cranes attached to her deck. The cranes could load and unload scrap and pig iron by means of magnets, or coal, sand, stone, and slag with the use of grab buckets. Her owners set her on a regular route between the industrial centers of Detroit and Cleveland. However, bad luck continued to plague the vessel. In August 1928, she grounded hard on Colchester Reef in western Lake Erie. Once lightered, she was towed to Detroit for repairs. Again she hit bottom, this time in 1933 while downbound in the Livingston Channel of the Detroit River. The crew managed to keep her pumped out while being towed back to Detroit, but on the approach to the Nicholson dock, the *Cort* sank. Once more, she was salvaged and put back into service.

On her last run for the 1934 season, the *Henry W. Cort*, commanded by thirty-five-year-old Captain Charles Cox, sailed up the lakes from Detroit to Lake Michigan. On Tuesday, November 27, she cleared Muskegon and headed for South Haven with a load of pig iron. In Chicago, the *Cort* picked up more pig iron, this time for the Holland Furnace Company. After departing Holland, she made for Gary, Indiana, to take on a cargo of structural steel, then head back for Detroit. But that Friday, November 30, while en route to Gary, the *Cort* ran into a heavy gale, with winds from the southwest clocked at forty-five miles per hour. As the intensity of the winds increased, the whaleback struggled to make headway. The fact that she was traveling light made the endeavor even more difficult for the blunt-nosed pigboat. The big cranes on her deck made her top-heavy, and Captain Cox weighed the risk of turning around in the heavy seas, fearing she might capsize. The winds built to gale force, shrieking across the wild lake at sixty miles per hour. When the *Cort* encountered monstrous waves near Michigan City Cox decided to make the turn and run before the storm. He figured he had a choice of either beaching his vessel at Little Sable Point or making for the shelter of Muskegon's harbor with its new arrowhead breakwater. He chose the latter.

About 10:00 that night, the *Cort* approached the harbor entrance. Just as the vessel was turning to line up for the passage between the two arms, backwash from the north breakwater rocks met an incoming breaker. The ship was lifted up and smashed against the outside of the north arm. The captain immediately ordered the ship backed up out of the channel entrance, but as she did so, the breakers caught the stern and pushed it around to the north. The *Cort*, mortally holed on her port side, now lay at a thirty-degree angle along the outside of the breakwater, heeling to starboard, with her bow pointing south. Water poured into the hold and engine room as her keel settled in the sand at the base of the rock pile. Just after impact, the ship's lights went out.

CHAPTER 4

The wreck of the whaleback *Henry W. Cort* on the Muskegon breakwater ([P83–313] Muskegon County Museum).

The Coast Guardsman on watch witnessed the *Cort*'s foundering and rang the alarm. Within minutes, Chief Boatswain's Mate John A. Basch mustered a crew of four and set out in the station's largest surfboat—a thirty-six-foot craft with a forty-horsepower engine—to rescue the ship's crew. As they encountered the tremendous seas, the men no doubt wished they already had the larger ninety-horsepower surfboat due to arrive by mid-December. They slowly made their way toward the stricken ship, with their boat pitched high by the huge waves, then abruptly dropped into the troughs. In the darkness it was nearly impossible to gauge the best passage through the crests, which became more violent as they approached the breakwater and the stranded whaleback. It only took an instant for one of the giant waves to toss three of the surfmen out of the boat, but while two of them—Charles Bontekoe and Roger Stearman—struggled back onto the craft, the third—young Jack Dipert—was swept away. The cry of "Man overboard!" rang out, but in the pitch-black night and the raging seas, the others could not find him. The twenty-three-year-old Dipert had been in the Coast Guard service in Muskegon since July. This fateful night was his first chance to participate in a rescue. The others frantically searched for the missing man, but within minutes their surfboat was swamped and lost power, and they had to look after their own lives. They decided to abandon the craft after it was blown around the end of the north breakwater and drifted closer to the beach. Edward Beckman, with a line tied around his waist, was the first to leave the boat and struggle to the shore. He pulled in John Basch next, with the other two following soon after. Nearly exhausted from their efforts, wet and cold, they nevertheless spread out to search the beach for their mate Jack Dipert.

Word of the shipwreck quickly ran through the Muskegon area, and despite the late hour, throngs of people drove to the beaches on both sides of the channel to witness the disaster and, if possible, aid in the rescue. At first, a rumor spread that a car ferry had run aground; later, the wreck was thought to be the steamship *Illinois*, hard on the breakwater. Only later did the truth come out that it was the *Cort*. Among those who turned out were men from the Civilian Conservation Corps whose barracks were located at Muskegon State Park. They joined Basch and the others in the search for the lost surfman.

Also arriving at the windswept shore were some reporters from the *Chronicle*, who interviewed John Basch, a twenty-five-year veteran of the Coast Guard service. They jotted down notes by the beam of a flashlight as he told them, "We lashed ourselves in the boat. Even then, it was difficult to stay with it. One of the big waves caught Dipert and hurled him over the side. We saw him for just a second and then he was gone. We drove back and forth until the engine was flooded and we lost our power. Then it looked as if all of us would lose our lives."[14] When the search for Dipert proved futile, the men were taken by ambulance back to the Coast Guard station for dry clothes and rest.

Hope of finding the *Cort*'s crew alive faltered. The would-be rescuers could barely see the outline of the darkened ship. Waves constantly topped the breakwater and washed over the deck, and no sign of life onboard could be detected. The hours spent waiting for daylight wore on those who kept vigil and aroused their worst fears. Word spread that all onboard the vessel were believed dead. Still, townspeople who gathered on the beach built bonfires in the hope that the crew, if alive, could see them and know that help was coming. The drivers who parked their cars along the nearby stretch of Scenic Drive signaled reassurance by flashing their headlights.

Meanwhile, the Muskegon Coast Guard realized more assistance was needed. The stations at White River and Grand Haven were contacted and both sent men. Grand Haven's Captain William Preston, the hero of the *Salvor* rescue, responded with a surfboat and a crew of six. Preston later recounted that the trip to Muskegon that night was one of the most harrowing he had ever encountered. The craft was pitching wildly through the rough seas, and several times he thought they would overturn when the waves pushed their boat on its beam's end. When entering the breakwater, they passed within one hundred feet of the *Cort* and noticed several lights emanating from within the ship. This gave them hope that the crew was still alive. The Coast Guard cutter *Escanaba* also came up from Grand Haven, arriving at 1:30 A.M. At a distance from the breakwater, the cutter trained powerful searchlights on the wreck, hoping to find evidence of life. In addition, Lieutenant Ward W. Bennett of the Tenth Coast Guard District drove up

CHAPTER 4

from Grand Haven to coordinate the rescue effort. He consulted with Preston and Basch and concluded that the rescue efforts would have to wait until dawn. Any further rescue attempts in the dark would put more lives at risk.

When daylight came Basch led a group of the Muskegon Coast Guard out along the north breakwater. The men, lashed together like mountain climbers, made painstaking progress along the jagged, ice-sheathed rocks as they inched their way 3,000 feet out to the stranded *Cort*. Waves still crested over the breakwater, drenching the men and threatening to wash them into the lake. Captain Preston and his Grand Haven crew had taken their surfboat out to position themselves north of the breakwater. If anyone had been washed off the rocks, they would have been there to pick them up. However, the open seas proved too rough and the boat returned to stand by in more protected waters.

When Basch and his men reached the *Cort*, they found the ship's crew emerging from their shelter onto the deck. Captain Charles Cox and his crew of twenty-four men had survived the night in relative comfort. Their immediate fear after the ship struck the breakwater and was holed was that the boilers might blow up in the rush of cold water. That danger passed, and the crew then took stock of their situation. In the dark they managed to find a lantern and some candles and then made their way to the galley. There, the coal-burning stove, which had been slightly damaged during the collision, was repaired and the cook prepared coffee and a meal from Thanksgiving leftovers. The crew passed the long night conversing, playing cards, or sleeping the best they could.

The Coast Guard shot a line to the wreck and the *Cort*'s crew descended the thirty feet from the tilted deck to the breakwater, the first few climbing down hand over hand, but the last twenty in an improvised breeches buoy. Captain Cox was the last to leave the ship. Those anxiously watching from the shore counted the men as they appeared and cheered each survivor.

The *Cort*'s crew, tired and cold, now faced the worst of their ordeal—walking along the icy, wave-swept breakwater to the shore. Tethered together in three groups and assisted by the Coast Guard, they made the treacherous journey over the rocks. Those who slipped on the crags were helped up and supported by the others. Only near the end of the trek did one man collapse from exhaustion. Several of his shipmates managed to carry him in a blanket the remainder of the way. Witnesses to the drama watched the slow procession of the survivors and their rescuers, with the men sometimes hidden from view by snow and spray. By 9:40 A.M., all were on the beach and the crowd burst into cheers. Two men were transported to Mercy Hospital for treatment of exposure and minor injuries. The others were taken to the Civilian Conservation Corps' barracks, where they could warm up and recuperate from their ordeal. Several days later, when the weather calmed, the crew was allowed to return to the wreck to recover their belongings.

Lieutenant Bennett praised the efforts of rescuers Preston, Basch, and the men in their crews, saying, "They performed in the best tradition of the lifesaving service."[15] He also acknowledged the assistance of a number of others, including the men of the Civilian Conservation Corps, and Mrs. John Basch and the other women who provided meals and hot coffee for the hardworking Coast Guard crew.

The *Cort*'s crew make their way along the icy breakwater (© *Muskegon Chronicle*).

Captain Cox expressed his indebtedness to the Coast Guard for their brave efforts in saving his men, and sorrow over the loss of the heroic Jack Dipert. In describing the last moments of the *Cort,* he blamed two key factors for her foundering: that the vessel was sailing light in such weather, and that a sudden shift in the wind forced him to change plans:

> The forecast was for a northeast wind and I believed we would encounter no great difficulty. Off Michigan City the wind shifted suddenly to the south and I decided there was one of two things to do. I could not control the ship as it dropped into the trough. I could beach the ship or try for Muskegon. It was decided to try for Muskegon and we were about to enter and fighting the storm, when the giant sea caught the ship and tossed it on the breakwater.[16]

He said that the vessel would have been easier to manage if she had been loaded. Instead, the bow of a whaleback rides high when headed into the wind and sailing light. He recalled encountering a storm on Lake Superior while traveling light: "The ship was whirled around four times in that storm."

Cox described the scene aboard the *Cort* when she hit the riprap: "We were making a good entrance when suddenly a great wave caught the boat and tossed it as though it was a cork on the north arm of the breakwater. There was a terrific crash and a big hole was made in the bottom. The stove was knocked down. There was no panic or disorder. We feared the boilers might explode and so we gathered in a forward compartment waiting for the fires to die down."[17] The young captain had spent his entire career on Great Lakes vessels, quickly working his way up from deckhand. For the past four years, he had been master of the *Henry W. Cort*. His brother, James Cox, was a fireman on the ship.

Captain Andrew H. Green, Jr., and C. H. Havill, president and secretary-treasurer of the Lake Ports Shipping and Navigation Company, owners of the *Cort*, arrived in Muskegon within a day of hearing the news of the wreck. They were told the vessel had two holes in its hull, but further inspection by divers had been hampered by bad weather. Until such inspections could be made, the owners refused to discuss the ship's future. The old whaleback was not insured, and considering her years of bad luck and the headaches she had caused the company, they had to evaluate whether to salvage her.

Upon hearing of the *Cort*'s foundering Friday night, Captain Green said he experienced a "terrible ordeal," not knowing the fate of Captain Cox and the crew. The news of the rescue reached him Saturday noon when he arrived in Muskegon by train from Detroit. He dismissed the loss of the ship, but rejoiced to hear that all the crew were safe, praising them as "truly worthy of the title of seamen." He added, "I didn't read the newspapers coming to Muskegon Saturday morning for I didn't want to believe my men were gone. I know them all."[18]

Green gratefully acknowledged the courage and dedication of the Coast Guard and others who helped in the rescue. Tears came to his eyes when he described the brave conduct and selfless concern the *Cort*'s crew showed each other from the time the vessel was caught in the storm to their perilous trek along the breakwater: "When they came to leave the ship, it was the oldest and weakest man who was given the first chance for his life and the captain who went overboard last. Then it was the younger mates who carried Harry Sutton, the cook, to safety. It showed their spirit, too, when they tied themselves together and all came ashore helping one another."[19]

Ultimately the company decided not to salvage the wreck, and she was left where she lay, stranded along the outside of the Muskegon breakwater. The bow soon broke off and sank. Dynamite was used to remove the upper cabin, which was deemed a navigation hazard. Today, only a pile of rubble lies at the *Cort* wreck site.

The *Henry W. Cort* had been involved in tragedy on an earlier visit to Muskegon that same year. On the afternoon of Saturday, June 2, at the eastern end of the channel, the whaleback collided with an outboard motorboat carrying three fishermen. Two of the three drowned; the third was saved when tossed a life ring by a crewman on the *Cort* and pulled to safety. Several weeks later the coroner's inquest was held, and eventually government inspectors cleared Cox and his crew of any blame.

Tragedy Averted: The Near-Wreck of the *Fred W. Green*

Only two years after the wreck of the *Cort*, Lake Michigan's raging seas sought to impale another ship on Muskegon's breakwaters. It was a close call, but the *Fred W. Green* managed to escape destruction thanks to the expert handling of her master, Captain Ole Jacobsen.

The *Fred W. Green*, a sand-and-gravel carrier, was a familiar sight in Muskegon's harbor. Built in Ecorse, Michigan, in 1918, the vessel, 255 feet long with a beam of 43 feet, was owned by John J. Roen, of Charlevoix.

On Tuesday, November 24, 1936, the *Green*, with a crew of twenty-seven and Captain Jacobsen at the helm, left Chicago on a run to Grand Haven to pick up a load of gravel. That afternoon, the vessel, traveling light, encountered one of the worst storms of the season—a gale with winds of forty miles per hour blasting in from the southwest. The rough seas caused her to roll heavily and hampered her attempts to enter Grand Haven's channel. Jacobsen decided to seek shelter in Muskegon's harbor.

The storm intensified as the ship headed further up the shore. At Muskegon's breakwater, huge waves smashed over the riprap, then rolled back in a treacherous backwash. As Jacobsen negotiated the entrance between the arms, the freighter was caught in the tugging backwash and then hurled against the north breakwater. The sharp rocks punctured a hole below the waterline and the vessel listed to port. However, another swell immediately pulled the ship free. Jacobsen realized the *Green* was damaged and made every effort to get her into the channel before the waves brought further destruction. He steered the crippled freighter toward the south breakwater, then straightened her out so she headed down the center of the channel.

The ship's crew, shaken when their vessel hit the rocks, quickly worked to contain the inrush of water by closing off the stern compartment. They also put three pumps to work but could not keep up with the flooding. Listing to port and with her stern sinking, the *Green* managed to reach the north revetment of the channel before the stern touched bottom in twenty-four feet of water.

The Coast Guard sent out a lifeboat to stand by until the *Green*'s crew had secured the ship to the wall. Jacobsen was taken to the Coast Guard Station to file his report of the incident. His skillful handling of the injured ship earned him praise from the community. What turned out to be a bad accident could have been a greater disaster in less competent hands.

With the help of centrifugal pumps provided by the Lyons Construction Company of Whitehall working along with the *Green*'s pumps, the crew managed to dry out the ship. A diver later made temporary repairs to the hull. He found the sharp breakwater rocks had punctured three holes in the bilge—two in the stern and one at midship. Once patched, the freighter was floated over to the old Pere Marquette car ferry slip on the channel's south side to await the decision of where she would be dry-docked for further repairs.

Coming Full Circle: The *Highway 16/LST 393*

Like the *Milwaukee Clipper*, the auto carrier *Highway 16* enjoyed an active and successful career, only to fall on hard times in the second half of the twentieth century. The *Highway*

CHAPTER 4

The freighter *Fred W. Green* loading steel (Historical Collections of the Great Lakes, Bowling Green State University).

16, however, was originally constructed for harder and more dangerous work when built in 1942. The shipyards at Newport News, Virginia, were busy producing vessels for the war effort, and among those to come out of dry dock was the ship christened the USS *LST 393*, launched on November 11. Built in accordance with other landing ship/tanks, she measured 328 feet long with a beam of 50 feet and was powered by twin 12-cylinder diesel engines. Servicemen who traveled onboard an LST found these vessels offered no pleasure cruise. The flat-bottomed hull made for a rough ride when the seas ran high. However, in the duties for which they were designed—bringing in troops and tanks to a beachhead—they acquitted themselves nobly. The *LST 393* performed her varied duties in Atlantic and Mediterranean waters, transporting personnel and vehicles, prisoners of war, and casualties. She also participated in some of the war's most dramatic and heroic events, most notably the Sicilian Occupation of July 1943 and Salerno Landings on September 15 and 21, 1943, and the massive Normandy invasion of June 1944. For her service, she earned three Battle Stars, one for each invasion. The war ended, and on March 1, 1946, the *LST 393* was decommissioned at New Orleans.

Two years later the vessel was sold to the Wisconsin and Michigan Steamship Company, which brought her up to the lakes via the Mississippi River. Converted into an auto carrier, she would transport new cars between Muskegon and Milwaukee. Because her role in cross-lake transportation was seen as an extension of the highway that crossed Michigan from Detroit to Muskegon and then picked up again in Milwaukee, the vessel was renamed the *Highway 16*.

The *LST 393* as the auto carrier *Highway 16* (© *Muskegon Chronicle*).

The former transport that once carried Sherman tanks now filled her hold with new General Motors autos made in Detroit for delivery to Milwaukee and points further west. On the return trip, she carried cars made in Kenosha by American Motors. Occasionally she helped the *Clipper* when there was no more room for passenger vehicles in the car ferry's hold. The *Highway 16* maintained a year-round schedule. Usually she could handle the harsh winters, but on two occasions, in January 1962 and January 1963, she became trapped in thick ice off Muskegon harbor, with her 1963 entrapment lasting seventy-two hours. Overall, the *Highway 16* performed admirably. Her former captain, Robert Priefer, recalled her years as an auto carrier: "She was built for getting onto the beach, discharging cargo and getting out. She wasn't made to be a ferry, but she did a very good job."[20] Her postwar career was tarnished by one tragedy. On July 4, 1959, while sailing inbound through Muskegon Channel at about 2:00 A.M., she ran down a cabin cruiser with eight people onboard, six of whom drowned.

After twenty-five years of civilian service, the *Highway 16* made her last voyage on July 30, 1973. Like the old car ferries, she had fallen victim to changes in the railroad industry. Improved rail service made it more economical to transport cars through the

CHAPTER 4

Chicago area than across the lake. The ship was sealed up and lay idle at the Mart dock for the next twenty-seven years. But the new millennium has other plans for the old vet. The *Highway 16* has been targeted for restoration and, together with several other historic vessels, should enjoy a renewed career as part of the new Great Lakes Naval Memorial and Museum on Muskegon Lake.[21] In ceremonies held on May 28, 2000, she was given her old name *LST 393* and dedicated to the memory of LST crews by members of the USS *Silversides* and Maritime Museum.

The historic significance of Muskegon's *LST 393* is clear. Nearly a thousand landing ship/tanks were built during World War II. Today, a few of them may be found in foreign waters, but only two such vessels that retain the profile of a true LST can be found in North American waters—the *LST 393* and the *LST 325*.[22] The museum organization made an agreement with the ship's owners to restore the vessel to her World War II glory, complete with a fresh coat of grey paint and armaments. The bow doors and ramps had been plated over during her conversion to an auto carrier; now they will be uncovered and restored. Otherwise, relatively little work needs to be done; her structure is sound, the engines are in working order, and the interior is in excellent condition. In 2002, the *LST 393* was opened for public tours.

Laid-Up Lakers: Steel Strikes of the 1950s

Muskegon's harbor remained lively for the first half of the twentieth century. The new industries required materials that could be transported most efficiently by the large Great Lakes freighters and tankers: coal, pulpwood, oil, and limestone. Sand and various manufactured products were shipped out. However, shipping activity around all the Great Lakes slowed significantly on two occasions in the 1950s when steel strikes idled many big boats. Both times, Muskegon Lake became a parking lot for a fleet of vessels waiting out the strike.

The nation's industries were crippled in July 1956 when union workers for the steel companies walked out in a labor dispute. As a result, three hundred ore carriers sought out harbors around the Great Lakes where they could drop anchor until the strike was settled. The port of Muskegon was unfamiliar to the ships of the steel fleets, but the deep channel and large lake harbor could provide ample space for a number of them. Arrangements were made for vessels of the Interlakes fleet, Hutchinson and Company, and Pittsburgh Steamship Company to spend their down time on Muskegon Lake.

At 9:30 A.M. on July 2, the first ore carrier of many—the 618-foot *J. L. Mauthe*, an Interlakes ship owned by the Pickands-Mather Steamship Company—sailed into Muskegon and tied up at the Municipal Marina property. The *Mauthe* was the flagship, the largest of the Pickands-Mather fleet. Workers were just completing the temporary anchorage facilities for the twenty-some vessels expected to dock along the waterfront when the next freighter, the Interlakes ship *H. G. Dalton*, arrived outside the breakwater that afternoon. Captain Frank VanDusen, the master of the *Mauthe,* telephoned the *Dalton* and highly recommended their new accommodations: "It's a good, clear harbor. Plenty of room here."[23]

More Interlake freighters entered Muskegon over the next several days: the *Frank Armstrong, William McLauchlan, Col. James Pickands, Samuel Mather,* and *Harry W. Croft.* The *Charles L. Hutchinson,* flagship of the Hutchinson and Company fleet, was an early arrival and anchored on the North Muskegon side of the lake, at the foot of Third Street. Before long, a total of twenty-eight large ore carriers lined the shore. Those on the Muskegon side were tied bow and stern to each other. At the beginning of the strike, the crews stayed aboard their ships, and mail and food service was provided by the Puhalski Food Market, which set up a water-borne delivery system. Later, the crews were allowed to go home. The month-long strike proved to be a boon for local ship supply and repair firms, which did business to the tune of $50,000. Thus, while the four-week work stoppage hurt the big industrialists, it helped some local businesses. It also was a Muskegon boat watcher's fantasy-come-true to see so many ships—and ones not normally seen in the local waters—in the harbor at one time. Not since the lumber schooner days had the Port City been so crowded with large ships.

On Saturday, July 28, news of the strike settlement instigated renewed activity around the lakes. In Muskegon, ship officers and cooks returned to the idled vessels that same day in preparation for sailing by mid-week. The crews got orders to report by Monday morning. Once the formal announcement came, the race would be on for the freighters, sailing light, to beat the other vessels to the ore docks of Lake Superior and make up for the twenty-eight days of lost time. On August 2, local boat enthusiasts enjoyed the major spectacle provided by the procession of the big boats down the lake and through the channel. They never expected to see such a sight again.

However, the situation repeated itself only a few years later. In mid-July 1959, the steel workers again took to the picket lines. This time it took four months for the sides to settle their differences. The ships affected by the strike headed for harbors around the Great Lakes to wait it out. Muskegon played host to eleven vessels during those months. Hutchinson and Company made arrangements for their ore carriers to tie up in Muskegon, with the *Clarence B. Randall, John T. Hutchinson,* and *James P. Walsh* the earliest arrivals, given space to berth at the Hartshorn Marina's lay-up slip. Another Hutchinson ship, the *J. J. Sullivan,* made port several days later on Monday, July 20. At that time, other ore carriers for the Interlakes and Pickands-Mather fleets were still making the rounds to different ports, hauling stockpiling ore, and were expected to lay up within a few more days, some at Muskegon.

The July 20 *Chronicle* noted that that weekend had seen exceptional activity in the harbor: "The local port with arrival of the lakers, heavy car ferry, coal and tanker traffic, and arrival and departure of three overseas vessels, experienced one of its busiest week ends. Muskegon Coast Guard station logged 37 major vessels in and out in the period 8 A.M. Saturday to 8 A.M. today plus scores of small craft."[24] The other ships to lay up

CHAPTER 4

Freighters at sunset, laid up during the 1956 steel strike (© *Muskegon Chronicle*).

along the Muskegon waterfront were the *W. H. McGean, Frank Billings, A. A. Augustus, John Stanton, William A. Paine, Harvard,* and the Hutchinson flagship, the *Charles L. Hutchinson.*

The strike stretched on through the summer and into the fall. Then an emergency arose that compelled two of the ships to leave their berths and head to Indiana Harbor. On the evening of November 3, a smoldering coal fire—apparently caused by spontaneous combustion—was discovered in the hold of the 640-foot *Charles L. Hutchinson* when deck plates were found to be hot. During the investigation, one of the hatch covers was lifted and black smoke billowed out. The captain decided to make a run for Indiana Harbor first thing the next morning where the 15,000 tons of hot cargo could be offloaded. The *William A. Paine,* carrying 7,000 tons of coal, was to follow the *Hutchinson* up the lake and discharge her cargo to prevent a similar incident.

It took some expert handling to free the vessels from the tangle of lines and cables that tied the ships to the moorings. The wind, gusting at thirty-five knots, made the job even more difficult, nearly driving the *Hutchinson* ashore at Hartshorn Light. Once free and traveling under emergency status, the ships made a run for the channel and Lake Michigan. Those seeing the two leave Muskegon and not aware of the situation speculated that the strike was over. The *Hutchinson* and *Paine* made it safely to Indiana Harbor, and once the coal was unloaded both ships returned to Muskegon to continue their lay-up.

Six of the eleven ore boats in Muskegon during the 1959 steel strike (left to right), *Clarence B. Randall, James P. Walsh, John Stanton, William A. Paine, A. A. Augustus,* and *Frank Billings* (© *Muskegon Chronicle*).

Within days of their return, however, the steel strike ended. On November 9, crews started heading back to the laid-up vessels to prepare for late-season runs to ports on Lakes Michigan and Superior. Five of the ships—the *Sullivan, McGean, Billings, Augustus,* and *Stanton*—had ore in their holds scheduled for delivery at Indiana Harbor. The *Hutchinson* and five others soon sailed for Duluth and other Lake Superior ports to pick up loads of iron ore. To stretch the season, officials at the Soo Locks announced that they would stay open past the closing date of December 15 so more loads could be transported to the steel mills on the lower lakes.

Breakwater Blues Reprise: The Ordeal of the *Makefjell*

Foreign ships could visit Muskegon only during the months when the St. Lawrence Seaway was open. During the 1960s the *Chronicle* would trumpet the arrival in port of the first salty of the season; if spring came early, a foreign vessel might make it through during the first week in April. Toward the end of the year, ship captains were under pressure to make it down the lakes and through the seaway before it closed in late November. The threat of the notorious November gales, which not only endangered ships on the open

CHAPTER 4

lakes but also caused delays in ports, added to the stress felt by foreign shipmasters as they kept to a tight late-fall schedule.

One salty on her final run of the season made local history as the last (to date) shipwreck in the waters off Muskegon. The *Makefjell* story is reminiscent of the *Henry W. Cort* wreck, minus the human drama, but rife with examples of poor coordination of salvaging efforts that dragged this Scandinavian saga out for a full week in late fall 1962.

The *Makefjell*,[25] a modern (three-year-old) Norwegian freighter of 452 feet, was bound for Muskegon from Milwaukee on Thanksgiving evening—November 22—with a heavy load of construction equipment and automotive parts. In Muskegon, she would add another 250 tons of cargo to her 5,000-ton load before heading out the seaway. Lake Michigan was rough that night, with winds of thirty miles per hour creating eight- to ten-foot waves. Somehow, the pilot misjudged the harbor entrance and the ship hit the outside of the south breakwater near the lighthouse at the end of the arm. The sharp rock ripped a seven-foot gash in her starboard side and water rushed into the No. 2 hold. While her bow was hard aground, her stern was free. But the wind and strong current pushed the vessel around until she lay alongside the rocky wall.

Captain Ernst Pederson and the crew of thirty-six were in no immediate danger and all remained aboard the ship while inspections were made to assess the damage and options were considered by several authorities on how best to free her. The crew tried pumping out the water but made little progress. The Coast Guard cutter *Woodbine* responded and tried pulling the vessel off with a nine-inch hawser, but the line snapped. By dawn, the salty *Prins Willem V*, sister ship to the *Makefjell*, arrived, offering to assist the *Woodbine* in a second effort. This time they would try a tandem towing hawser, with a line connecting the stern of the *Makefjell* to the stern of the *Woodbine*, and another line connecting the bow of the cutter to the stern of the *Prins Willem*. But before they could attempt the operation, Captain Oglestaadt, the ship owner's representative from Chicago, arrived and halted any further attempts to free the ship. The *Makefjell*'s captain was concerned that his vessel might have lost her stability; there was no certainty she would float if pulled off the rocks.

The pressure was on to free the ship before the seaway closed November 30. The *Prins Willem* was released from salvaging duties and ordered to take on the cargo at Muskegon's Mart dock intended for the *Makefjell*. At least one of the two Fjell-Oranje Line ships would make it through the seaway in time.

Heavy seas pounded the stranded vessel Friday night, the waves breaking over her stacks. The *Woodbine*, which had held a line on the big ship to keep the stern from hitting the rocks, had to leave the *Makefjell* when it was decided that salvage operations would be needed to save the vessel. (Regulations state that the Coast Guard can provide no further assistance to a stranded vessel once commercial salvaging operations begin.) However, the wave action caused the freighter to lift and settle repeatedly, gradually moving her further into the harbor entrance. The captain called the *Woodbine* back and a line was again attached, but the strain was too much and the line broke. The cutter's Lieutenant

The Norwegian freighter *Makefjell* hard on the south breakwater (© *Muskegon Chronicle*).

Commander Joseph Fox, seeing that his boat and crew were in danger from the rough seas and heavy snow on the deck, returned to port.

In the meantime, strategies were outlined to help free the *Makefjell*. The authorities involved had to consider a number of factors in trying to determine the best course of action. Complicating matters was the weight of the ship's cargo, which, combined with the water in the hold, would make it nearly impossible simply to pull her off the breakwater. Offloading some of the cargo was deemed necessary. However, tugs and barges for lightering the ship were not readily available; it would take several days for them to reach Muskegon, and that was if the weather held. In addition, a lightering operation would be hazardous if the surf was running high. If the vessel was pulled free from the rocks but sank, she might block the harbor entrance, disrupting shipping traffic. If a major storm blew up, she might be pounded on the rocks and damaged further.

While the ship's predicament was a headache for the maritime authorities, it provided great excitement for the locals. In Muskegon, the Thanksgiving holiday weekend looked more like the Fourth of July as hundreds of townspeople gathered on the beach at Pere Marquette Park to view the *Makefjell* wreck. The crowds swelled into the thousands as they were joined by visitors from around western Michigan and even out of state. During the first three days an estimated 150,000 thronged the shoreline. Cars slowly cruised

CHAPTER 4

the parking area and found empty spaces scarce. Muskegon police were busy keeping people from making their way out onto the south breakwater to get a closer view. After a snow fence was trampled down, the police erected a sturdy barricade as a more effective deterrent. Those who had just put their boats into storage for the winter brought them out again and, weather permitting, tried to get as close as possible to the Norwegian ship and other vessels assisting her. The owner of a fishing tug even bought time on local radio stations, offering excursions to the wreck site for $1.50 per person. He was quickly put out of the tour business by the Coast Guard. The stranded ship held the people's interest for an entire week.

That weekend some progress was made, but not enough. The seas moderated after Friday's storm. Barges and additional pumping equipment had been brought in from various ports, and this allowed stevedores to lighter about 250 tons of cargo. The ship's crew drove wedges and wadded-up burlap into the gash on the starboard side, partially patching the hole, and managed to pump out some water. But bad weather moved in Sunday night and halted the lightering operations.

On Monday tugs, including Muskegon's own *Willard L.*, were able to move the vessel slightly. But the *Makefjell* remained firmly grounded amidships, her bow, with the gash patched up, extending two hundred feet out from the breakwater and her stern free of the rocks. The salvaging operation had settled down to a steady routine of lightering and pulling.

By Tuesday, November 27, the authorities involved in the operation concocted an ambitious plan. A number of vessels, including the Coast Guard cutters *Woodbine*, which had been on duty in Saugatuck, and *Sundew*, brought down from Charlevoix, and the Grand Trunk car ferry, the *City of Milwaukee*,[26] along with the tugs, now joined by the largest tug on the lakes, the 142-foot *John Purves*, would jointly pull the *Makefjell* free. Time was running out; the seaway would close in a few days. Even though the seaway officials offered to extend the deadline as long as the unusually mild weather held, there were no guarantees the injured freighter could make it through in time. Initially the *Makefjell*'s owners accepted the offers made by Grand Trunk and the Coast Guard, and the vessels were on their way to the scene. But before they arrived, representatives of the Norwegian ship's owners unexpectedly cancelled the plan and opted to continue the lightering and pulling operation.

The resulting confusion and wasted efforts led to frayed tempers. *Chronicle* reporter Bruce D. McCrea, who had been following the *Makefjell* story all week, wrote about the frustration felt by those involved:

> Responsible is a combination of exhausted men, a dangerous job . . . and what appears to be lack of what maritime men know as a "salvage master." This is the person who makes the final decision and rises or falls with the results.
>
> The Makefjell situation hasn't lacked for direction. There are any number of able, trained and extremely competent men at the scene. But as one weary operator, who had gone 38 hours without sleep, put it, "it's the old case of all chiefs and no Indians."[27]

On Wednesday the Ninth Coast Guard District at Cleveland, which the day before had deemed the *Makefjell* "a menace to navigation,"[28] gave the ship's owners an ultimatum: they could no longer count on the Coast Guard's assistance unless a major effort to free the ship took place before dawn on Thursday, November 29. Immediately the workers involved redoubled their energies to lighter as much cargo as possible before midnight. In the early morning hours all available tugs, along with the cutter *Woodbine*, would combine their forces to pull the vessel off the sand at the base of the breakwater.

This final operation was a success. By 2:00 A.M. Thursday morning, the *Makefjell* was afloat and under her own power, pushed and pulled to freedom by the *John Purves* and three other tugs. Onshore, the night shift of onlookers sitting in their cars blasted their horns in a salute to the ship. Stevedores continued to unload the ship's cargo while teams of divers inspected the hull fully for the first time since the accident happened. It looked like the *Makefjell* would make it through the seaway by the December 4 deadline.

The ship did make it through the seaway, and just in time. Shortly after she cleared the last lock near Montreal, a wintery storm struck, bringing the seaway shipping season to an abrupt end. The *Makefjell* underwent hull repairs in Quebec and later in her home port of Oslo.[29]

The full, official report of what happened to the Norwegian ship on the evening of November 22 had not been made during the time she was stranded at Muskegon. Seaman Edward Whalen, who was on duty at the Muskegon Coast Guard Station, saw the vessel hit the breakwater. However, the Ninth Coast Guard District Headquarters at Cleveland would not allow him to make any public statement pending a possible hearing. Another witness had observed the *Makefjell* approaching the harbor from the south. Normally, ships approaching Muskegon in rough weather enter from the north, taking into account the wind and wave action that might push a vessel south and thus allow a margin of safety. It is possible the freighter misjudged the effect of the elements and was pushed onto the breakwater.

Three years later the *Makefjell* returned to Muskegon for the first time since her accident. In a lavish reception onboard the ship, her captain, Isak Isakson, and crew welcomed the community, port, and Coast Guard officials who had participated in her rescue. Kenneth Dusing, vice president in charge of operations for Great Lakes Overseas, the Fjell-Oranje Line's U.S. agent, praised the people of Muskegon and spoke highly of the Port City: "The Fjell-Oranje Line has a special affection for the Port of Muskegon. This vessel was in deep trouble here three years ago, and this community turned itself inside out to support her. I know this will get back to other ports, but we should be fair. The Port of Muskegon has the best deep water facilities of any U.S. port on the Great Lakes."[30]

Museum Ships: The USS *Silversides* and the USCGC *McLane*

The ships of Muskegon—from the lumber schooners to the passenger steamers—have actively worked in the harbor, participating in local trade and tourism. However, two

CHAPTER 4

Four tugs attempting to pull the *Makefjell* free (© *Muskegon Chronicle*).

of the more recent vessels to become a part of Muskegon's maritime history are retired, having spent their active years on saltwater in wartime and government service and on the Great Lakes as training vessels. Both the USS *Silversides*, a World War II submarine, and the U.S. Coast Guard cutter *McLane*, a former "rum chaser," found a new home along the south wall of Muskegon Channel as part of the USS *Silversides* and Maritime Museum, later renamed the Great Lakes Naval Memorial and Museum.

The 312–foot *Silversides* entered the war within months of the attack on Pearl Harbor and served in the Pacific fleet throughout the conflict, targeting supply vessels bound for Japan. Thirty enemy ships were sunk and fourteen crippled by the *Silversides* on her fourteen war patrols, ranking her as one of the highest scoring submarines of the war. Her illustrious service gained her numerous awards and medals, including the Presidential Unit Citation for four patrols. Today the *Silversides* is the only remaining World War II sub of the elite group that scored the highest in tonnage sunk.[31]

After her heroic war performance, the *Silversides* was decommissioned from active service in 1946. Like the other veteran, the *LST 393*, she was towed up the Mississippi River to enter the Great Lakes for continued service, this time stationed in Chicago as a naval reserve training vessel. Finally, in June 1969, she was taken off the Naval Register. She lay idle for the next three years, this time facing enemy action from vandals and looters. However, in 1973, plans to have the old sub scrapped were thwarted when a group of supporters, including a number of former submariners, stepped in to save her for posterity. Led by the *Silversides*' former forward torpedoman Richard R. Freitag, the group, under the name USS *Silversides* and Maritime Museum, invested their own funds and countless hours toward the extensive restoration job.

In 1985, the sub's supporters sought another port for the restored vessel. Muskegon businessman Robert G. Morin, Sr., proposed Muskegon as the submarine's new home. After several years of negotiation among politicos, the navy, and the groups in Muskegon and Chicago, arrangements were made to tow the *Silversides* to her new berth in Muskegon Channel. The sub's midnight arrival on August 7, 1987, was greeted by thousands of well-wishers gathered along the channel and bobbing in small craft on the water. Later, on September 19, a colorful celebration saw the *Silversides* named a National Historic Landmark. The event, attended by former submariners from around the country, also gave solemn remembrance to lost submarines and their crews.

Docked along the south side of the channel, the *Silversides* as a museum ship draws thousands of visitors each year, including scout groups, which have booked overnight stays aboard the vessel. The U.S. Navy transferred the care and maintenance of the historic sub to the Great Lakes Naval Memorial and Museum, but the navy still has ownership and regularly conducts inspections of the submarine.

Besides visitors, the *Silversides* has attracted the attention of the film industry. In 1993, a television crew from the BBC visited Muskegon to film the sub for a documentary. Included in the footage is a reenactment of a depth-charge attack as it would have been experienced by the sub's crew. Then, in late June 2001, a film production crew from Miramax spent a week in Muskegon shooting footage of the *Silversides* for the movie *Below*, which is about a fictional submarine mission set during World War II. For certain periods of time that week, Muskegon Channel was closed to all shipping traffic so that tugs could tow the submarine into Lake Michigan in preparation for filming the scenes.

The retired USCGC *McLane* joined the *Silversides* when she was towed into Muskegon in May 1993. The *McLane* had led a varied and exciting life since she was built in 1927, but like so many old vessels she had fallen on hard times in later years. The sleek 125–foot cutter was commissioned during the height of Prohibition, one of thirty-three such vessels to patrol U.S. waters and intercept the rumrunners of the day. In addition, for nearly fifteen years the vessel was used for search-and-rescue operations out of New London, Connecticut, Oakland and San Pedro, California, and Morehead City, North Carolina.

With the coming of World War II, the *McLane*, now relocated to Ketchikan, Alaska, participated in U.S. Navy patrols on the Bering Sea while still crewed by Coast Guard personnel. During this time the cutter was involved in a daring and dangerous expedition to search for and destroy a damaged Japanese sub. The mission, carried out in rough seas, was successful, but only after the *McLane* barely escaped being torpedoed by the enemy. The *McLane*, commanded by Lieutenant Ralph Burns, and another Coast Guard–manned naval boat, YP-251 (a converted halibut boat, the *Foremost*) under the command of Lieutenant Niels P. Thomsen, pursued the sub and finally dropped the fatal depth charges.

In the years after the war until 1969, the cutter carried out patrol duty in the waters off Alameda, California, and later Brownsville, Texas. That year, she was decommissioned. Her retirement was short-lived, however, and a new career opened up when the Marine Navigation and Training Association (MNTA), a private nonprofit group based in

CHAPTER 4

The submarine USS *Silversides* at sunset during the filming of *Below* (Great Lakes Naval Memorial and Museum).

Chicago, bought her. She sailed through the seaway and Great Lakes to Chicago, arriving April 19, 1970. In her new home, the *McLane* was renamed *Manatra II* and served as a training vessel, teaching seamanship and navigation to young sailors. When funding and low interest forced the MNTA to close, the training vessel was laid up. Old and without regular maintenance, she succumbed to deterioration, which reduced her to a partially sunken wreck.

Again, Muskegon's Bob Morin stepped in. As chairman of the USS *Silversides* and Maritime Museum, he saw potential in the aging cutter and had her towed to Muskegon, where extensive repairs were made and restoration done by the Grand Rapids Naval Reserve and a number of volunteers. Given her former name *McLane*, the Coast Guard cutter now serves as a museum ship and, in conjunction with the *Silversides*, provides additional sleeping quarters for the overnight youth groups.

The *Halcyon*'s Days in Muskegon: From Seaside to Scrapheap

Starting in the early 1970s, concerns about the environmental health of the Great Lakes prompted the U.S. government not only to clean up the worst pollution destroying the lakes' ecosystem but also to conduct studies and monitor conditions on the Inland Seas. Vital to this effort are research vessels, fitted out as floating laboratories, which patrol the lakes to test and study their condition. These small ships are owned by the federal government's Great Lakes Environmental Research Laboratory, which is supervised by the National Oceanic and Atmospheric Administration (NOAA).

In 1996, the forty-three-year-old R/V *Shenehon* was due to retire after more than twenty years of service. Another research vessel, the ten-year-old *Halcyon*, was brought up

The USCGC *McLane* (Great Lakes Naval Memorial and Museum).

from the East Coast to Muskegon in October that year to take over the *Shenehon*'s duties on Lake Michigan. The *Halcyon*, a sixty-foot steel craft with twin aluminum hulls, had been used by the U.S. Army Corps of Engineers to map depths of the Atlantic Ocean along the eastern seaboard. Once in Muskegon, she was secured at the Mart dock to be renovated and fitted out with research equipment, then winterized for the season.

When Mart dock personnel came to work around 7:00 A.M. on Monday, December 2, they found the stern of the *Halcyon* underwater, her prow angled high. The ship was slowly sinking in waters twenty-six feet deep. The ship's master, Bill Burns, was immediately summoned, and emergency services called. The U.S. Coast Guard responded, as did local police, fire departments, and the Muskegon County Sheriff's Department, but initially they could offer little help. However, members of Muskegon County's Hazardous Materials Response Team arrived by 8:15 and immediately set out floating booms to contain the diesel fuel leaking from the boat.

The cause of the sinking could not be immediately determined. The vessel seemed fine when last checked by dock personnel at 4:00 P.M. the previous day. When the boat's

CHAPTER 4

crew was aboard her on Friday, November 29, they found nothing out of order. Captain Burns announced that once the *Halcyon* was raised and dried out, a full inspection would reveal what had caused her to sink. He believed the vessel could be fully repaired and put back into service.

The effort to raise the *Halcyon* took days and the combined efforts of Coast Guard personnel, divers, wrecker and crane operators, hazardous materials personnel, and Muskegon firefighters. That Monday, marine contractors and fire department personnel partially pumped out the half-submerged boat with the help of a fire truck, and raised her two feet by hooking up her bow to a large crane and two wrecker trucks. Divers then connected chains and cables to cleats on the submerged stern. They found one of the stern cleats—used when she was tied to the dock—had broken from the strain when the stern went down. The external part of the motor and the propeller assembly were next hooked up. While three men continued to work the pumps onboard the vessel, the cables strained to raise her. The job was long and tedious, but they managed to dry out the bottom cabin, the galley, and meeting room.

Just when the operation appeared to be a success, the lake took the upper hand. Jay Kersman, who led the hazardous materials team, explained: "Eventually, we thought we could get it to float, but one of the cleats on the front all of a sudden just let go. At that time, we had three people on the boat working the pumps. The boat shifted dramatically. It lunged about three feet and started to lean. They knew immediately they had to get off. We grabbed arms and pulled them off the boat and watched it sink."[32] This time, the *Halcyon* slowly and completely sank to the lake bottom until only the roof of the pilothouse was visible above the water.

NOAA officials spent the next day finding a salvage contractor who could lift the *Halcyon* from the depths. They lined up two Muskegon firms—Erickson's Rigging and Millwright Services and Andrie, Inc.—to provide 100-ton cranes to raise the vessel. The two Erickson cranes would be stationed on the dock, the Andrie crane on a barge. The operation was set to take place on Monday, December 9. In the meantime, workers from the various agencies involved prepared the ship for raising. One major task was handled by Marine Pollution Control, a Detroit firm, which came in to pump 2,400 gallons of diesel fuel out of the vessel and into a tanker truck. Only a small amount of fuel had spilled when the *Halcyon* initially sank and it was contained by absorbent booms. Again, water would be pumped out as the ship was carefully raised by the giant cranes. As U.S. Coast Guard Lieutenant Greg Case explained, "It's full of water. If you just pulled up, you could snap cables, injure people, crack open the hull and spill fuel."[33]

The operation began as scheduled but stalled when a load-measuring device on one of the cranes malfunctioned. Efforts resumed the next day. This time, the *Halcyon* was successfully raised and loaded onto a barge. There she remained for the next few months while subjected to thorough inspections that brought forth some startling discoveries as well as incriminating accusations. Her relatively undramatic foundering, at first seen as laughable by the locals who followed the story, took a more serious turn and served to throw light on repeated negligence by government agencies, which nearly resulted in disaster.

An independent marine architect, Robert A. Ojala, was hired by the NOAA to conduct a thorough examination of the *Halcyon* following the accident. He found the vessel's hull was less than watertight and subject to internal flooding, which compromised her ability to stay afloat. In a December 24 letter to the NOAA, Ojala wrote: "In my opinion, you are lucky (the *Halcyon*) sank at the dock. If a minor casualty had occurred out in Lake Michigan, you may have sunk out there with the (boat's) poor watertight integrity."[34]

The *Muskegon Chronicle* conducted its own investigation and found the history of the *Halcyon* was riddled with numerous problems from as far back as 1990, along with coverups and denials that potentially endangered those who sailed the vessel.

The *Halcyon* was built in 1985 for $1 million, and right from the start mistakes were made. She was constructed of a heavy steel that exceeded the weight requirements for the vessel's particular design, and the extra 18,000 pounds made her sit low in the water. In 1994, work done on the vessel's engine and propulsion system resulted in stress fractures in the aluminum outer hull. In addition, zinc plates meant to control corrosion in the hull were poorly installed and allowed water to seep into the rear compartment of one of the ship's two pontoons. These problems did not go unnoticed by the vessel's crew. The *Chronicle* gained access to the *Halcyon*'s logs for the years she was operated by the U.S. Army Corps of Engineers and found numerous reports of flooding in the hull.

The NOAA thought they had a real bargain when they acquired the *Halcyon* for free; the agency had not been able to obtain funding for a new vessel from the government and had checked out the lists of government surplus vessels. When NOAA officials first inspected the boat, she was in the water and they did not notice any leaks. In his report, Ojala stated that flooding was not easily detected because the *Halcyon* lacked proper monitoring equipment: "In some cases, there were no means of determining the presence of water (in the hull) under any circumstances with the vessel afloat."[35] However, early in 1996, an independent consulting firm alerted the NOAA to the *Halcyon*'s structural defects, leaks, and an inadequate drainage system that trapped water in the hull. Despite this knowledge, the agency felt these problems posed no danger to the crew that would sail the boat to the Great Lakes, and thus did nothing to make the vessel seaworthy before it was sent up from Norfolk, through the seaway, and into the lakes to Muskegon.

Ojala's findings were not well received by the NOAA. The agency had sent its own investigators to inspect the ship after the sinking, and they reported that the crew members who were preparing the *Halcyon* for winter lay-up had made mistakes which caused the accident to happen while the boat was tied up at the dock. According to a Washington-based NOAA official, the crew had placed too heavy a load on the rear deck, allowing Muskegon Lake's choppy waves to swamp the boat. The assistant director of the NOAA's Great Lakes Environmental Research Laboratory in Ann Arbor, David Reid, defended this position by saying, "The vessel made it into the Great Lakes. There wasn't any threat to the personnel on the way in."[36] (As one might expect, the NOAA had forbidden the vessel's crew from speaking to reporters.)

Beyond all the finger-pointing and blame-placing, the question of whether the *Halcyon* could eventually be repaired and readied for duty on Lake Michigan became

CHAPTER 4

more problematic as the costs were tallied. The government had already spent $150,000 to fit out the vessel for research purposes. Added to this was the $270,000 to recover the boat from Muskegon Lake. The anticipated cost for making the necessary repairs to the vessel's highly defective hull and resultant damage from the sinking ran from $500,000 to $1 million.[37]

The troubling story of the *Halcyon* was brought to the attention of ABC News correspondent John Martin, whose featured segment, "It's Your Money," informed viewers of cases where tax dollars have gone to waste. Martin visited Muskegon for several days in early March 1997 to do an exposé on the *Halcyon*, detailing the exorbitant and needless costs incurred through gross mismanagement of the research ship. Thus, news of the fiasco reached a national audience.[38]

After the flurry of activity and controversy died down, the hapless *Halcyon* was transported by barge to Bay Shipbuilding in Sturgeon Bay. Repairs were never made and the vessel remained in storage, finally being declared government surplus in July 1999.

With modern navigational aids, safety features, and trained personnel, the loss of a ship to shipwreck is rare these days. Most often, old ships that have outlived their use on the lakes are either sold off to some foreign company for further service in distant ports, or they fall victim to a cutting torch. Such an end is unfortunate, but expected. But when a modern vessel sees only ten years of service before she is tossed on the junk heap, especially when the cause of her demise is solely due to gross and repeated human error, a greater feeling of loss prevails, infused with a certain sense of outrage. Although the *Halcyon*'s stay in Muskegon was brief and her loss pathetic, her story deserves a rightful place in the city's maritime history.

More important, it offers a critical lesson that demands wider circulation and attention from those in positions of authority. Was the *Halcyon*'s case unique, or are there other *Halcyon*s out there, known to be defective but afloat only until a minor accident or major disaster prove their unseaworthiness? The *Muskegon Chronicle* not only covered the loss of the vessel and subsequent findings as news items but also printed editorials highlighting the broader, more disconcerting issues. An editorial of February 20, 1997, concluded with this concern: "What worries us, in addition to the costs incurred as a result of the Halcyon sinking, is that this kind of sloppy work could be repeated elsewhere. It is terrifying to consider a similar incident with far more serious results, affecting possibly a Navy or Coast Guard ship, that would put the lives of members of the military at risk due to the same bungling that sunk the Halcyon."[39] Another editorial put the incident in perspective in this way:

> The Halcyon debacle really only amounts to a dot of ink in the vast federal budget, a tale of a few millions of misspent dollars in a sea of hundreds of billions spent annually by the federal government.
> One question that begs to be asked, then, is how many Halcyon-type blunders have been committed over and over and over again?
> Another is, will anyone in authority learn anything from this embarrassing, and potentially fatal, episode?[40]

CHAPTER 5

Muskegon Today

New Ships and Old

Commercial shipping in Muskegon has slowed considerably over the last few decades. While foreign vessels often came to call in the 1960s, hardly any do so now, their owners wanting to avoid the extra expense incurred in making frequent stops around the Great Lakes. Lakers enter the port on the average of four or five times a week, unloading coal for the B. C. Cobb generating plant or Sappi Fine Paper[1], or stone at the Verplank dock and cement at the Lafarge dock. Avid boat watchers take special note when a rare visitor arrives. In late November 2000, the *Arthur M. Anderson*, a 767–foot freighter of the USS Great Lakes Fleet, docked at the Mart for repairs to her boilers. Freighters of the USSGLF rarely visit Muskegon's harbor.[2]

But as Muskegon enters the new millennium, city leaders are discussing several proposals to reinvigorate maritime life in the Port City. One is establishing a commercial shipping zone at the east end of Muskegon Lake. A fifty-three-acre waterfront site near the Cobb plant, currently zoned "lakefront recreational," if rezoned, could draw greater shipping activity. Another plan calls for the reestablishment of ferry service between Muskegon and Milwaukee, possibly using high-speed catamarans to carry several hundred passengers and approximately sixty-five vehicles. Several outfits have offered their plans, but to date no firm deal has been struck. Initial feasibility studies have shown that some form of cross-lake transport has good market potential, but the details are still in the works. One concern, however, is finding adequate docking space for any such vessel in both Muskegon and Milwaukee, although the old *Milwaukee Clipper* dock by the Mart is being considered as a possible terminal in Muskegon. In addition to this, the Lake Michigan Carferry Company of Ludington, which operates the *Badger,* is moving ahead with plans for cross-lake service between Muskegon and Racine, Wisconsin, aboard the *Badger*'s sister ship, the *Spartan*.[3] The 410–foot *Spartan* is undergoing major refurbishing, which will convert the old ferry into a luxury vessel complete with several restaurants, two movie theaters, conference rooms, and a total of thirty-six state rooms. Once readied, she will be re-christened the *Wisconsin Clipper.* In recent years, cruise ships have made a

CHAPTER 5

modest comeback on the Great Lakes, and in time Muskegon may benefit as a port of call for both foreign and American visitors.

Other maritime activities have helped to enliven the lakefront, most focusing on the important statewide business of tourism. Muskegon was one of six Great Lakes ports selected to host the 2001 Great Lakes Tall Ship Challenge.[4] During several summers in the 1990s, a few tall ships visited the port, bringing back in some small way the graceful and romantic Age of Sail. However, with the event of 2001, a scene more reminiscent of the port's lumber schooner days was created when a total of twenty sailing vessels— primarily schooners, brigs, and barquentines—arrived in Muskegon Lake August 9–12 and docked at a specially constructed marina at Heritage Landing in the city's downtown. The festivities were capped by the Parade of Sail as the ships left the harbor and people, many with cameras and camcorders, jammed the shorelines and channel to witness and record the departing white-winged fleet. The event was widely publicized and over 100,000 visitors from around Michigan and nearby states came to the city for the festive occasion. The crowds were not as large as those in other cities on the ships' itinerary, but the excitement and enthusiasm ran high and gave Muskegon a much-needed boost. Future tall ship festivals are expected to become part of the Port City's summer events every few years.

Prior to the 2001 event, the first tall ship in recent memory to enter Muskegon's harbor was the 237–foot *Christian Radich,* which toured the lakes and U.S. seacoasts in 1976 as part of the nation's bicentennial. However, an even earlier—and unexpected— visit to Muskegon by a famous tall ship and by an historic naval vessel took place in August 1913. To mark the one hundredth anniversary of Commodore Perry's victory in the Battle of Lake Erie (September 10, 1813), the recently raised and reconstructed brig *Niagara,* which had been Perry's flagship, was towed to various ports on the Great Lakes to be featured at festivals commemorating the historic event. Towing the *Niagara* on her tour was the *Wolverine* (formerly the *Michigan*), an iron-hulled naval gunboat. The *Wolverine,* built in 1843 to patrol the waters of the Great Lakes, had served in various capacities, including as a naval recruitment ship.[5] One of the most lavish celebrations was offered by the city of Chicago, where the two historic vessels were the centerpiece of its Perry Centennial Exhibition.

After leaving Chicago, the ships headed for Cheboygan, Michigan, to participate in another Perry event. However, around 2:30 A.M. on August 22, they were near Ludington when a violent gale tore down the lake from the north, endangering both vessels, especially the fragile *Niagara.* Battling the raging seas was futile, and so Richard Bos, a former Muskegonite who was chief master and navigator of the *Wolverine,* convinced Captain William F. Morrison, the commander of the expedition, to turn back and seek shelter at Muskegon.

The 600–foot towline was taut, but it held as the ships sailed back up the lake. At the channel, the *Wolverine* sent a wireless message requesting a tug, but no tug came to assist them. A stiff north-northeast wind was blowing across the piers, and it was feared the *Niagara*—bobbing "light as a cork"—would be swept across the channel and dashed against the south pier. But expert seamanship prevailed, and late that night both safely entered the harbor on their own. The vessels remained in Muskegon for several days, waiting for calmer weather before continuing to Cheboygan. During that time, the townspeople were given the chance to step aboard and tour the famous ships.[6] Muskegon had not been on the itinerary, but on this occasion the forces of nature brought about a special windfall for the port.

Only two of the many ships wrecked in the waters off Muskegon are relatively intact and can be easily reached by scuba divers. The battered remains of the *Henry W. Cort* can still be seen resting alongside the north arm of the breakwater, and the broken hull of the barge *Salvor* lies in approximately twenty feet of water several miles north of the channel. Other wrecks, particularly wooden schooners and steamships, have left no obvious traces; their timbers were smashed to pieces with scavengers carrying off souvenirs and the sands burying the skeletal remains in unmarked graves. Little is left of these ships for divers to explore. However, officials of the West Michigan Artificial Reef Society plan to deliberately sink a small ship in the waters off Muskegon. Several aging boats, including a fifty-year-old research vessel, the *Cisco*, are being considered for this project. Not only will the wreck attract divers for sport; she will also provide researchers with information on the area's fish population, help them study the zebra mussels that have plagued the Great Lakes in recent years, and measure environmental changes that occur around artificial reefs. The vessel selected will be the third boat deliberately sunk on the Great Lakes; the others are in the waters off the Upper Peninsula.[7]

If all goes well with the plans for the historic ships of Muskegon, visitors will soon step back into maritime history onboard three naval vessels: the USS *Silversides*, the *LST 393*, and the USCGC *McLane*. All three will be part of the new Great Lakes Naval Memorial and Museum at a docking site being developed on Muskegon Lake just west of the Mart. Plans to develop the site were on hold for about a year as a result of a dispute over water rights between the nearby Grand Valley State University's Water Resources Institute and the West Michigan Dock and Market Corporation. When an agreement amicable to both sides was reached in 2001, the museum's project moved forward. The museum board, working with the Mart's president, Max McKee III, secured a twenty-five-year lease to occupy the waterfront. The LST, owned by the Mart, will be donated to the museum in return for a percentage of the gate receipts. The site is expected to draw 100,000 visitors annually. In addition, the *Milwaukee Clipper* could well become a major attraction for visitors to the area and serve as a reminder of the days when steamship travel flourished on the Great Lakes.

The glory days of Muskegon's shipping era may be past, but with these current projects and a renewed interest by maritime history enthusiasts—local, regional, and national—the Port City may still conjure up the spirits of the HMS *Felicity, Lyman M. Davis, Alabama,* and all the other ships that graced this lake harbor and sailed the waters beyond the windswept dunes.

THE GOOD CAPTAIN

Ships and maritime life on the Great Lakes have inspired many poets and songwriters over the years. In July 1915, William D. Totten, an attorney from Seattle, was a passenger aboard the Goodrich steamer *Alabama,* at that time commanded by Captain W. E. Franklin. He later penned a poem titled "The Good Captain," which he dedicated to the shipmasters of the Goodrich line. When Goodrich received the poem, the company's vice president and general manager, H. W. Thorp, made copies of it and sent it to all the ship captains. I found it in the Stufflebeam collection at the Muskegon County Museum archives and received permission to publish it.

The Good Captain

Beneath a clouded midnight sky
When angry waves ran mountains high,
A captain paced the deck
And through the darkness peered ahead,
While o'er the deep his vessel sped
Avoiding shoal and wreck.

The sleeping passengers below
His many trials could not know,
On him they well relied;
And when the dreary night had passed
They saw the stately ship made fast
In port—her master's pride.

In many a voyage he'd set sail
From port to port through storm and gale,
And brought her safely through;
But he alone was made aware
Of burdens of a Master's care
For hardships well he knew.

THE GOOD CAPTAIN

He always did his duty well
And his admirers proudly tell
Of all his virtues fair,
His sweet reward is honest fame,
A record clean, an honored name
And praises rich and rare.

Life's work well done, its race well run,
When gleamed for him its evening sun.
At peace with all mankind,
Still masterful he saw afar,
The gleaming of God's evening star,
Which all good seamen find.

    Wm. D. Totten
    November 22, 1915
    Seattle

APPENDIX A

Angus Linklater/The *Granada*

Angus Linklater, one of the three survivors of the lumber schooner *Granada*, wrecked off Muskegon's harbor during the terrific storm of October 15, 1880, told the story of the ship's last run and tragic loss to a *Muskegon Daily Chronicle* reporter. His harrowing account appeared in the October 18 edition of the paper.

My name is Angus Linklater. I reside in Chicago, am a brother of the captain of the schooner. We left this port Friday evening with a lively breeze, bound for Chicago. When about half way over, the storm came up, and shortly afterwards the schooner lost her steering apparatus. The storm became more severe and we were obliged to drift about at the mercy of the gale, expecting each moment would be our last. Two schooners and a barge passed us, and so close, too, that I could read their names. They did not offer to assist us in any way, but passed us by.

At the time they went by, I was engaged in tying canvas about the boys. Saturday morning we had a little lunch. About noon, the steward and a sailor died from exposure. The steward was badly frightened; his eyes were almost turned around in his head and his arms were as black as coal from the cold. After he died, I did the body up in canvas and left it.

My brother, the captain, was very brave, and all of us kept up good spirits, hoping and praying for safe deliverance. Oh how long the hours were! The scene, sir, cannot be described. Alone on the raging waters with no help near, and expecting each moment to be dashed into eternity. I, myself, (although having been shipwrecked three times before) prayed to God that one of the masts might fall and crush me. We were not lashed to the rigging as there was great danger there, but all stayed on deck trying to keep warm.

About noon Sunday, we sighted land and our spirits revived a little. I should judge it was half past two when the vessel struck the beach. We then commenced to make rafts. The vessel being old, she soon began going to pieces. We could see the people on the beach, see the life boat make attempts to reach us. Soon I noticed the body of a sailor [having been on the boat only one trip and did not know the names of the crew] between the places where the vessel had parted, being chawed up into pieces, and crying, "For God's sake, boys, move me!" I removed him, and wrapped canvas about him, and could hear him groan. That's the last I saw of him.

Finally the mate [William Bissett] and a sailor made a raft and started for shore. The Captain and I being brothers, talked over family matters, and then made a raft and started out. When we had gone a little way, the raft parted, and the Captain went down. When he came up, I seized him and tried to save him. I got him on to the lumber and again was he washed off. That's the last I saw of him. When I pulled him upon the lumber the last time, my hand was jammed in the timbers; I thought my whole arm was off. I clung to the raft till washed off, and then swam. When near the shore, I was picked up by the gallant volunteer crew who went out with the life boat. I was taken to a house and kindly cared for. I had had nothing to eat from the time we had lunch on the boat until I came ashore Sunday night, nearly 11 o'clock.

APPENDIX B

Capt. J. D. Dunbar/The *R. B. King*

After his schooner, the *R. B. King*, was lost on the Muskegon piers during a November gale, Captain J. D. Dunbar talked to a reporter for the *Muskegon Daily Chronicle*. The account of the shipwreck and Dunbar's report appeared in the November 9, 1885 edition under the headline "A Schooner Wrecked." The following is Dunbar's statement.

We left Chicago at 9 o'clock Saturday morning [November 7] and made a flying trip across. The wind was blowing at a lively rate and a heavy sea was rolling. One hour after we sighted the lights at this harbor, we struck the north pier. The vessel immediately filled with water. Three of the men at once fastened themselves in the main rigging and I got into the fore rigging. In a few minutes, her mast went out and then she capsized. We were then all in the water and were forced to let go. At this time, the life saving crew fired a rocket to let us know that our situation had been discovered, and to encourage us, if possible, to hold out until they could come to our rescue. In a few minutes, I managed to get hold of the foreboom. I had just obtained a good hold with my arm under the foot stops when the life saving boat was over me. I told them I had a good hold, and that they should save the other boys first. In a second or two, another tremendous wave came and I almost regretted what I had said. I "ducked" and in about two minutes the boat was over me. They grabbed me and pulled me into the boat. Charles Anderson, a Dane, who lives in Chicago, and who was mate of the schooner, was next rescued. We were placed on shore and told where the life saving house was and the crew went back to rescue the other two sailors. They were not found and my impression is that they were injured or struck on the head when the schooner went over. The Life Saving Crew is entitled to an abundance of praise for their gallant work in rescuing us—in fact, you cannot say too much in their praise. The night was so dark that the only way they could find us was by listening to our shouts. At the station we were supplied with dry clothes and made as comfortable as possible.

APPENDIX C

Frank Dulach/The *Waukesha*

The *Waukesha*'s sole survivor, Frank Dulach, gave the following account of the shipwreck in a sworn statement before Muskegon's Justice of the Peace Peter W. Losby and others on November 8, 1896. It was published in the *Muskegon Morning News* on November 10.

His Sworn Statement

We left Ludington Friday, Nov. 6, 1896, between 4 and 5 P.M. bound for South Chicago with salt and twenty-five barrels of apples. The wind was northerly. After a while the wind shifted to go around into the west. It was about 10 or 11 o'clock at night when we saw what we thought were the Grand Haven lights. The captain said, "That's not the Grand Haven light." We went a little farther up and after the wind died off altogether. We stood to and the captain said: "We'd better stand off on the other tack." The vessel started leaking about 6 o'clock that afternoon. It was about 12 o'clock in the night when we couldn't get one more suck from the pump, and started pumping on the forward pump and after pump. All were at work except the captain. He called once, and after a while the mate went into the cabin with the sailor by the name of Fred. He gave them drink altogether. About 2 o'clock Saturday morning we met two seas, one from the southeast and another from the west-southwest. The boat started leaking worse, and we kept both pumps going all we could. About 9 o'clock we told the captain me and my watch partner, he had better put the boat on the beach wherever he could get her, as we could not stand to pump all night and day. He said to us he would go about and tack the ship for the land. We answered back we wanted to see the land first so we could know where we were, and not go like a fool without knowing.

The Captain Master

The captain said he was the captain of the vessel and knew what he was doing. My partner answered him back that he knew what he was doing with a jug of whisky in him. The mate jumped up and said: "You're going to pump; that's all you have to do. We have officers on board to do the rest." I answered him: "If you are the man to look after everything, I am going to look after my life." The mate stood there a moment, then went aft and, turning to the captain, told him he had better go and find out where we were before night. This was about 10 o'clock Saturday morning. We kept off in the northeast. We saw land about 1 P.M. on my watch. It was Little Point Sauble. We started to keep off again, and jibed over, heading straight south along the shore. Then we saw some piers. Some said it was Grand Haven, others Muskegon. The captain was very drunk, didn't know whether it was Muskegon or a chicken in the air. When we got a little bit closer, between me and my partner we found it was Muskegon.

The captain, mate and one other sailor started kicking, saying it was neither Grand Haven nor Muskegon, and he didn't know where we were. I told the captain he had better put the boat in between the piers and let her go, no matter where she went. He said he was sure there was no water, wouldn't put her in, and wanted to go to anchor, pump her dry all he could that night, fix her up and go on the way in the morning for South Chicago. I told him rather than let go the anchor he had better go out in the lake under canvas. We were about a mile and a half from the beach.

The Harbor Lights

About five minutes after we let go the anchor we started to see the harbor lights. I said to my partner: "That sure is Muskegon." I was cursing and swearing because the captain wouldn't try to make the harbor rather than stay at anchor. After he let go the anchor we put fastenings in to keep the foresail from thrashing and going to pieces.

Then we started to pump her out again. We sounded the pump and it was 4 feet six inches in the hold. The captain came forward to the cabin door and called all hands to luncheon. Everybody went and asked him, while eating, what he calculated to do. He said he intended to do the best he could for all. I answered: "That's not the way to do, to lie there at anchor, because by 11 o'clock she will go to pieces." Right after luncheon we started pumping again. About 5:30 or 6 the captain came forward again and said: "The yawl boat and stern tackle are gone." The bow davit went a moment later, and the captain said that it was "too bad." I told him the boats were no good. We went to pump her out again, and the captain came back and sung out: "Get aft and calk her down." She was opening up. I told him it was no use, and at the same time I tried to do the best I could to calk her. I went to my partner, where he was pumping, and told him to go to the captain and ask for a torch for the life boat to come. The sailor, who was drunk, said: "There's no danger here." I said: "No danger for you, but there is for me." I knew what I was talking about. My partner said he would go after the torch. I told him to wait a while. I went and asked the cook for the torch, and he said the captain had it. The captain asked me why I wanted it, and I said: "To signal the lifeboat." He said he didn't believe the lifeboat would come, and told us to wait until morning, when we could hoist a flag, and then they wouldn't come until 9 or 10 o'clock.

The *Waukesha*

Tried to Calk

I went down and tried to calk after the captain went to his room, shut the door and refused to give me the torch. I had a lantern to go below to see to calk, and the captain, when I tried to signal with the light, stopped me before I had it three inches from the rail. I then went down and started fixing her up.

When I got through, it was 8:45. I went forward with my lantern, looked around and said to my partner: "The best way is to slip the cable and let her go on the beach." My partner went aft to take off the cable shackle. The captain heard the noise, went aft and picked up two life preservers, one for him and one for the mate. They went up in the forward rigging and had life preservers with them. The mate had his on, and the captain his in his hand. My partner jumped in the forecastle and threw three life preservers on the deck, keeping one himself. We picked them up, and all hands went up to the fore rigging. After the big cable let go the little one held, but not enough, and we started dragging. We got up only a little way when the boat started to go down on the port side. When she had a list of about three feet the forward mast went over and we all fell off the mast. The cook and Fred, who was the sailor drunk with the captain, were swept off the rigging by a sea. The captain and mate and the Swede sailor got again on the foremast. Me and my partner went in the main rigging on the lee side. I hung to the fore part of the main rigging and my partner on the after part. As we hung, the main topmast went and, together with the cross trees, fell over on us. I was hit on the shoulder, a glancing blow. The cook was struck on the leg and head, which was the last I saw of him.

On the Fore Rigging

I got back on the fore rigging, grabbed the floating foremast and foreyard and lashed them together so the sea wouldn't roll me over. My partner wanted to go on the mizzen rigging and protect himself by the topsail. I called him back. He came. The mizzenmast went in another moment. The five left tried to keep on the raft we had made. The captain was in the fore part, my partner next to the captain, the mate third, I the fourth, and the Swede the fifth, all hanging on. The Swede was so far gone he couldn't help himself. I caught him by the collar and pulled him up all I could. The mate helped me take him up.

The captain began drinking from the bottle he had with him and passed it to the mate, who took a drink. Then the captain took the bottle back. The captain was helplessly drunk. The mate let go the Swede when he took the drink. I held on as stoutly as I could without myself slipping off. I asked the mate why he let go the Swede and he said nothing. I saw then the Swede was dead. I held him with my feet between his legs, but after a while I let go. I am not sure whether his life-preserver was fastened on or not. That was about 9:30 or 9:45.

The captain started jabbering to himself and my partner caught him as he started to fall. I tried to help the captain. We put him astride the yard and tried to hold him, but he lay down helpless.

My partner let go to fix his scarf and the captain fell from my grasp. He came up between the two spars. My partner grabbed him and lifted his head out of the water. I tried to lash him. I said: "There's no more use to help him." This was about 10:30. The washing cut the line and the captain sank, having no life-preserver on.

The Mate Went

About 10:45 the mate went, washed off, though we tried our best to save him. I tried to cheer my partner by saying we were nearing land, and we hung on. About 5 in the morning my partner began freezing. I tried to put his feet in one of the spar lashings and in this way I kept him till daylight, when he fell away. I tried to lash his head above the water and told him the boat was coming. He moaned, tried to get up, said "No use," and fell into the water.

About half an hour after that the lifeboat came and took me off.

When we came along shore to anchor we had a fly up for a tug. No other signals were given, and no signals of distress or for help were given from the vessel at any time.

This is my own story of the wreck of the Waukesha, and is made voluntarily on my part and without any influence of any kind being exerted.
Frank Dulach
Subscribed and sworn to before me this 8th day of November, A.D. 1896.
Peter W. Losby
Justice of the Peace of Muskegon City, Mich.
In presence and hearing of Herbert E. Johnson, D. C. Wickham and A. F. Temple.

APPENDIX D

Frank Dulach Reiterates

In his sworn statement concerning the wreck of the *Waukesha,* Frank Dulach claimed the ship's captain, Duncan Corbett, had been drinking heavily the night the vessel went down. The captain's family and supporters were shocked by what they said was a lie, contending that Corbett was not a drinking man. Dulach stood by his original account and finally felt compelled to prepare a statement to be published in the *Muskegon Weekly Chronicle.* It appeared in the November 19, 1896 edition under the headline "Reiterates!" The entire statement reads as follows.

A Statement from Frank Dulach

After having read the papers of the last four days it seems almost necessary for me to make an apology for not having drowned with the rest of the crew of the ill-fated Waukesha. But I assure you that the responsibility for my being here rests alone with the crew of the Muskegon life saving station. It was them that snatched me from the jaws of death on the morning of November 8, 1896, when they rescued me from the piece of wreck upon which I had been fighting for life for twelve long hours and was well nigh exhausted and about ready to surrender. But they bore me to the station, warmed and nursed me back to strength, for which I am profoundly grateful.

As soon as I had gained sufficient strength to talk I was plied with queries as to how we came to be in such condition without having asked for assistance when it was so near at hand. I related the facts to a reporter and in explaining the reason for not having signaled for help—which strong and willing hearts stood on the shore ready to lend at the first intimation of our situation, it was not possible for me to draw the mantle of charity over the faults and foibles of an erring ship mate, which I would gladly have done but had to tell the facts, for which I have been charged with mutiny, calumny and branded a liar. To excite the sympathy of the public the friends of the captain of the ill-fated vessel have held up the bleeding hearts and wounded feelings of friends of his family. But there is a reverse side to this picture, there are other families and other friends who have hearts and feelings.

It may not be out of place here to note the twelve hours of mental agony and bodily torture that the survivor was compelled to endure through the error of this man whom so many of his friends come and brand me a felon and a liar and then forced me to tell what they don't know about the captain's drinking. They had the evidence of the truth or falsity of my narrative in their possession, the bodies of sailor Fred and mate who I said drank with the captain after the vessel came to anchor, and the traces of alcohol could have been found in their stomachs or my story [is] not true.

Now cease your prattle about what you don't know and if anything more is to be said give us some proof and if those who contributed so freely to the fund for my prosecution would so willingly spend some of it to ascertain the facts about this matter I will go with them where they will find other sources of evidence that my story is true.

Frank Dulach

APPENDIX E

Toronto Evening Telegram/The Lyman M. Davis

The demise of the schooner *Lyman M. Davis* in a blazing spectacle on the Toronto waterfront on June 29, 1934, marked a singular end for one stalwart veteran of the lumber era. A writer for the *Toronto Evening Telegram* witnessed the scene and described it, not only with an eye for the event but with insight into the meaning of the loss of this particular ship. The account, which appeared in the June 30, 1934 edition of the Toronto paper, was sent to the *Muskegon Chronicle,* which reprinted it on July 5 ("Last of Old Lumber Schooners Is Burned").

The Lyman M. Davis, which rode triumphant through Great Lakes gales for more than [a] half-century, was destroyed early today as the feature show in a Sunnyside holiday spectacle.

Burned to the water's edge and wracked by the explosions of powerful fireworks, the stout little schooner, which was born in a Muskegon shipyard 61 years ago, was towed to deep water shortly before 2 A.M. and sunk by a dynamite charge in her bottom.

Only when the final act sent the vessel, hot and steaming, beneath the quiet ripples of the outer bay did the last of the many thousands of persons leave the amusement park. For more than an hour the great crowd stood fascinated by the roaring flames. They were more than firestruck. They were held by the same type of spell which in older days drew morbid crowds to the public Toronto hangings.

Even the most thoughtless of the watchers saw in the sinking vessel something more than the destruction of an inanimate thing. They had a feeling that out in the center of the oil-fed flames, the bursting bombs and roaring rockets, a personality and what, until then, had been a living memory of inland sailing fleets, was quickly dying.

As a spectacle, the schooner's burning was eminently satisfactory. The deck and holds had been piled high with dry wood and tinderlike crates on Thursday, from a Western Gap pier head. Even in that, the vessel's destruction had the character of an execution. She was made to take that last short voyage even as a condemned person is made to walk to the gallows, and she did in the ignominious tow of a sooty tug.

On the deck and in the rigging fireworks experts had placed powerful bombs and rockets. The last property for the fire set was placed late last night when men poured eight barrels of coal-oil through the ship.

Shortly before midnight a tug towed the *Lyman M. Davis* from the Sunnyside anchorage, the spot she occupied last summer and through the long reprieve from destruction gained by those most interested in seeing her preserved as a monument to lakes sailing, to a point about 30 yards beyond the sea-wall. The tug held her there at the length of a great cable.

The fire was set almost on the hour and in a few short moments the flames had roared along the oil trail from stem to stern and to the tops of her slender masts. As the fire burned into her vitals, the bombs and rockets were ignited. The explosions fanned out great sheets of flames and sparks and out from the burning ship rockets rose high and cut into the blackness of the upper sky.

All that remained of the schooner was towed out into deep water before the flames reached the waterline. To the late-stayers there came the sound of a muffled explosion. The fire again flamed high and then quickly died into blackness.

The Lyman M. Davis had ceased to amuse.

APPENDIX F

Frank Blakefield/The *Erie L. Hackley*

When the small passenger and packet steamer *Erie L. Hackley* foundered in northern Lake Michigan in the early evening of October 3, 1903, only eight of the nineteen crew and passengers aboard her survived. Among those lost was the ship's owner and captain, Joseph Verous. The vessel's purser, Frank Blakefield, was one of the exhausted survivors picked up by the steamer *Sheboygan* at about 7:00 the next morning. He gave the following account, which appeared in the October 5 edition of the *Muskegon Daily Chronicle*.

The squall struck us about 6 o'clock as we were just north of Green Island. It came suddenly and with terrific fury. I was in the pilot house with the captain, who had just said the elements looked threatening and that he would try to run to port. When the first fierce gust hit us, the captain tried to throw the boat up into the wind, but his efforts to do so were unavailing. Then I joined him at the wheel, but our combined efforts were not sufficient to make her mind the wheel.

Then, of a sudden, she listed and began to fill with water. With that the passengers and crew were panic-stricken and I left the captain in the pilot house and ran aft to let down the lifeboat. By the time I got aft, the Hackley was filling so rapidly that it was apparent it would be impossible to launch any boats. There came another fierce blast and the upper works went by the board. Then the steamer began to sink rapidly and it was apparent her setting on the bottom would be a question of only a few moments. Eighteen of the nineteen persons aboard were gathered on the deck, most of them in a state of panic. The situation was made particularly heart-rending by the women, who shouted hysterically, imploring the men to save them, and accompanied their appeals for assistance with prayers.

As the boat sank it was clear that there was only one hope of anyone being saved, and that was by clinging to the wreckage. I gave orders for the men to put the women on it first. The did so and behaved bravely. It was then a wild scramble on the part of each man to get such pieces of planking as he could secure and cling to it.

Every man found something to float on except the captain who remained in the pilot house to the last, doing his best to right the boat. He finally went down with her.

We floated on different pieces and for a few minutes we were in sight of each other, but soon darkness came on and we separated.

The last persons that I saw, except for those with me, were the two Vincent girls from Egg Harbor, who were floating together. They seemed to have recovered entirely from their first fright and were making a brave struggle for their lives, a struggle which now seems to have been in vain.

Three of us who were fortunate enough to escape clung to the wreckage all night, bitten by the cold wind and benumbed by the colder water, and the surprise is that we did not all die of exposure. Each drifted, I know not where, until picked up by the Sheboygan.

APPENDIX G

"Doc" Ray Cooke/The *Alabama*

"Doc" Ray Cooke of Chicago regularly sailed between White Lake and Chicago as a passenger on ships of the Goodrich Line. He wrote an account of a trip he made in 1927 onboard the *Alabama*. The two other passengers he mentions are "Doc" Herbert S. Ray and "Gov" W. B. Jarvis, both members of the White Lake Yacht Club. The article was first printed in the *White Lake Yacht Club News* in March 1928 and later reprinted in Daniel Yakes's *Muskegon: First Hand*.

When I went aboard the S. S. Alabama on Saturday, March 3rd, the weather was perfect for that time of year. There was no ice along the west shore of Lake Michigan and the Goodrich Company, in answer to my inquiry, stated that they were encountering no difficulty with ice. Mr. Lyons was at the Purser's window with his usual cheerful greeting, and as I went up the companionway I found Pete Malone at his customary station ready to exchange news for tickets.

He said, "There are a couple of White Lakers on tonight. You will find 'Doc' Ray and 'Gov' Jarvis forward in the dining room."

I thanked him and went up.

Doc was just finishing his dinner and as the ship plowed along with absolutely no motion we three smoked, drank the ship's coffee, and swapped lies until time to turn in. Events at White Lake for the past twenty years were reviewed and when it came my turn to add something to the conversation, I told them how I had crossed the lake in February, 1925, with the temperature 10 below zero and a gale blowing. On that occasion the tossing of the ship awoke me about 7 A.M. Everything was loose on board, and when I lurched into the dining room to get breakfast, I found all the tables upside down and in confusion. Pete was the only man in the galley. He had managed to brew some coffee and together we sat on the edge of a pantry shelf and drank the coffee and ate a piece of hard tack.

On that trip we were six hours late getting to the ice off Grand Haven. We couldn't make port so ran up to Muskegon and found the same ice condition. Returning to the Haven, we approached to within a mile of the piers, shut off the engines and froze in. The next afternoon I walked ashore and froze an ear while doing it. The ship remained in the ice for three days that time.

"That must have been a great experience," said Doc, "I wish it would happen to me sometime."

Pete promised to call us at 6:30 A.M.

I awoke to find the engines shut off. Thinking we were at Grand Haven, I looked at my watch. It was four o'clock. Something wrong somewhere. The ship was rolling slightly and a cold wind filled the stateroom. The shutter stuck, but it came down, and in the light of a full moon I took in the situation at a glance. We were stuck in a polar sea, with snow crusted cakes of ice as far as the eye could reach.

"Damn Doc Ray and his wish," and I went back to bed, pulling the blankets up to my ears.

Pete didn't call us.

We had breakfast at 9 A.M. and then sent wireless messages ashore. It hurt to have to pay for the name, address, and signature as well as the message.

Looking out, we saw two miles of ice between us and Grand Haven and a quarter of a mile behind us. A black cloud was in the northwest, and as we watched we could see spray being shot into the air from the water beyond the ice, like puffs of smoke that traveled along and then dissolved.

A Grand Trunk car ferry and later a second one hove in sight. There was a gale blowing by now and the ferries were in the trough of the sea. As they approached we could see them roll. When they rolled our way, we could see their entire deck as plainly as if we had been perched on the top of their masts.

Pete ventured a sea-going remark: "They are rolling the tacks right out of their carpets."

All day long the two ferries belched smoke and steam, backing and crushing into the ice trying to break their way through. We made one attempt and then shut off the engines and saved the coal.

The crew broke into the cargo and we had our Sunday papers. A greasy pair of cards were borrowed from the forecastle and the game started. With their usual interest in the comfort of their passengers, the Goodrich Company furnished meals and Tom Wickham, the steward, couldn't do enough for us to help make the best of the situation. Every meal was excellent. Jarvis said, he didn't care if we stayed a week.

Just after dark someone reported that the car ferries were in. Our engines started, our hopes arose and Doc Ray wished that we could get in port that night.

We moved back and forth a dozen times making a gradually lengthening groove in the ice and finally got enough momentum to keep on backing towards open water, then a half mile away, the propeller helping to break a track.

The ice had been "making" all day and it was interesting to watch the change in formation as we backed through it. Where we had been during the day, the ice looked like thousands of large tarts all wedged together. These were about twenty feet in diameter, perfectly round with a rim of white snow around the edge and dark water or ice in the center. These tart formations kept getting smaller and smaller until within a hundred feet of open water where they were just starting to "make." Here they were about the size of lily pads, but of the same shape and general formation as those nearer shore. I had always thought that the lake froze when smooth, gathered snow, and then broke up into big chunks whenever there was a storm.

As our stern reached open water, spray came over the deck as there was still a big sea running. We headed up the shore until we reached the track that the car ferries had worked so hard to open and then went through without any trouble, arriving in Grand Haven about thirteen hours late.

The funny part of it was, Doc got both his wishes. He and Jarvis had spunk enough to come back the next night on the boat. Has anybody seen them since?

APPENDIX H

Guy E. Jones/The *Naomi*

On the morning of May 21, 1907, Guy E. Jones returned to Muskegon and his home on Ada Street. Only hours before, he had narrowly escaped the inferno that claimed the Crosby steamer *Naomi*, becoming one of the last to leave the ship. Jones, who had worked as a painter on the *Naomi*, spoke with a reporter from the *Muskegon Chronicle*, recounting his escape and the scenes he had witnessed. His story appeared in that day's edition of the paper.

I was awakened at 1:25 [A.M.] by a violent coughing spell. The room was full of smoke. I could smell it although I couldn't see it. It was still pitch dark at that hour. There had been a call from the cabin watch at every door. But I slept so soundly that I suppose I did not hear it.

The lights were all out and the electricity refused to work. I made a dive for my clothing, got part of it and went immediately on deck. I was without underclothing and hosiery and was lucky to escape with as much as I did.

Arriving on deck I found a large crowd of passengers, some fully dressed, others half dressed, and others still in their night clothes.

By that time lots of smoke was pouring out of the doors and windows of the cabin. A small flame was coming through the floor of the forward deck. Three streams of water were being directed towards it.

All of the passengers, especially the women, were very orderly and level-headed. There was, of course, a good deal of suppressed excitement. The women were asking if the fire was being subdued and the men were reassuring their wives.

When it was seen that the fire was well under way the captain ordered the women folks into the boats. These were lowered by the crew and some of the passengers very promptly. Two boat loads were filled with the women, a couple of children who were on board, and some of the men, and put out into the lake so as to avoid the flames.

By that time, the fire had reached the middle part of the steamship.

The Naomi, in the meantime, had called for help and two passenger steamers and a coal barge were soon in sight. Eleven or twelve of us stayed on board, but only four were lowered, the rest of us waiting for help. When the coal barge came alongside, we simply walked on board.

As we stepped off the fire was completely over the upper deck of the Naomi and the cabin was all aflame. Five minutes later there was very little chance left for anyone to stand on board that vessel without being burned.

I saw one of the men who was burned. Before we left the ship he stuck his head out of the port hole and cried for help.

It was dark then, but from the reflection of the light of the fire from within we could see his head. His voice was full of agony. They told him that there was no chance of getting through the fire to him and asked him his name. He gave it, and said that his partner was dead. When they counted up afterwards, however, four men were found missing.

From the coal barge we were transferred to the Kansas, which is accustomed to meet the Naomi at that point in the line of crossing the lake. The Kansas picked up the others from the life boats and took us on board. For an hour we remained watching the burning vessel. It was a solid mass of flames above its steel hull. Then they took the refugees below and fed and cared for us.

APPENDIX I

Capt. Edward Miller/The *Muskegon*

Captain Edward Miller was one of the first to give his testimony at the federal inquiry held after the Crosby steamer *Muskegon* was wrecked on the pier of Muskegon. His noteworthy career record and professional handling before and during the crisis absolved him from blame. Here is his statement, as published in the November 1, 1919, issue of the *Muskegon Chronicle*.

First, I want to say that a captain and his crew is usually condemned by the reading public in such a disaster as this before the true facts are known. But my conscience is clear because I did all that any man could have done in such an emergency. I followed all the rules of good seamanship, my crew obeyed my orders to the letter. The gale was the worst I have ever encountered during my 35 years of sailing the lakes. The ship was fated, I guess. The facts prove it. My heart goes out to those who lost their lives, and to their relatives. I would have gladly sacrificed my own to have prevented a soul on board being lost.

It was all done in a moment and nothing could have saved my ship. Mechanical agencies were powerless against those mountain high waves, the wind and the undertow that caught us. The wireless would have been of no avail, as the coast guards' boat could not have lived in those waves to reach us had I wirelessed for help.

Besides, the thrashing waters extinguished the fires, put the dynamos out of commission and left the ship in darkness a moment after we struck the pier. Darkness made the rescue work hazardous and consequently costly in lives.

We left Milwaukee at nine o'clock Monday night. I never leave port until I have received the official forecast of the weather from the government or have read the official barometers in the newspapers. When we left Milwaukee the weather report read "Moderate wind." No storm signals had been issued.

I read my barometer. It indicated fair sailing weather and no storm. Had the barometer registered lower, I would have held the Muskegon in port and not ventured out.

An hour after leaving port the barometer read 29.3. At 11 o'clock it recorded 29.4, indicated better weather conditions. It remained at 29.4 until we reached mid-lake about midnight. At 12:30 A.M. I again read the barometer, which I closely followed on account of the unusual calmness of the mid-lake. The lake there was like a mirror. Then the barometer showed 29.3 and at 1 o'clock it had dropped to 29.2.

APPENDIX I

Suddenly from out of the nor'-west came a terrific gale. The wind tossed the waves mountain high. We had no warning. I weighed the question of returning to Milwaukee, but we would have foundered had I tried to turn the boat around in that sea. We were riding the gale easily although the waves were breaking over our decks. Running with the wind and waves was safer than being caught in the trough of the seas.

When we left Milwaukee I decided to remain in the pilot house with my wheelsman during the trip across the lake. Something seemed to tell me that I would encounter rough weather in spite of the government report to the contrary.

I called Ted Mique of Lowell, a wheelsman, from his berth to the pilot house. He was the best of my two wheelsmen, and I could rely on him in any emergency. He was an able and experienced seaman.

"We are going to have a bad gale, Ted," I said to him as he entered the pilot house.

"It certainly is getting rough, captain," he replied. "We can't turn back in this sea though. She's riding it well."

We tested the ship by the rudder often, and she responded quickly. The wind veered from the nor'west to nor'-nor'west. Every moment the gale increased in velocity. In all my 35 years of sailing I never encountered such a sea.

When an hour out of Muskegon, I asked Mique what he thought of running along the east shore to Holland, and then scooting farther inland back to Muskegon by bucking the waves. He said the boat had done it before, but that the channel at Muskegon could be easily made, as the boat was running a true course, despite the wind and waves.

We had an extension made to the rudder last summer after that May accident, and it had improved her steering wonderfully.

When the channel at Muskegon was sighted the waves were tossing us like a cork. I gave orders to have the oil tanks on the port and starboard bow opened to quiet the waves while we were some distance from the entrance of the channel. The oil had no effect on the waves, which continued to break over our bow.

With the wind and waves beating across our quarter, I saw that only full speed ahead would drive us into the channel entrance. I telephoned to Chief Engineer Johnston to give her full speed ahead and to be ready to back her at the same speed. He replied, "Aye, aye, sir."

We were soon making between 12 and 13 miles an hour. As we neared the channel I again ordered the oil tanks opened. Still no effect was noticed on the seas.

As we entered the channel, I had Ted, the wheelsman, hug the north pier to work against the wind and waves, which were breaking over the piers and foghorn house.

We started straight in, nicely, and it seemed that our battle against the hurricane had been won when without warning a great wave struck our port bow and carried us across the channel against the south pier. The wind aided the waves, and a terrific undertow caught us. Let me say here that the Muskegon channel is noted for having the worst undertow on the east shore.

We were lifted against the south pier in a twinkling of an eye. I heard the cabin and upper works crash as we struck.

I got out my life preserver, intending to put it on, but said to myself, "The hell, I won't wear it! I'll die first."

Mique said, "Captain, I would put it on if I were you," while he was adjusting his own life belt. "It may come in handy. We'd better." I followed his advice and put it on.

Then another big wave hit the boat and the cabin was crushed.

Things were happening instantly and the waves were breaking the ship to pieces like a giant human with a great ax. Cracking timbers and crashing of wreckage against the pier were heard above the roar of the waves and the howl of the wind. The water flooded the engine room, stopped the dynamos and left the ship in darkness.

Then the stacks fell. How we escaped from being crushed to death in the pilot house when the smokestacks fell is a miracle.

The upper works of the boat began to go to pieces as soon as we hit the pier and the starboard of the boat was lifted onto it, where her paddle wheel guard caught.

When she struck I telephoned Engineer Johnston to back full speed, but she refused to respond because her paddle wheels were caught on the pier. I knew she was doomed then.

I gave orders to get everybody out of the staterooms, especially the women. Second Mate Steffens carried out my orders. I ordered everybody to jump for the piers. Lifeboats could not be used nor the life rafts in those waves.

I asked Steffens if all the women had been saved. He said, "Yes, captain, as far as I could find out in the darkness. The upper works are going overboard rapidly."

Then a huge wave hit the ship and carried the pilot house overboard. Steffens clung to it. He was carried 600 feet up the channel where the coast guards threw him a lifeline and pulled him onto the pier.

Note: Wheelsman Edward (Ted) Mique survived and was the first to give testimony at the inquiry. Chief Engineer Brant Johnston also survived, but his mother, Mrs. Kate Johnston, who was a passenger onboard the ship, was one of the thirty-one casualties of the wreck.

APPENDIX J

Lyman Nedeau/The *Salvor*

While writing this book, I learned that one of the survivors of the *Salvor* wreck, Lyman Nedeau, was still alive. I reached him at his winter home in Florida with the help of mutual friends and found he was very willing to share his memories of the experience. The following account is not verbatim but written from notes taken during several phone conversations. I sent the narrative to Mr. Nedeau after each revision for his corrections and approval. In June 2002 I met him in person and learned a few more details, which I added to his account.

Lyman Nedeau has lived around water most of his life. He was born on Beaver Island in northern Lake Michigan, the son of a commercial fisherman. When he was still young, his family moved to the Port Sherman area of Muskegon, their home less than a block from the channel. Here his father, Israel Nedeau, continued to work in the fishing industry. The Nedeau family grew to include eight children—seven boys and one girl.

In 1930, at the age of seventeen, Nedeau went to work for the T. L. Durocher Company. His father had become friends with the company's owners, who were based in De Tour, Michigan. This connection helped Nedeau get a job on the stone barge *Salvor*. While some of the men on the vessel had more specialized work as firemen and crane operators, Nedeau took on various duties—deckhand, wheelsman, and dishwasher in the galley—and enjoyed the time he spent onboard. At the Muskegon breakwater site, the stone barges would anchor in the channel. A temporary railroad track had been built along the beach to the shore end, and a hopper, once filled with stone from the barge, would run along the track and deposit its load at the end of the growing arm.

On September 25, the *Salvor* was loaded at Gill's Rock with 2,800 tons of stone. The heavy cargo—half of which was stowed in the forward hold and half in the stern—gave the barge a draft of 30 feet. The following morning, when the *Salvor*, towed by the tug *Fitzgerald*, was heading for Muskegon, Nedeau, along with another crewman, George Secord, was on duty in the pilothouse. It was his turn at the wheel. Although the barge had no engines and was towed by a tug, it was still necessary to steer the vessel, and the men on the *Salvor* took turns as wheelsmen. When the storm hit, the *Fitzgerald* and *Salvor* struggled through the huge waves whipped up by the sixty-five-miles-per-hour winds. Nedeau counted nine waves to the mile. He recalled how the five-hundred-foot towline—a steel cable one-and-a-half inches thick—connecting the vessels was "taut as a fiddle string" when both the stern of the tug and the bow of the barge rode high on the wave crests. Under such conditions, the larger vessel severely hindered the tug, which could barely make headway. The waves would push the *Salvor* toward the shore, and the tug would be pulled back along with it. Nedeau said because they were in such heavy seas and shallow water, the *Salvor*'s crew realized they were not going to make it to Muskegon harbor.

When the cable snapped under the strain, waves turned the barge around so the bow was pointed north. About half a mile from shore, the barge struck bottom and her keel broke amidships under the tons of the stone, which weighted both ends of the ship. After tying down the wheel, Nedeau and George Secord came down from the pilothouse in the stern, and Nedeau worked his way along the boom, or crane, which lay lengthwise on the vessel, bracing himself against it or lying flat on the deck whenever a wave broke over the barge. He reached the base of the A-frame at midship and clambered up the framework to the "rooster" on top, following two other crewmen—Clifford Lane and Harry Smith—who went aloft. Nedeau explained that the "rooster" was the nickname for the system of pulleys atop the A-frame that handled the cables for the cranes. Crewmen—himself included—had to climb up to the "rooster" every six hours to keep the pulleys greased when the machinery was in operation. Both Smith and Nedeau had on their life preservers; however, Lane was not wearing one. With two extra people—Mrs. Ida Olmstead and her son—onboard, there were not enough life preservers to go around. Lane gave his to nine-year-old Lornie Olmstead, who, with his mother and aunt, took to the *Salvor*'s life raft. The life raft was washed off the boat when it hit a leg of the A-frame. While three of the four on the raft made it to shore, Lornie was the one lost in the roaring breakers.

Nedeau witnessed the power of the raging seas as the waves battered the stranded barge. The steel bars of the boom's lattice-work were bent up, and some steps leading to the A-frame were flattened out by the pounding surf. He mentioned that if he, Smith, and Lane had delayed in climbing up the A-frame, the steps to it would have been damaged and useless in helping them reach the upper works.

Nedeau recalled that the worst part of their ordeal was the cold wind. Getting drenched by the waves, which broke high enough to wet them with spray, was preferable, since Lake Michigan was still fairly warm at that time of year. But the fierce winds stung with a bitter, life-threatening chill. The newspaper account states that the men tied themselves to the A-frame, but Nedeau refutes this; they had no lines they could use for such purposes. Instead, they wedged themselves in among the beams and hung on. Nedeau sat between Smith's legs, and they had hoped Lane would make it down to their beam and join them as they huddled to keep warm. Little conversation passed between the men, mainly comments about activities they could see along the shore as a crowd of people gathered there and the Coast Guard made attempts to rescue the *Salvor* crew.

By morning, Captain William Preston and his men from the Grand Haven Coast Guard arrived and prepared to pick up the two survivors on the A-frame. Nedeau recalled their boat rode right over the submerged deck of the *Salvor* as they got into position. Smith was the first to jump into the raging water. He landed in the trough of a wave, narrowly missing the many cables strung on the barge. If he had not jumped right, the cables would have severely cut or killed him. Nedeau plunged in next, landing in a cresting wave well clear of the cables, and was immediately picked up by the Coast Guard crew.

It was a rough ride back to Grand Haven in the Coast Guard's powerboat. As the boat pitched wildly through the waves, both survivors, sitting in the forepeak, were offered hamburgers and hot coffee, which they drank straight from the thermos. Nedeau remembered how he held his sandwich so tightly that his clenched fingers broke through the soft bread. Harvey Nedeau, Lyman's brother, had heard about the shipwreck while in Detroit and immediately drove to Grand Haven. He met the boat when it came in and drove his brother and Smith to Mercy Hospital in Muskegon.

The two spent approximately ten days in the hospital recovering from their ordeal. Hundreds of people stopped by to see them and the press interviewed them at length. Once he left the hospital, Smith rented a car and left town and Nedeau never heard from him again. He went back to work for the Durocher Company. When the U.S. Army Corps of Engineers declared the *Salvor* wreck a hazard to navigation, he returned to the wreck site on a Durocher Company vessel and assisted the team as they first removed the machinery and superstructure, and later dynamited the hull of the barge. He recalls how the dynamite blast killed dozens of fish in the water nearby. The men took advantage of the unexpected harvest and had only to collect the fish and prepare them for dinner.

In spite of his brush with death on Lake Michigan, Lyman Nedeau could not stay away from the sea—freshwater or saltwater. He served fifty-six months in the U.S. Navy and later continued to work on various Great Lakes freighters and tugs for a number of years, with Muskegon or nearby towns serving as home base. In more recent years, Nedeau has divided his time between Michigan and Florida. Throughout his life, he has maintained a love for the lakes and yet this feeling is infused with a deep respect for their power, which he experienced firsthand.

NOTES

Chapter 1

1. Mahan and Mahan, *Wild Lake Michigan,* 11–15.
2. John Gasman, "From New York to Wisconsin in 1844," trans. and ed. Carlton C. Qualey, *Studies and Records of the Norwegian-American Historical Collection* (Northfield, MN, 1930), 5:45. Quoted in Yakes, "Common Men," 3:11.
3. The term, which literally translates to "woods runners," refers to unregulated fur traders who would sell their pelts to the highest bidders, often of rival nationalities, such as the English or Dutch. Dunbar and May, *Michigan: A History of the Wolverine State,* 22.
4. Yakes, "Common Men," 1:10.
5. Johnston, "From Bark Canoe to Bulk Carrier," 62.
6. James P. Barry, *Ships of the Great Lakes* (Holt, MI: Thunder Bay Press, 1996), 23.
7. Catton, *Michigan: A History,* 52–54.
8. Yakes and Hornstein, *The Many Lives of Muskegon,* 3:24.
9. Armour and Widder, *At the Crossroads,* 124–25.
10. Excerpt from the log of the HMS *Felicity,* quoted in Kyes, *Romance of Muskegon,* 8; Quaife, *Lake Michigan,* 293–94.
11. Quaife, *Lake Michigan,* 103–5.
12. Banner, "The Riddles of *Felicity,*" 62–63.

Chapter 2

1. Until about 1840–50, the settlement's name was known under several variations: Muskeego, Maskego, Maskegon, or Muskego.
2. Yakes, "Common Men," 1:14–15.
3. Catton, *Michigan: A History,* 103; Yakes and Hornstein, *The Many Lives of Muskegon,* iv–3.
4. Yakes, "Common Men," 1:29.
5. Kyes, *Romance of Muskegon,* 25.
6. Yakes, "Common Men," 1:51.
7. "Muskegon 50 Years Ago."
8. Yakes, "Common Men," 1:119.
9. Kyes, *Romance of Muskegon,* 41.
10. Yates, "Shipping History."
11. Karamanski, *Schooner Passage,* 29–30.
12. Charles Hackley was involved with a number of partners in his lumber business. In this study, the focus is on Hackley and McGordon (1867–81) with James McGordon, and the partnership that followed, Hackley and Hume (1881–1905), with Thomas Hume.
13. Harms, "Life after Lumbering," 74.
14. Ibid.
15. Harms, "Life after Lumbering," 141.

16. Ibid.
17. "Muskegon 50 Years Ago."
18. Harms, "Life after Lumbering," 141–42.
19. Ibid., 288–89.
20. "Beached," *The News and Reporter*, November 3, 1875. Muskegon did not have a life saving service until 1878.
21. Harms, "Life after Lumbering," 169.
22. Ibid., 289. The Hume family took care of another one of their captains. In 1941, Captain Peter DeBlake, former master of the schooners *Rouse Simmons* and *Cape Horn*, had fallen on hard times. George A. Hume, the son of Thomas Hume, and others arranged to pay for his entrance fee to the Old People's Home (now the Hume Home for Assisted Living), founded by his father (Hackley and Hume Collection).
23. Yakes, "Common Men," 1:177.
24. Harms, "Life after Lumbering," 142.
25. Yakes and Hornstein, *Muskegon: First Hand*, 100.
26. Harms, "Life after Lumbering," 83.
27. Yates, "Ships Also Dotted Muskegon Lake."
28. Harms, "Life after Lumbering," 236.
29. Letter to John M'Donnell, Collector, *Detroit Daily Advertiser*, September 20, 1838, p. 2. The *Advertiser* refers to him as Captain Homans, but the U.S. naval records list him as a lieutenant. Thanks to Davis Elliott, information technology specialist, Navy Department Library, for this correction.
30. Kyes, *Romance of Muskegon*, 98.
31. Witherell, obituary.
32. Ibid.
33. Kyes, *Romance of Muskegon*, 98; Witherell, obituary.
34. Kyes, *Romance of Muskegon*, 42; statistical information supplied by Mike Spears.
35. Kyes, *Romance of Muskegon*, 94.
36. Harms, "Life after Lumbering," 152.
37. Kyes, *Romance of Muskegon*, 94.
38. Quaife, *Lake Michigan*, 333.
39. Yates, "Ship Repair Projects Date Back 67 Years."
40. *Marine Directory of the Great Lakes*, individual entries.
41. Before the village was named Port Sherman in 1866 (after Union General William T. Sherman), the area was simply known as "the Mouth."
42. Kyes, *Romance of Muskegon*, 84.
43. Yakes and Hornstein, *The Many Lives of Muskegon*, viii, 5–6.
44. Yates, "Know Muskegon," *Muskegon Chronicle*, April 22, 1950, p. 18.
45. Fuller, *Historic Michigan*, 47.
46. Kyes, *Romance of Muskegon*, 59.
47. Fuller, *Historic Michigan*, 47–48.
48. Yates, "Coast Guard Forerunner."
49. Point Solitude was an earlier name for Little Sable Point.
50. Letter, *Detroit Daily Advertiser*, December 10, 1839, p. 2.
51. Ibid.
52. The steamship *Lexington* burned off Eaton's Neck, New York, on January 13, 1840, with the loss of 140 lives.
53. *Detroit Daily Advertiser*, April 9, 1840, p. 2.
54. Lillie, *Historic Grand Haven and Ottawa County*, 189.

Notes to Chapter 2

55. "Dangers of Lake Navigation."
56. This sudden and devastating storm became known as the "*Alpena* storm" from the loss of the passenger steamer *Alpena* with over seventy passengers and crew. See "Lost to the Depths: The Wreck of the *Alpena*" in chapter 3 of this volume.
57. "A Terrible Voyage."
58. Ibid.
59. "Recalls a Brave Act."
60. Ibid.
61. Bruce D. McCrea, "Pete Cardinal Clears Mystery of Graves of Indians and Wreck of Lumber Vessel," *Muskegon Chronicle*, September 25, 1953, reprinted in Bluffton Historical Committee, *Shifting Sands*.
62. "Beached," *Muskegon Daily Chronicle*. It should be noted that the *Annie Nelson* was listed in the log at the Life Saving Station as the *Emma A. Nelson*.
63. "The Waleska Safe."
64. In 1897, the surfmen were paid $65 a month, with an extra $3 for any off-season work.
65. "Their Labors Ended."
66. Ibid.
67. The two crewmen lost in the wreck of the *R. B. King* were twenty-six-year-old Fingle Fringelson, who had sailed with Captain Dunbar for three seasons, and twenty-one-year-old Andrew Olson. Olson had been onboard the *King* for only three months. He was unmarried but had a widowed mother living in Chicago who depended on him for financial support.
68. "Their Labors Ended."
69. "Lost in the Gale."
70. "The Blizzard," *Muskegon Daily Chronicle*, November 19, 1886, p. 2.
71. *South Haven Sentinel.*
72. In September 2002, the wreckage of a scow schooner, 90 feet long, was discovered in shallow water about two miles north of Muskegon Channel and sixty feet from shore. Brendan Baillod and Ross Richardson of the Great Lakes Shipwreck Research Foundation were called in to investigate the hull. While the vessel's identity cannot be proven beyond doubt, they believe it is the *Helen*.
73. Henderson and Peterson sent two investigators to the wreck site ("Another Wreck"). The *Daily Chronicle* reports are not clear on whether David Smith was one of the investigators, or whether he made the journey on his own ("Washed Up by the Waves").
74. "Relics of the Wrecks," *Muskegon Daily Chronicle*, November 26, 1886, p. 3.
75. "Driven to Destruction."
76. "Another Wreck."
77. "Forty-Seven Lives Lost."
78. *Muskegon Daily Chronicle*, November 20, 1886, p. 2.
79. Statistics from "History of the Great Lakes," Hackley and Hume Collection.
80. Hollister, "Loss of the Christmas Tree Schooner," 82. Hollister claims another note found in a bottle, allegedly from Captain Schuenemann, was a hoax. It read: "Friday. Everybody goodbye. I guess we are all through. Seas washed over our deck load Thursday. During the night the small boat was washed over. Ingvald and Steve fell overboard Thursday. God help us. Herman Schuenemann." The names of the *Rouse Simmons* crewmen are known and no one named Ingvald or Steve was aboard at the time of the ship's loss.
81. How rough is a matter of debate. One Chicago captain, John Hea, claimed it was a "thunder squall" ("What Captain Hea Thinks"). Overall, compared with the other theories put forth at that time, the bad weather was not considered a major factor in the loss of the *Hume*.
82. "The Missing Schooner," *Muskegon Chronicle*.

83. "The Missing Schooner," *Muskegon Daily Chronicle*.
84. Ibid.
85. Gebhart, "The Mystery of the *Thomas Hume*," 21–22; Boyer, *Strange Adventures of the Great Lakes*, 58.
86. Letter from Thomas Hume, May 29, 1891, Hackley and Hume Collection.
87. "With All on Board."
88. The discrepancy in the length of the *Hume* (132 feet) and the mystery vessel (175 feet) would contradict Culbert's suggestion.
89. "Frenchman, he don't lak to die" is the opening line of a folksong of the lumber era.
90. The following is a compilation of Dulach's statement and other information that later came to light and was reported in the *Muskegon Chronicle*. See appendix C in this volume for Dulach's full statement.
91. "Foundered!"
92. "Inquest on the Sailors," *Chicago Tribune*, November 10, 1896, p. 4.
93. A friend of the Gayton family sent a telegram to confirm that the body of the black man was indeed the *Waukesha*'s cook, Thomas Gayton. He arrived by train to escort the body back to Gayton's home in Benton Harbor. Gayton, who was in his early twenties, left behind a wife and young child. Mrs. Albert Foster of Chicago heard about the *Waukesha* disaster and sent a telegram asking if one of the unidentified bodies had certain distinguishing marks: two tattoos, one of a large anchor on the right arm, and another of a small rope and anchor on the left wrist. From the response, she determined that her husband, twenty-two-year-old Albert Foster, known to Frank Dulach as "Irish," was indeed among the dead. Albert Foster had come from a wealthy New York family, and to his parents' disappointment, the "independent and wayward boy" left his elegant home in New York City to become a Great Lakes sailor. His parents often tried to persuade him to return and enjoy a life of privilege and a profitable career, but the young man, preferring the rigors of shipboard life, never accepted their offer. The day he left was the last time he saw his home. He was only fourteen at the time. From "Reiterates!"
94. "Six Men Drowned," 7.
95. Palmer, "Last of the Great Lakes Schooners," 4.
96. Ibid., 5.
97. Ibid., 12.
98. Ibid., 5.
99. Ibid., 5, 11.
100. Ibid., 9–10.
101. Ibid., 13.
102. "Last of Old Lumber Schooners Is Burned," 1.
103. Curwood, *The Great Lakes*, 52–53.

Chapter 3

1. Kyes, *Romance of Muskegon*, 111.
2. Harms, "Life after Lumbering," 238–39.
3. Ibid., 246–47.
4. Yates, "Boat Company Had Big Plans in 1903."
5. Ibid.
6. James L. Smith, "Loading and Shipping Lumber," in Yakes and Hornstein, *Muskegon: First Hand*, 102.

7. John Torrent, "The Life and Times of John Torrent" (interview in *Muskegon Chronicle*, January 20, 1900), reprinted in Yakes and Hornstein, *Muskegon: First Hand*, 98ff.
8. Elliott, *Red Stacks over the Horizon*, 17ff.
9. Ibid., 23.
10. *Muskegon Reporter*, May 4, 1860 (quoted in Elliott, *Red Stacks over the Horizon*), 26–27.
11. Elliott, *Red Stacks over the Horizon*, 27.
12. Ibid., 41.
13. Ibid., 50–51.
14. LaFayette, "SS Virginia Kept Busy with Muskegon Runs."
15. "The Steamer Nyack."
16. Ibid.
17. Kohl, *Titanic*, 248.
18. Truscott, "Carrie A. Ryerson Had Popular Reign."
19. Creviere, *Wild Gales and Tattered Sails*, 199.
20. Kyes, *Romance of Muskegon*, 71.
21. The DGH&M Railroad sold off its two steamships in 1896. The *City of Milwaukee* went to the Graham and Morton Line, and the *Wisconsin* was bought by the Crosby Transportation Company.
22. "Steamboat Collision."
23. "Recalls a Brave Act."
24. Elliott, *Red Stacks over the Horizon*, 31–33.
25. The "*Seabird* disaster" resulted in the loss of one hundred lives, with only two survivors.
26. "A Hungry Sea."
27. "Wind's Wreck."
28. "A Hungry Sea."
29. The *Muskegon Daily Chronicle* reported "eighty-seven marine disasters have been at noon today [October 20] reported on Lakes Erie, Huron and Michigan." Of them, sixteen were total losses.
30. Because accurate passenger lists were not kept at the time, the exact number of lives lost on the *Alpena* is uncertain. Estimates have ranged from seventy to one hundred. This figure (seventy-three) is from the "Great Lakes Vessel Index" of the Historical Collections of the Great Lakes.
31. *Muskegon Daily Chronicle*, October 25, 1880, p. 1.
32. Ibid.
33. Ibid.
34. The mayor of Muskegon, Frank Jiroch, had planned to take the *Alpena* to Chicago on a business trip the night of October 15 and had bought his ticket for the voyage. But when the city council called a meeting for that night and required the mayor's presence, he reluctantly canceled his trip and stayed in town. Doubtless, Mayor Jiroch counted his blessings when the news of the *Alpena*'s fate reached him. The ticket he had bought has been preserved by his family through the years. Yates, "Goodrich Ship Lost."
35. Captain Albert E. Goodrich died in September 1885, and his son took over as company president in 1889.
36. The name was changed in 1923 when Goodrich merged with the Graham and Morton Company of Benton Harbor.
37. Letter from Robert Stufflebeam. This is generally acknowledged in several sources, although it cannot be completely verified due to inaccurate records.
38. Elliott, *Red Stacks over the Horizon*, 149–50.
39. Letter from Robert Stufflebeam.
40. Letter from Robert Stufflebeam (*South Haven Daily Tribune* citing *Chicago Tribune* article).

41. "Beloved Captain Known as More Than Ship's Pilot," *Muskegon Chronicle*, September 17, 1938, p. 1.
42. "The New Steamer."
43. "Propeller Milwaukee Sunk by a Collision in Lake Michigan."
44. The two were the *Lawrence* and the *Champlain*, which were bought by the Northern Michigan Line and continued to serve as passenger and freight steamers on Lake Michigan (File, Herman G. Runge Collection, Milwaukee Public Library).
45. "Propeller Milwaukee Sunk by a Collision in Lake Michigan."
46. "Further Particulars Concerning the Loss of the Milwaukee."
47. "The Steam-Barge Milwaukee Sunk in the Lake, with One of the Crew," *Chicago Times*, July 10, 1886, p. 7.
48. Ibid.
49. Ibid.
50. "Marine Intelligence: Steambarge Milwaukee Sunk to the Bottom by the Steambarge Hickox."
51. "Sunk in Midlake."
52. *Muskegon Daily Chronicle*, July 10, 1886, p. 2.
53. In some sources, the ship is given the misnomer *City of Muskegon*.
54. La Bonville, "The 'Muskegon' Wreck," 42.
55. All of the following comments by Robinson are in "Had Hunch Something Wrong on 'Muskegon,'" 1, 5.
56. "Had Hunch Something Wrong on 'Muskegon,'" 5. Local historian Pete Caesar, in his self-published book *Lake Michigan Wrecks III*, dismisses Robinson's claim: "When the pilot-house of the steamer was lifted off by the waves and pier collision, wires to the auxiliary lights and horns were also severed!" (66).
57. "Was Captain Miller in Fear for Safety of Doomed Ship."
58. "Crosby Company Gives Aid to the Sufferers," *Muskegon Chronicle*, October 29, 1919, p. 12.
59. "Death of Captain Miller."
60. Dowling, "The Illinois and Missouri," 31.
61. In 1934, the Wisconsin and Michigan Transportation Company merged with the Pere Marquette Line Steamers under the name Wisconsin and Michigan Steamship Company. The merger affected four ships: the *Virginia, Illinois, Missouri,* and *Nevada*. Later the company acquired the *Juniata/Milwaukee Clipper*.
62. On September 8, 1934, the *Morro Castle* burned off the New Jersey coast with the loss of 134 lives.
63. "Odds and Ends."
64. "Aqua(RAM)a Still Playing Bump'sa Daisy."
65. "A Great Car Ferry."
66. "Shenango."
67. Ibid.
68. Yakes and Hornstein, *The Many Lives of Muskegon*, ix, 15.
69. "3 Fires Damage Mothballed Ferry."
70. Steele, "Railroad Ferry Will Harbor Guests."
71. Ibid.

Chapter 4

1. Kyes, *Romance of Muskegon*, 153.
2. Elve, "Pigeon Hill," 5.
3. Woodruff, "5,000 Here Greet Danish Freighter," 2.

Notes to Chapter 4

4. LaFayette, "Many Foreign Ships Steamed into Muskegon's Port," 4B.
5. Yakes and Hornstein, *The Many Lives of Muskegon*, ix, 17.
6. Wolff, *Lake Superior Wrecks,* 149–50.
7. "Body of Youth Is Taken from Barge Derrick," *Muskegon Chronicle,* September 29, 1930, p. 2. Clarence Brunett's body was recovered on October 9, 1930, near Duck Lake Channel.
8. "Three Suffer during Night aboard Barge," 17.
9. "Coast Guard Wins Praise," 1, 12.
10. Ibid., 12.
11. Ibid.
12. Ibid.
13. Ibid.
14. "All Aboard Safe as Freighter Cort Wrecks."
15. "Praise Given Coast Guards."
16. "Blames Light Load in Wreck," 1, 13.
17. Ibid.
18. "Cort's Future Is Uncertain," 1, 11.
19. Ibid.
20. Walsh, "The Two Lives of the LST," 1, 2.
21. In 2001, the USS *Silversides* and Maritime Museum changed its name to the Great Lakes Naval Memorial and Museum to better reflect the variety of vessels under its aegis.
22. Several other former LST ships are in U.S. waters, but their structures have been significantly modified for their current use and do not resemble true LSTs (phone conversations with John Waite and Bob Morin, Sr., of the Great Lakes Naval Memorial and Museum, August 29, 2000). A group of World War II vets sailed the *LST 325* over to the United States from Greece in December–January 2000–01. The vessel is scheduled to be restored as a museum ship in Mobile, Alabama.
23. "Ore Carriers Docking Here for Steel Strike."
24. "Arrival of Another Ship Boosts Ore Fleet to 11."
25. This *Makefjell* was the third Fjell Line ship of that name. The first *Makefjell* visited the Great Lakes several times in 1933. She participated in the Normandy invasion and in 1946 returned to the lakes. After she was sold to another company and renamed, a second *Makefjell* was built for the line in 1948. Gillham, "Old Friends from the Fjell Line."
26. Grand Trunk was eager to be involved in this project as the stranded ship endangered their car ferries' passage in and out of Muskegon harbor.
27. McCrea, "Patience Runs Thin on Waterfront."
28. Ibid.
29. Woodruff, "Port City Welcomes Return of Makefjell!"
30. "Makefjell Toasts Its Rescuers, Port."
31. *Great Lakes Naval Memorial and Museum.*
32. Alexander and Medendorp, "Lake Won't Give Up Research Ship."
33. "Raise the Halcyon: New Try Planned."
34. Alexander, "Halcyon: A Shipwreck Waiting to Happen," 2A.
35. Ibid.
36. Ibid.
37. "Will Any Heads Ever Bounce as a Result of the Halcyon Fiasco?"
38. Hausman, "RV Halcyon Debacle To Be Subject of TV News Story," 1Aff.
39. "Will Any Heads Ever Bounce as a Result of the Halcyon Fiasco?"
40. "Halcyon Should Never Have Been Purchased At All."

Chapter 5

1. Formerly the Central Paper Company and later the S. D. Warren division of Scott Paper Company.
2. Those who know the story of the *Edmund Fitzgerald* shipwreck will recall that the *Arthur M. Anderson* was the ship that followed the *Fitzgerald* and had the last radio contact with her just before she went down in Lake Superior on November 10, 1975.
3. Service was originally planned between Muskegon and Milwaukee, but Milwaukee has shown little interest in the Lake Michigan Carferry Company venture. "Passenger Vessels and Ferries," *Great Lakes/Seaway Log* 29.25.
4. The other ports were Kingston, Ontario; Port Colborne, Ontario; Cleveland; Detroit/Windsor, Ontario; and Bay City, Michigan.
5. The *Michigan/Wolverine* visited Muskegon in 1886, 1904, and 1907 to recruit men for service in the U.S. Navy.
6. "Famous Flagship Niagara Driven into Muskegon Harbor," 1, 5.
7. "Research Ship to Get New Life as Artificial Reef." This information is also from a phone conversation with Bob Morin, Sr., Sept. 19, 2002.

GLOSSARY

abaft Toward stern.

aft At, in, or toward the stern.

amidships In or toward the middle of a ship, or the part midway between stem and stern.

barge An unpowered vessel used for transporting freight.

bateau (pl. bateaux) A light boat, especially one having a flat bottom and tapering ends.

beam The side of a vessel, or the direction at right angles to the keel.

"On her beam ends" So far inclined on one side that the deck beams are practically vertical.

bilge In general, the bottom of a ship. Specifically, the "corner" where the bottom meets the side.

boiler Steam generator. Large iron drum to create steam to drive machinery.

boom (n.) A long pole or spar used to extend the foot of certain sails; a spar or beam projecting from the mast of a derrick, supporting or guiding the weights to be lifted; (v.) to confine floating timber.

booming tug Tugboat used to pull rafts of logs in booms.

bow Front of a ship.

bowsprit A large spar projecting forward from the bow of a ship.

breeches buoy A lifesaving device using a harness suspended from overhead lines to lift survivors from shipwrecks. The lines are fired out to the wreck with a Lyle Gun.

bridge A raised platform from side to side of a ship above the rail, for the officer in charge.

brig A two-masted vessel square-rigged on both masts.

cableshackle Used to join lengths of cable, "U" shaped with a pin to close the open end.

car ferry A ship built specifically to transport railroad cars or automobiles in the hold.

catwalk Narrow walkways on piers or on a vessel.

centerboard Relatively thin board that can be lowered through the keel, used to counteract the tendency of a sailing ship to move sideways.

clipper schooner Type of schooner with sharp lines and speed of a clipper ship with the flat-bottom design and cargo-carrying capacity of a schooner.

crosstree One of the horizontal transverse pieces of timber or metal fastened to the head of a lower mast or topmast to support the top, spread the shrouds, etc.

davit Small fixed derrick used to raise and swing out lifeboats.

dockwalloper (slang) A laborer about docks or wharves.

downbound (on the Great Lakes) Heading out of the lakes' system. On Lake Michigan, a ship traveling downbound would be headed north.

draft The depth a vessel sinks in water.

drop keel *See* centerboard.

fly A signal pennant.

fore-and-aft Running in a back-to-front direction. Schooner rigged, as opposed to square-rigged sailing vessel.

forecastle (or fo'c'sle) Raised portion of a ship's bow, used mainly for crew quarters in nineteenth-century vessels.

foremast The mast nearest the bow of a ship.

foresail The principal sail on the foremast of a schooner.

foreyard The lower yard on the foremast.

founder To fill and sink; to swamp.

Fresnel lens A large lens with a surface composed of many small lenses arranged to focus light on a single point. The order of lenses range from first order (largest) to seventh order. Great Lakes lighthouses used second- to fifth-order lenses.

hatch Deck opening, usually for loading cargo.

hawser Anchor line or towing line; heavy rope, cable, or chain.

heel (v.) To lean to one side; to cant; tilt.

hold Portion of ship's hull used for carrying and stowing cargo.

hooker/lumber hooker A ship especially designed for transporting wood and wood products.

hooks Anchors.

hull The frame or body of a ship, exclusive of masts, yards, sails, and rigging.

hurricane deck The highest deck.

jibe To shift from one side to the other when running before the wind, as a fore-and-aft sail or its boom; to alter the course so that the sail shifts in this manner.

jib sail Headsail. Small triangular sail carried forward of ship's foremast.

keel The backbone of a ship. A girder that runs down the centerline in a ship's bottom.

lee The side or part that is sheltered or turned away from the wind.

lifeboat A boat, provisioned and equipped for abandoning ship, carried in davits so it may be lowered quickly.

light (as in "sailing light") Without cargo.

lighter (v.) To remove cargo.

log boom String of logs tied end-to-end for enclosure of a log raft.

master A ship's captain.

mate A captain's assistant.

mizzenmast Third mast in a three-masted sailing vessel.

oakum Loose hemp fibers, often soaked in water repellents, used to caulk the seams of ships.

pigboat Another name for a whaleback.

pilothouse Compartment on the bridge in which the controls and navigation instruments are found and the location of the personnel involved with the vessel's navigation.

port Left side of a ship when facing ship's bow.

Glossary

powerboat A boat propelled by mechanical power.

propeller Screw used to drive a ship through the water; type of ship driven by a screw.

purser Ship's officer responsible for passenger tickets and ship's books.

quarterboard One of the boards raising the bulwarks of the quarter (the side of a vessel, from amidships to the stern).

reef (v.) To shorten sail by reducing the area exposed.

revetment A facing of masonry or the like, especially for protecting an embankment; a retaining wall.

rigging (main rigging; forerigging) Wire or hemp rope used to support masts or operate sails.

riprap A foundation or wall of stones thrown together irregularly to form a protective shield for a seawall, lighthouse, or other structure that is occasionally buffeted by the sea.

rudder quadrant The fitting on the rudder stock to which the rudder cables are attached to control the rudder.

salty A foreign ship, i.e., a saltwater vessel.

schooner Sailing craft with two or more masts, rigged with fore-and-aft sails, 60 to 200 feet long.

scow Square-built vessel with flat sides, usually a flat bottom.

scow schooner Type of schooner with a boxy appearance and a shallow draft.

shrouds A set of strong ropes extended from the mastheads to the sides of a ship to help support the masts.

side-wheel steamer A steamboat propelled by two large paddle wheels, one on each side.

slip keel *See* centerboard.

sloop Sailing craft with one mast, usually no more than forty feet in length.

spar A pole or mast used to support or spread sails or to carry lights or flags.

square-rigged Having square sails as the principal sails.

stack A steamship's funnel.

starboard Right side of a vessel when facing ship's bow.

steam barge A small wooden ship used for carrying lumber products. Single-decked steamer of 130 to 200 feet with raised poop deck.

steering vane A small rudder attached to the main rudder controlled by a wind vane.

stem Foremost portion of the bow of a ship.

stern After (rear) end of a ship.

steward Officer in charge of passengers' meals and accommodations.

strand To run ashore or aground; to become stuck on an obstruction or a beach.

superstructure Cabins or "upper works" of a vessel. The part that projects above the hull.

surfboat A long, heavy boat meant to be launched in the surf from a beach, carried on a beach cart or trailer, usually horse-drawn. Powered by oars or a small gasoline engine.

tack (n.) The direction or course of a ship in relation to the position of her sails; a course obliquely against the wind; one of the series of straight runs that make up the zigzag course of a ship proceeding to windward; (v.i.) To change the course of a ship by bringing her head into the wind and then causing it to fall off on the other side.

topmast Upper portion of a two-piece mast.

transom Any of several transverse beams or timbers fixed across the sternpost of a ship, to strengthen and give shape to the after part.

trough The low point between two waves.

upbound (on the Great Lakes) Heading into the lakes' system. On Lake Michigan, a ship traveling upbound would be headed south.

weather side Of or pertaining to the side or part, as of a ship, that is exposed to the wind.

"went missing" Term used to describe a vessel that is overdue and presumed by its owners to have been lost at sea.

whaleback Unusual ship design with steel hulls and rounded decks introduced by Captain Alexander McDougall of Duluth, Minnesota, in 1888. McDougall's American Steel Barge Company built whaleback barges and steamers between 1888 and 1896.

yard A long cylindrical spar with a taper toward each end, slung crosswise to a mast and suspending a square sail, lateen sail, etc.

yawl Small skiff or lifeboat.

BIBLIOGRAPHY

"Alabama Is Held during Night in Blocked Channel." *Muskegon Chronicle,* January 19, 1924, p. 17.
Alexander, Jeff. "Cabin of Research Ship Breaks Surface." *Muskegon Chronicle,* December 10, 1996, B1.
———. "Halcyon: A Shipwreck Waiting to Happen." *Muskegon Chronicle,* February 9, 1997, pp. 1A+.
———. "Officials Preparing to Raise Sunken Ship." *Muskegon Chronicle,* December 6, 1996, B1.
Alexander, Jeff, and Lisa Medendorp. "Lake Won't Give Up Research Ship." *Muskegon Chronicle,* December 3, 1996, B1.
"All Aboard." *Muskegon Chronicle,* November 24, 1962, p. 17.
"All Aboard Safe as Freighter Cort Wrecks." *Muskegon Chronicle* (early ed.), December 1, 1934, p. 1.
Alpena, Vessel Data Sheet, Great Lakes Vessels Online Image Database, Historical Collections of the Great Lakes, Bowling Green State University, 2000. http://www.bgsu.edu/colleges/library/hegl/vessel.html
"Another Wreck." *Muskegon Daily Chronicle,* November 22, 1886, p. 3.
"Aqua(RAM)a Still Playing Bump'sa Daisy." *Muskegon Chronicle,* July 21, 1959, p. 2.
Area Development Department, Consumers Power Company. *Port and Harbor Facilities: Piers, Wharves, and Docks.* Jackson, MI: Consumers Power Company, 1975.
Armour, David A. and Keith R. Widder. *At the Crossroads: Michilimackinac During the American Revolution.* Lansing, MI: John Henry Co., 1986.
"Arrival of Another Ship Boosts Ore Fleet to 11." *Muskegon Chronicle,* July 20, 1959, p. 2.
Banner, Melvin E. "The Riddles of the Felicity." *Telescope* 18 (1968): 61–64.
"Barge Death Toll Five: Narratives of Heroism Recorded in Two Wrecks." *Muskegon Chronicle,* September 27, 1930, pp. 1+.
"Barge Salvor Twice Re-Christened So Seamen Were Uneasy." *Muskegon Chronicle,* September 29, 1930, p. 2.
"Beached." *Muskegon Daily Chronicle,* November 16, 1883, p. 3.
"Beached." *The News and Reporter,* November 3, 1875, p. 1.
"Believed 21 Lost Lives in City of Muskegon Wreck." *Muskegon Chronicle,* October 28, 1919, pp. 1+.
Bennet, Orlie, comp. "Shipping of the Port of Grand Haven, 1821–1900." *Telescope* 19 (1970): 134.
"Blames Light Load in Wreck." *Muskegon Chronicle* (final ed.), December 1, 1934, pp. 1+.
"The Blizzard Aftermath." *Muskegon Daily Chronicle,* November 20, 1886, p. 3.
Bluffton Historical Committee. *Shifting Sands: The Story of the Bluffton Area.* Muskegon: Bluffton Historical Committee, 1976.
Bluffton School PTA Historical Committee. *Sand in Their Shoes: A Story of the Bluffton Area.* Muskegon: Bluffton School PTA Historical Committee, 1996.
Bowen, Dana Thomas. *Shipwrecks of the Great Lakes.* Cleveland: Freshwater Press, 1995.
Boyer, Dwight. *Ghost Ships of the Great Lakes.* New York: Dodd, Mead, 1968.
———. *Ships and Men of the Great Lakes.* Cleveland: Freshwater Press, 1977.
———. *Strange Adventures of the Great Lakes.* Cleveland: Freshwater Press, 1974.

Bibliography

"Broken on the Shore." *Chicago Times,* November 18, 1886, p. 15.

Burkert, Rebecca. "Michigan Profiles: Charles H. Mohr." *Michigan History* 76:6 (November/December 1992): 62–63.

Burns, Robert C. "History in the Making." *Muskegon Chronicle,* October 1, 2001, pp. 1A+.

C. Hickox, Vessel Data Sheet, Great Lakes Vessels Online Image Database, Historical Collections of the Great Lakes, Bowling Green State University, 2000. http://www.bgsu.edu/colleges/library/hegl/vessel.html

Caesar, Pete. *Lake Michigan Wrecks III.* Green Bay, WI: Great Lakes Marine Research, 1989.

"Captain Miller Tells Dramatic Story of His Battle to Save Ship." *Muskegon Chronicle,* November 1, 1919, pp. 1+.

"Captain Preston Arrives with Crew of Six." *Muskegon Chronicle* (early ed.), December 1, 1934, p. 1.

"Captain Saves Ship; Dashed on Breakwater." *Muskegon Chronicle,* November 25, 1936, pp. 1+.

"Capt. Stufflebeam Is Found Dead in River." *Muskegon Chronicle,* September 17, 1938, p. 1.

"Carferry City of Milwaukee." *Association for Great Lakes Maritime History Newsletter* 16.3 (May/June 1999): 7.

Catton, Bruce. *Michigan: A History.* The States and the Nation Series. New York: W. W. Norton, 1984.

"Channel and Beach Are Choked with Great Mass of Flotsam from Wreck." *Muskegon Chronicle,* October 28, 1919, p. 1.

Charrney, Theodore S. "The *Rouse Simmons* and the Port of Chicago." *Inland Seas* 43 (winter 1987): 243–46.

Chicago Times, July 8, 1886, p. 7.

"The Christmas Tree Ship." *A Most Superior Land.* Through the Local History Collection, Milwaukee Public Library.

"Clipper Trapped Three Miles Out." *Muskegon Chronicle,* January 22, 1962, p. 15.

"Coast Guard Wins Praise, Survivors of Barge Say They Do Not Deserve Criticism." *Muskegon Chronicle,* September 29, 1930, pp. 1+.

"Cort Sank Near Detroit Year Ago." *Muskegon Chronicle* (final ed.), December 1, 1934, p. 1.

"Cort's Future Is Uncertain." *Muskegon Chronicle,* December 3, 1934, pp. 1+.

Creviere, Paul J., Jr. *Wild Gales and Tattered Sails: The Shipwrecks of Northwestern Lake Michigan from Two Creeks, Wisconsin to Dutch Johns Point, Michigan and All of the Bay of Green Bay.* [DePere, WI]: P. J. Creviere, 1997.

"Crew of Our Son Taken from Historic Ship in Thrilling and Daring Show of Seamanship." *Muskegon Chronicle,* September 27, 1930, pp. 1+.

"Crosby Steamer, Nyack, Practically Destroyed by Fire at Muskegon Dock." *Muskegon Chronicle,* December 30, 1915, pp. 1+.

Curwood, James Oliver. *The Great Lakes: The Vessels That Plough Them: Their Owners, Their Sailors, and Their Cargoes.* New York: G. P. Putnam's Sons; Knickerbocker Press, 1909.

"Damaged Ship Is Raised by Repairs." *Muskegon Chronicle,* November 27, 1936, p. 2.

"Dangers of Lake Navigation." *Muskegon Daily Chronicle,* November 17, 1883, p. 2.

"Death of Captain Miller Recalls Tragic Sinking of City of Muskegon Here 31 Years Ago with Loss of 31 Lives." *Muskegon Chronicle,* January 15, 1951, p. 2.

Derler, John C. "Grand River Pageant." *Telescope* 17 (1968): 3–11.

Detroit Daily Advertiser, December 10, 1839, p. 2.

Detroit Daily Advertiser, April 9, 1840, p. 2.

"Double Rites for Victims of Lake Tragedy." *Muskegon Chronicle,* June 4, 1934, pp. 1+.

Dowling, Edward J. "The Illinois and Missouri." *Steamboat Bill,* June 1948, pp. 31–32.

———. "Red Stacks in the Sunset." *Illinois State Historical Journal* 40 (1946): 176–99.

———. "The Ships That Made Milwaukee Famous." *Inland Seas* 4.2 (1948): 83–95.

"Dreadful Shipwreck and Loss of Life." *Detroit Daily Free Press,* December 10, 1839, p. 2.

Bibliography

"Driven to Destruction." *Chicago Tribune,* November 23, 1886, p. 6.
Dunbar, Willis F., and George S. May. *Michigan: A History of the Wolverine State.* 3d. ed. Grand Rapids, MI: Eerdmans, 1995.
Elliott, James L. *Red Stacks over the Horizon: The Story of the Goodrich Steamboat Line.* Ellison Bay, WI: Wm. Caxton, 1995.
Elve, Steve. "Pigeon Hill." *Telescope* 44 (1996): 3–5.
———. "The Wreck of the Muskegon." *Telescope* 25–26 (1977): 156–59.
"Enlisted in Navy: Three Recruits Accepted." *Muskegon Chronicle,* August 30, 1904, p. 5.
"Erie L. Hackley: Well-Known Steamer Foundered." *Muskegon Daily Chronicle,* October 5, 1903, p. 5.
"Expect Ore Ships to Berth Here." *Muskegon Chronicle,* July 14, 1959, p. 2.
Fairbanks, C. T. "The Burning of the Naomi and Rescue of the Passengers." *Muskegon Daily Chronicle,* May 22, 1907, p. 1.
"Famous Flagship Niagara Driven into Muskegon Harbor by Terrific Gale." *Muskegon Chronicle,* August 23, 1913, pp. 1+.
"The Favorite." *Muskegon Weekly Chronicle,* June 21, 1888, p. 2.
"Ferry Planned for Muskegon." *Detroit Free Press,* May 23, 2001, p. 5B.
"Fire-Struck Thrill Seekers Watch End of Old Schooner." *Toronto Evening Telegram,* June 30, 1934, p. 20.
"Forty-Seven Lives Lost." *Chicago Tribune,* November 22, 1886, p. 7.
"Foundered!" *Muskegon Weekly Chronicle,* November 12, 1896, p. 1.
"Four Crosby Boats." *Muskegon Weekly Chronicle,* November 19, 1896, p. 1.
"Four Muskegon Firemen and Youth Die in Poison Gas-Filled Hold of Old Ship." *Muskegon Chronicle,* March 17, 1945, pp. 1+.
"Freighter Cort Was Involved in Fatal Accident Here Last Summer." *Muskegon Chronicle* (early ed.), December 1, 1934, pp. 1+.
Fuller, George N., ed. *Historic Michigan: Land of the Great Lakes—Muskegon County.* Ed. James L. Smith. Vol. 3. [Dayton, OH]: National Historical Association, 1935.
"Further Particulars Concerning the Loss of the Milwaukee." *Muskegon Daily Chronicle,* July 12, 1886, p. 2.
Gebhart, Richard. "The Mystery of the *Thomas Hume.*" *Inland Seas* 57.1 (2001): 18–22.
Gillham, Skip. "Old Friends from the Fjell Line." *Telescope* 40.6 (1992): 143–47.
"Grand Haven People Stirred by Word of Lake Tragedy." *Muskegon Chronicle* (final ed.), December 1, 1934, p. 11.
"A Great Car Ferry!" *Muskegon Weekly Chronicle,* October 7, 1897, p. 3.
Greater Muskegon Chamber of Commerce. *A Civic and Industrial Survey of the Muskegon Area and Western Michigan.* Muskegon: Greater Muskegon Chamber of Commerce, 1938.
Great Lakes Naval Memorial and Museum. Muskegon, 2001.
"Guards Halt Wreck Looting by Greedy Mob." *Muskegon Chronicle,* October 29, 1919, pp. 1+.
Hackley and Hume Collection. Shipping Ledgers. University Archives and Historical Collections, Michigan State University.
"Had Hunch Something Wrong on Muskegon." *Muskegon Chronicle,* October 29, 1919, pp. 1+.
"Halcyon Should Never Have Been Purchased At All." *Muskegon Chronicle,* March 14, 1997, p. 5A.
Harms, Richard Henry. "Life after Lumbering: Charles Hackley and the Emergence of Muskegon, Michigan." Ph.D. diss., Michigan State University, 1984.
Hausman, John S. "RV Halcyon Debacle To Be Subject of TV News Story." *Muskegon Chronicle,* March 9, 1997, pp. 1A+.
Hausman, John S., and Jeff Alexander. "Research Vessel Sinks at Mart Dock." *Muskegon Chronicle,* December 2, 1996, pp. 1+.
Helen. Ship Information and Data Record. Herman G. Runge Collection, Milwaukee Public Library.

Bibliography

"Heroic Fight of Crew Told by Survivor: George Secord Describes Boat's Struggle to Gain Piers." *Muskegon Chronicle*, September 27, 1930, pp. 1+.

"Heroism Marks Rescue Attempt." *Muskegon Chronicle* (final ed.), December 1, 1934, pp. 1+.

"Historical Background on the Milwaukee Clipper." *http://www.milwaukeeclipper.com/historic.htm.*

Hollister, Fred. "Loss of the Christmas Tree Schooner." *Sea Classics* 10.1 (1977): 6+.

"Hull of Salvor Is Broken in Two." *Muskegon Chronicle*, September 30, 1930, pp. 1+.

Hume Papers. Comp. Jean Hume Browning and Jean Hume Tomanica.

"A Hungry Sea." *Chicago Times*, October 18, 1880, p. 1.

"Identified!" *Muskegon Weekly Chronicle*, November 12, 1896, p. 6.

"Inquiry on Shipwreck Is Opened." *Muskegon Chronicle*, October 29, 1919, pp. 1+.

"Inquiry on Wreck Big Topic Now." *Muskegon Chronicle*, October 31, 1919, p. 1.

Johnston, Joseph E. "From Bark Canoe to Bulk Carrier." *Telescope* 59.3 (2001): 59–67.

Karamanski, Theodore. *Schooner Passage: Sailing Ships and the Lake Michigan Frontier*. Detroit: Wayne State University Press, 2000.

Knoth, Donna Quaife. "Steaming in Style." *Michigan History* 76:6 (November/December 1992): 32–36.

Kohl, Chris. *Titanic: The Great Lakes Connections*. West Chicago: Seawolf Communications, 2000.

Kyes, Alice Prescott. *Romance of Muskegon*. Muskegon: Muskegon Heritage Association, 1974.

La Bonville, William. "The 'Muskegon' Wreck." *Telescope* 15 (February 1966): 38–43.

LaFayette, Tressa. "'Favorite' Was the First to Offer Ferry Service." *Muskegon Chronicle*, June 14, 1992, p. 3B.

———. "Fire Spelled Doom for the SS Missouri." *Muskegon Chronicle*, May 21, 1989, p. 6B.

———. "For Several Years the Wolverine Was Assigned to Duty in Muskegon." *Muskegon Chronicle*, July 4, 1993, p. 3C.

———. "Icebound Ships Dotted Local Harbor in 1962." *Muskegon Chronicle*, January 25, 1987, p. 3B.

———. "Many Foreign Ships Steamed into Muskegon's Port." *Muskegon Chronicle*, June 3, 1990, p. 4B.

———. "Rouse Simmons Sank 77 Years Ago." *Muskegon Chronicle*, December 10, 1989, p. 3B.

———. "SS Virginia Kept Busy with Muskegon Runs." *Muskegon Chronicle*, April 27, 1986, p. 3B.

"Last of Old Lumber Schooners Is Burned." *Muskegon Chronicle*, July 5, 1934, p. 1.

"Last Water Cargo of Pulpwood Lost." *Muskegon Chronicle*, September 27, 1930, p. 2.

LeMieux, Dave. "Found! Teacher Discovers 1886 Shipwreck." *Muskegon Chronicle*, September 16, 2002, p. 1A ff.

Lillie, Leo C. *Historic Grand Haven and Ottawa County*. Grand Haven, MI: Leo C. Lillie, 1931.

"Lost in the Gale." *Chicago Times*, November 20, 1886, p. 2.

"The Lost Schooner." *Muskegon Daily Chronicle*, May 29, 1891, p. 2.

"The Lost Steamer." *Muskegon Daily Chronicle*, October 22, 1880, p. 1.

"The Lost Steamer." *Muskegon Daily Chronicle* (2d ed.), October 23, 1880, p. 1.

"The Lost Steamer." *Muskegon Daily Chronicle*, October 25, 1880, p. 1.

Lowell, Jon. "The Biggest Show in Years." *Muskegon Chronicle*, November 26, 1962, p. 27.

"Low Power Boat Hampers Work at Muskegon Station." *Muskegon Chronicle* (early ed.), December 1, 1934, p. 1.

Mahan, John, and Ann Mahan. *Wild Lake Michigan*. Stillwater, MN: Voyageur Press, 1991.

"Makefjell Toasts Its Rescuers, Port." *Muskegon Chronicle*, July 20, 1965, p. 4.

Marine Directory of the Great Lakes: 1888. Detroit: R. L. Polk, 1888.

"Marine Intelligence: The Missing Schooner Conway Wrecked off Fowler [sic] Creek, Mich., and Five of Her Crew Lost." *Chicago Times*, November 23, 1886, p. 6.

"Marine Intelligence: The Steam-Barge Milwaukee Sunk in the Lake, with One of the Crew." *Chicago Times*, July 10, 1886, p. 7.

Bibliography

"Marine Intelligence: Steambarge Milwaukee Sunk to the Bottom by the Steambarge Hickox." *Chicago Inter Ocean*, July 10, 1886.

"Mariners Book of Days 2001." January 13.

McCrea, Bruce D. "Freighter Aground Here: Norwegian Vessel on Breakwater Rocks." *Muskegon Chronicle*, November 23, 1962, p. 1.

———. "Makefjell Pulled Free, Plans Dash for Seaway." *Muskegon Chronicle*, November 29, 1962, p. 1.

———. "Order Use of Car Ferry in Try to Free Vessel." *Muskegon Chronicle*, November 27, 1962, p. 1.

———. "Patience Runs Thin on Waterfront." *Muskegon Chronicle*, November 28, 1962, A13.

———. "Race to Save Norwegian Ship: Crew Safe on Vessel." *Muskegon Chronicle*, November 24, 1962, p. 1.

———. "Ship Salvage Effort Gains: Huge Tug Due Today." *Muskegon Chronicle*, November 26, 1962, p. 1.

Middleton, Edward N. "The Steamer Virginia." *Telescope* 24 (1975): 35–40.

Miller, John F. "Lyman M. Davis." *Telescope* 10 (1961): 194–95.

"A $1,000,000 Loss? When the Makefjell Salvage Bills Are in, They May Easily Top That Figure." *Muskegon Chronicle*, November 26, 1962, p. 19.

Milwaukee. Ship Information and Data Record. Herman G. Runge Collection, Milwaukee Public Library.

Miramonti, David. "This Lady Never Had a Chance." *Telescope* 43 (1995): 125–127.

"The Missing Schooner." *Muskegon Chronicle*, June 11, 1891, p. 7.

"The Missing Schooner." *Muskegon Daily Chronicle*, June 2, 1891, p. 7.

"The Missing Schooner." *Muskegon Weekly Chronicle*, June 11, 1891, p. 7.

"More Vessels Wrecked." *Muskegon Daily Chronicle*, November 23, 1886, p. 1.

"Museums and Restorations." *Great Lakes/Seaway Log* 27.8 (April 12, 1999).

"Museums and Restorations." *Great Lakes/Seaway Log* 27.16 (August 2, 1999).

"Museums and Restorations." *Great Lakes/Seaway Log* 27.24 (November 22, 1999).

"Museums and Restorations." *Great Lakes/Seaway Log* 28.3 (January 31, 2000).

"Museums and Restorations." *Great Lakes/Seaway Log* 28.9 (April 24, 2000).

"Museums and Restorations." *Great Lakes/Seaway Log* 28.12 (June 5, 2000).

"Museums and Restorations." *Great Lakes/Seaway Log* 29.14 (July 2, 2001).

"Museums and Restorations." *Great Lakes/Seaway Log* 29.22 (October 22, 2001).

"Muskegon 50 Years Ago." *Muskegon Daily Chronicle*, January 26, 1901, p. 8.

"Muskegon Lake Criss-Crossed by Ferryboats." *Muskegon Chronicle* (centennial ed.), June 22, 1957, sec. 4, p. 5.

"Muskegon Vessel Passage." http://www.boatnerd/passage/muskegon.htm

Muskegon Chronicle, June 4, 1891, p. 7.

Muskegon Chronicle, June 11, 1891, p. 7.

Muskegon Daily Chronicle, July 10, 1886, p. 2.

Muskegon Daily Chronicle, November 20, 1886, p. 2.

Muskegon Weekly Chronicle, June 4, 1891, p. 4.

Neumiller, James H. "Aquarama/Marine Star." http://members.theglobe.com/algomedic/aquarama.htm

"New All-Steel Steamship to Succeed Nyack." *Muskegon Chronicle*, December 31, 1915, p. 1.

"New Name Added to Hero Roll." *Muskegon Chronicle*, September 30, 1930, p. 1.

"The New Steamer: New Barry Boat Arrives from Gotham." *Muskegon Daily Chronicle*, September 14, 1901, p. 7.

"Nightmare Is Ended for the Makefjell." *Muskegon Chronicle*, November 30, 1962, p. 6.

North Muskegon Historical Committee. *A Pictorial Record of the Muskegon Lumbering Era: The Brinen Lumber Company Prints*. North Muskegon: North Muskegon Historical Committee, 1976.

Bibliography

"No Word from the Hume." *Muskegon Daily Chronicle,* May 30, 1891, p. 3.

"Odds and Ends." *Great Lakes/Seaway Log* 27.18 (August 30, 1999).

Oleszewski, Wes. *Ghost Ships, Gales & Forgotten Tales: True Adventures on the Great Lakes.* Marquette, MI: Avery Color Studios, 1995.

"Only as Sea Gives Up Dead Will Total of Lives Lost Be Certain." *Muskegon Chronicle,* October 29, 1919, pp. 1+.

"Ore Carriers Docking Here for Steel Strike." *Muskegon Chronicle,* July 2, 1956, p. 1.

"Ore Ship Sails with Cargo Afire." *Muskegon Chronicle,* November 4, 1959, p. 1.

"Ore Ships Prepare to Sail." *Muskegon Chronicle,* November 9, 1959, p. 1.

Palmer, Richard F. "The Last of the Great Lakes Schooners: The *Lyman M. Davis.*" *Inland Seas* 51.1 (1995): 2–15.

"Passenger Vessels and Ferries." *Great Lakes/Seaway Log* 27.7 (March 29, 1999).

"Passenger Vessels and Ferries." *Great Lakes/Seaway Log* 27.7 (April 26, 1999).

"Passenger Vessels and Ferries." *Great Lakes/Seaway Log* 29.4 (February 12, 2001).

"Passenger Vessels and Ferries." *Great Lakes/Seaway Log* 29.11 (May 21, 2001).

"Passenger Vessels and Ferries." *Great Lakes/Seaway Log* 29.20 (September 24, 2001).

"Passenger Vessels and Ferries." *Great Lakes/Seaway Log* 29.25 (December 3, 2001).

"Perish in the Storm." *Chicago Daily Tribune,* November 9, 1896, pp. 1+.

Peterson, Howard. "The Grand Trunk Carferries in Muskegon." *Telescope* 44 (1996): 153–56.

———. "The Milwaukee Clipper: Boat of the Future." *Telescope* 45 (1997): 31–37.

———. "The Milwaukee Clipper Part II." *Telescope* 45 (1997): 69–72.

———. "Rescue of the Cort." *Muskegon Magazine* 5:2 (February/March 1989): 38–39.

———. "USCG McLane (WMEC 146)." *Telescope* 44 (1996): 93–95.

———. "'City of Milwaukee' and 'A Great Lakes Icon.'" *Telescope* 46 (1998): 9–11.

———. "M.V. Highway 16 (USS LST 393)." *Telescope* 43 (1995): 93–95.

———. "Submarine U.S.S. Silversides (SS236)." *Telescope* 42 (1994): 8–11.

———. "The Wreck of the Muskegon." *Telescope* 48 (2000): 8–11.

"Plans for Rebuilding Uncertain." *Muskegon Daily Chronicle,* May 22, 1907, p. 1.

Plumb, R. G. "The Goodrich Line." *Inland Seas* 1.2 (1945): 18–24.

"Port of Muskegon Has Record-Breaking Year." *Muskegon Chronicle,* April 23, 1960, p. 5M.

"Ports." *Great Lakes/Seaway Log* 28.4 (February 14, 2000).

"Praise Given Coast Guards." *Muskegon Chronicle,* December 3, 1934, p. 1.

"Preston Again Defies Gale at Distress Call." *Muskegon Chronicle* (final ed.), December 1, 1934, p. 1.

"Preston Praised for Saving Pair." *Muskegon Chronicle,* September 27, 1930, p. 18.

"Propeller Milwaukee Sunk by a Collision in Lake Michigan." *Muskegon Daily Chronicle,* July 9, 1886, p. 3.

Quaife, Milo M., ed. *Lake Michigan.* The American Lakes Series. Indianapolis: Bobbs-Merrill, 1944.

"Raise the Halcyon: New Try Planned." *Muskegon Chronicle,* December 4, 1996: B1.

"Ran in for Shelter." *Muskegon Daily Chronicle,* November 26, 1886, p. 3.

"Recalls a Brave Act." *Muskegon Daily Chronicle,* February 2, 1903, p. 1.

"Reiterates!" *Muskegon Weekly Chronicle,* November 19, 1896, p. 1.

"Relatives Crowd Beach as Guards Continue Search." *Muskegon Chronicle,* October 29, 1919, pp. 1+.

"Remembering the Clipper." *Muskegon Chronicle,* August 7, 2000, pp. 1D+.

"Rescue Try Is Marked by Heroism." *Muskegon Chronicle* (early ed.), December 1, 1934, p. 1.

"Rescued Sailor, Aide, Resting in Mercy Hospital." *Muskegon Chronicle* (final ed.), December 1, 1934, pp. 1+.

"Research Ship to Get New Life as Artificial Reef." *Detroit Free Press,* October 22, 2001, p. 5B.

"Rudderless Ship Is Rescued from Crushing Floes." *Muskegon Chronicle,* January 28, 1924, pp. 1+.

"The Saga of the Makefjell." *Muskegon Chronicle,* November 26, 1962, p. 26.

Bibliography

"A Schooner Wrecked." *Muskegon Daily Chronicle,* November 9, 1885, p. 3.
"Seek Body of Coast Guardsman as Crew of 25 Aboard Cort Rescued." *Muskegon Chronicle* (final ed.), December 1, 1934, pp. 1+.
"Shenango! The Big Freight Carrier Arrives in Muskegon." *Muskegon Weekly Chronicle,* December 9, 1897, p. 1.
"Silversides Museum Acquires LST." *Association for Great Lakes Maritime History Newsletter* 16.6 (November/December 1999): 1+.
"Six Men Drowned." *Muskegon Morning News,* November 10, 1896, pp. 3+.
"Six Ships Caught in Ice Field Here." *Muskegon Chronicle,* January 23, 1962, p. 9.
"Six Vessels Still Trapped in Big Ice Pack." *Muskegon Chronicle,* January 24, 1962, p. 1.
Smith, Robert H. *Maritime Museums of North America, Including Canada.* New York: Finley-Greene Publications, 1998.
South Haven. Ship Information and Data Record. Herman G. Runge Collection, Milwaukee Public Library.
South Haven Sentinel, May 8, 1886, p. 3.
"Speed Ship Salvage Efforts under Coast Guard Prodding." *Muskegon Chronicle,* November 28, 1962, p. 1.
"S.S. Milwaukee Clipper Preservation Inc." *Association for Great Lakes Maritime History Newsletter* 16.1 (January/February 1999): 5.
"S.S. Milwaukee Clipper Preservation Inc." *Association for Great Lakes Maritime History Newsletter* 16.4 (July/August 1999): 4.
"S.S. Milwaukee Clipper Preservation Inc." *Association for Great Lakes Maritime History Newsletter* 16.6 (November/December 1999): 4.
"Steambarge Milwaukee Sunk by Collision." *Marine Review,* July 15, 1886, p. 2.
"Steambarge Milwaukee Sunk to the Bottom by the Steambarge Hickox." *Chicago Inter Ocean,* July 10, 1886.
"Steamboat Collision." *Muskegon Weekly Chronicle,* June 21, 1888, p. 7.
"Steamer Missouri Afire at Dock." *Muskegon Chronicle,* May 11, 1939, p. 1.
"The Steamer Nyack." *Muskegon Chronicle,* April 26, 1894, p. 2.
"Steamship Naomi Burns on Lake Michigan; One Passenger and Four Deck Hands Die." *Muskegon Daily Chronicle,* May 21, 1907, pp. 1+.
"Steel Fleet in Harbor Here Now 8; More Coming." *Muskegon Chronicle,* July 5, 1956, p. 2.
Steele, Lori Hall. "Railroad Ferry Will Harbor Guests." *Detroit Free Press,* July 1, 2001, p. 4F.
Stonehouse, Frederick. *Haunted Lakes: Great Lakes Ghost Stories, Superstitions and Sea Serpents.* Duluth: Lake Superior Port Cities, 1997.
―――. *Haunted Lakes II: More Great Lakes Ghost Stories.* Duluth: Lake Superior Port Cities, 2000.
"Storm and Wreckage." *Muskegon Daily Chronicle,* November 18, 1886, p. 3.
"Strike Ends, Ore Fleet Here Prepares for Colorful Race to Steel Ports." *Muskegon Chronicle,* July 28, 1956, p. 2.
Stufflebeam Collection. Muskegon County Museum Archives.
"Sunk in Midlake." *Chicago Tribune,* July 10, 1886, p. 14.
"Surfman Who Gave Life Son of Service Veteran." *Muskegon Chronicle* (final ed.), December 1, 1934, p. 1.
Swayze, David. "Great Lakes Shipwreck File." *http://www.boatnerd.com/swayze/shipwreck/h.htm.*
"Swept by Violent Gales." *Chicago Tribune,* November 19, 1886, p. 1.
"A Terrible Voyage: A Ship Disabled in the Middle of Lake Michigan." *Muskegon Daily Chronicle,* October 18, 1880, p. 2.
"Their Labors Ended: Close of the Season at the U.S. Life Saving Station." *Muskegon Weekly Chronicle,* December 9, 1897, p. 9.

Bibliography

"3 Fires Damage Mothballed Ferry." *Milwaukee Sentinel*, October 14, 1987, p. 4.
"Three Suffer during Night Aboard Barge." *Muskegon Chronicle*, September 27, 1930, pp. 1+.
"Toll of Friday's Storm on Lake Michigan Now 11 Deaths and Loss of Three Vessels." *Muskegon Chronicle*, September 29, 1930, pp. 1+.
Truscott, Charles. "Alabama Suffered Few Serious Mishaps." *Muskegon Chronicle*, December 18, 1969, p. 51.
———. "Alabama Was Well Equipped for Winter." *Muskegon Chronicle*, December 4, 1969, p. 63.
———. "Carrie A. Ryerson Had Popular Reign." *Muskegon Chronicle*, April 30, 1970, p. 21.
———. "Goodrich 'Sister' Fleet Doomed by Misfortune." *Muskegon Chronicle*, October 30, 1969, p. 18.
———. "Ice Changed Ship's Trip into a Mercy Mission." *Muskegon Chronicle*, December 11, 1969, p. 17.
———. "Milwaukee Clipper." *Telescope* 19 (1970): 123–28.
———. "Old Steamer 'Juniata' Now Sailing as Proud Milwaukee Clipper." *Muskegon Chronicle*, February 19, 1970, p. 32.
———. "Once Proud Alabama Presently Being Used as Tow Barge." *Muskegon Chronicle*, 25 December 1969, p. 50.
———. "Steamship Once Ruined by Fire Returned to Useful Service." *Muskegon Chronicle*, November 27, 1969, p. 23.
———. "'Virginia' Was a Proud, Beautiful Big Lake Ship." *Muskegon Chronicle*, November 20, 1969, p. 5.
"Tug Appeared Doomed as She Floundered Near Port." *Muskegon Chronicle*, September 27, 1930, pp. 1+.
"Two Sifts of Lake Tragedy Hinted by Officials." *Muskegon Chronicle*, September 27, 1930, pp. 1+.
U.S. Department of Commerce. *Light List Great Lakes: United States and Canada*. U.S. Department of Commerce, Lighthouse Service, 1934.
"U.S.S. Silversides and Maritime Museum." *Association for Great Lakes Maritime History Newsletter* 17.1 (January/February 2000): 4.
U.S.S. Silversides and Maritime Museum. Muskegon, 2000.
"Vessel Burns; Crew Safe." *Duluth Evening Herald*, December 6, 1906.
"The Waleska Safe." *Muskegon Daily Chronicle*, November 16, 1883, p. 3.
Walsh, Michael G. "The Two Lives of the LST." *Muskegon Chronicle*, May 27, 2000, p. 1+.
"Was Captain Miller in Fear for Safety of Doomed Ship All Night before Tragedy?" *Muskegon Chronicle*, October 30, 1919, p. 1.
"Washed Up by the Waves." *Muskegon Daily Chronicle*, November 24, 1886, p. 3.
"Watched Helplessly While Sailor Burned." *Muskegon Daily Chronicle*, May 21, 1907, p. 2.
"What Captain Hea Thinks." *Muskegon Daily Chronicle*, June 4, 1891, p. 7.
"Will Any Heads Ever Bounce as a Result of the Halcyon Fiasco?" *Muskegon Chronicle*, February 20, 1997, p. 9A.
"Wind Shift Frees Icebound Shipping." *Muskegon Chronicle*, January 26, 1962, p. 11.
"Wind's Wreck." *Chicago Times*, October 19, 1880, p. 1.
"With All on Board: The Schooner Thomas Hume Lost on Lake Michigan." *Muskegon Daily Chronicle*, May 28, 1891, p. 2.
Witherell, John. Obituary. *Muskegon Daily Chronicle*, January 9, 1907, pp. 1, 7.
Wolff, Julius F., Jr. *Lake Superior Wrecks*. Duluth: Lake Superior Port Cities, 1990.
Woodruff, Charles H. "5,000 Here Greet Danish Freighter." *Muskegon Chronicle*, May 1, 1958, p. 2.
———. "Port City Welcomes Return of Makefjell!" *Muskegon Chronicle*, July 19, 1965, p. 13.
"Work of the Storm." *Chicago Times*, November 21, 1886, p. 5.
"Wreck of Muskegon Boat Found Near New Buffalo." *Muskegon Daily Chronicle*, October 10, 1905, p. 2.

Bibliography

"Wrecked by the Gale." *Chicago Tribune,* November 18, 1886, p. 1.

Yakes, Daniel J. "Common Men, Uncommon Wealth: Socio-Economic Inequality, Mobility and Power in Two Michigan Communities." 3 vols. Ph.D. diss., University of Kansas, 1990.

Yakes, Daniel J., and Hugh A. Hornstein. *The Many Lives of Muskegon.* Muskegon: Muskegon Community College, 1979.

———. *Muskegon: First Hand.* Muskegon, 1985.

Yates, Charles H. "Barry Brothers Prominent Ship Operators Here in Early 1900's." *Muskegon Chronicle,* April 5, 1958, p. 6.

———. "Boat Company Had Big Plans in 1903." *Muskegon Chronicle,* April 9, 1955, p. 6.

———. "Coast Guard Forerunner." *Muskegon Chronicle,* December 31, 1960, p. 7.

———. "Early Steamer Pride of Lakes." *Muskegon Chronicle,* July 15, 1961, p. 7.

———. "Goodrich Ship Lost in Terrific Gale Here 75 Years Ago Today." *Muskegon Chronicle,* October 15, 1955, p. 6.

———. "Harbor Here Voted $50,000 in 1867." *Muskegon Chronicle,* March 5, 1955, p. 6.

———. "January of 1924 Was Rough Month for Snow and Ice in This Area." *Muskegon Chronicle,* February 8, 1958, p. 6.

———. "Know Muskegon." *Muskegon Chronicle,* August 6, 1949, p. 19.

———. "Know Muskegon." *Muskegon Chronicle,* April 22, 1950, p. 18.

———. "Lake Steamers Had Tough Competition." *Muskegon Chronicle,* April 16, 1955, p. 6.

———. "Marine Star's Trip Recalls Era of Passenger Ships." *Muskegon Chronicle,* September 12, 1953, p. 26.

———. "Muskegon-Milwaukee Boat Service Goes Back to 1888." *Muskegon Chronicle,* July 31, 1954, p. 6.

———. "Old and Present Coast Guard Stations." *Muskegon Chronicle,* October 8, 1949, p. 5.

———. "Ship Repair Projects Date Back 67 Years." *Muskegon Chronicle,* November 14, 1953, p. 9.

———. "Shipping History Here Goes Back to First Lumber Cargo in 1839." *Muskegon Chronicle,* March 31, 1956, p. 6.

———. "Ships Also Dotted Muskegon Lake Back during the Lumbering Days." *Muskegon Chronicle,* August 18, 1956, p. 6.

———. "Steamer Illinois Made Many Trips Here." *Muskegon Chronicle,* July 2, 1955, p. 6.

———. "Str. Carrie Ryerson Had Popular, Long Career on Muskegon Lake." *Muskegon Chronicle,* November 1, 1958, p. 6.

INDEX

A. A. Augustus (ore carrier), 138–39
A. C. Van Raalte (excursion steamer), 67–69
Adams, James *(Hubbard)*, 13
Aims, Dick, 28
Alabama (passenger steamer), 62, 74–80, 155, 171
Alabaster, Michigan, 32
Albrightson, Harry *(Thomas Hume)*, 41, 43
Algoma (steamer), 17
Alice Getty (tug), 16
Alice Stafford (passenger steamer), 82
Alpena (side-wheel steamer), 34, 70–73, 187n. 56, 189n. 30
"Alpena" storm, 32, 187n. 56
American Fur Company, 4
American Shipbuilding Company, 101
Anchor Line, 101
Anderson, Charles *(R. B. King)*, 31, 159
Andrew Jackson (schooner), 10, 32, 39
Andrie, Inc., 148
Ann Arbor Railroad, 110
Annie Dall (schooner), 32–33
Annie F. Morse (schooner), 20
Annie Nelson (schooner), 28–29, 187n. 62
Apprentice Boy (schooner), 86–87
Aquarama (passenger steamer), 104–6
Arendall (schooner), 56
Arizona (passenger steamer), 59, 95, 96
Arms, George, 65
Armstrong, William *(Milwaukee)*, 83, 84, 86
Arnold, Joseph P. *See* Arnold Company
Arnold Company (shipbuilding), 19, 20, 48–49, 65
Arthur M. Anderson (freighter), 151, 192n. 2
Astor, John Jacob, 4
Atlanta (passenger steamer), 59, 82–83, 84
Avalon. See Virginia
Avery Newell (tug), 20

Badger (car ferry), 151
Baillod, Brendan, 187n. 72
Ball, Daniel, 17
Barnes, Frederick N. *(Lyman M. Davis)*, 49–50
Barry, Jack, 69
Barry, Miles E., 68, 81, 82
Barry Brothers Line, 67, 82
Basch, John A., 128–31
Bay City, Michigan, 18, 78
Bay Mill, 16, 39, 64, 65
Bay Shipbuilding, 150
B. C. Cobb (generating plant), 151
Beardsley, Paul R., 114
Bear Lake, 2, 9, 65; Channel, 4, 17
Beckman, Edward, 129
Beerman, Byron, 28
Belleville, Ontario, 88
Below (movie), 145
Belt Line (railroad), 108
Ben Calvin (freighter), 115
Bennett, Lieutenant Ward W., 129–30
Berrien (propeller steamer), 83
Bessemer Steamship Company, 126
Betsie, Point, 32
Betsy, Point. *See* Betsie, Point
Bissett, William *(Granada)*, 27–28
Black Peter, 4
Black River (South Haven), 34
Black River, Ohio. *See* Lorain, Ohio
Blakefield, Frank *(Erie L. Hackley)*, 169
Blodgett and Byrne (lumber company), 67, 115
Bluffton, 20, 24, 29, 33, 65
Bontekoe, Charles, 128
Bos, Richard *(Wolverine)*, 152
Boss (tug), 17
Boyle, Clyde *(Muskegon)*, 96–97
Brigham (schooner), 37
Brinen Lumber Company, 51, 56
British: control of the lakes, 3

Index

Brown, Ira, 27
Brown (engineer on the *Favorite*), 69
Brun, J. *(Waleska)*, 29
Brunett, Clarence *(Salvor)*, 121–22, 191n. 7
Brunswick-Balke-Collender Company, 61
Buffalo, New York, 25, 55, 62, 70, 101, 105
Buffalo and Black Rock Company, 9
Burns, Bill *(Halcyon)*, 147–48
Burns, Lieutenant Ralph *(McLane)*, 145

Caddie, D. *(Alpena)*, 72
Caesar, Pete, 190n. 56
Caldwell (propeller steamer), 24, 58
Califf, O. W., 66
California, 53, 61
Calkin, William *(Muskegon)*, 97
Campbell, Wyant and Cannon, 114, 126
Cape Horn (schooner), 10, 39, 186n. 22
Cardinal, Peter, 28
car ferries, 106–8, 110
Carolina. See *Charles H. Hackley*
Carrie A. Ryerson (coastal steamer/ferry), 39, 63–65
Carrie Ryerson (tug), 44
Carrie Mather (propeller steamer), 20
Case, Greg, 148
Cavanaugh, John (*City of Milwaukee* car ferry), 109
C. B. Kerr (freighter), 89
Celeste (schooner), 9
Centennial (ferry), 65
Central Paper Company, 124, 192n. 1
Central Wharf, 65, 70
Challenge (schooner), 10
Champlain (steamer), 190n. 44
Charles H. Hackley (passenger steamer), 80–83, 84
Charles L. Hutchinson (ore carrier), 137–39
Charlevoix, Michigan, 98, 133
Chase Brothers Piano Company, 54
Chase-Hackley Piano Company, 61. See also Chase Brothers Piano Company
Cheboygan, Michigan, 69, 152, 153
Chicago: as lumber market, 8–9, 14–15; Goodrich office in, 57; immigration to, 18–19
Chicago and Muskegon Transportation Company, 81
Chicago and Western Michigan Railroad, 108

Chicago, Racine and Milwaukee Line, 79
Chicago Times, 32, 87
Chicago Tribune, 35, 37, 38, 42, 88
Chicago Vessel Owner's Association, 10
C. Hickox (steam barge), 84–88
Christel Heering (freighter), 116
Christian Radich (tall ship), 152
Christie, George L., 66
"Christmas Tree Ship." See *Rouse Simmons*
City of Grand Haven (schooner), 124
City of Grand Rapids, 32
City of Holland, 63, 91–92. See also *Muskegon* (Crosby side-wheel steamer)
City of Kalamazoo (steamer), 78
City of Miami. See *E. G. Crosby* (passenger steamer)
City of Milwaukee (car ferry), 109–12, 142
City of Milwaukee (side-wheel steamer), 67, 91, 189n. 21. See also *Muskegon* (Crosby side-wheel steamer)
City of Muskegon, 190n. 53. See also *Muskegon* (Crosby side-wheel steamer)
City of New York (steam barge), 87
City of Racine (passsenger steamer), 59
Civilian Conservation Corps, 129–30
Clarence B. Randall (ore carrier), 137, 139
Clark, George Rogers, 3
Cleghorn, Alex *(Favorite)*, 67–68
Cleveland, Ohio, 25, 26, 59, 85, 11, 104, 105, 115, 127
Colchester Reef (Lake Erie), 127
Col. James Pickands (ore carrier), 137
Comet (side-wheel steamer), 57–58
Comet (tug), 18, 20
Commodore Jack Barry (tug), 81, 83
Constant, Pierre, 4
Continental Motors, 61
Cooke, "Doc" Ray, 171
Cora Fuller (tug), 20
Corbett, Duncan *(Waukesha)*, 45–48, 165
coureurs des bois, 2–3
Cox, Charles *(Henry W. Cort)*, 127, 130–32
Cox, James *(Henry W. Cort)*, 132
Crosby, Edward G., 57, 61–63
Crosby, Frederick G., 63
Crosby Transportation Company: founding of, 61–62; reorganized as Wisconsin and Michigan Transportation Co., 98, 114

Index

Culbert, George, 43, 188n. 88
Curwood, James Oliver, 52

Daryaw, Henry, 51
Davis and Company, C., 8
Davis, Charles, 48
DeBlake, Peter *(Rouse Simmons, Cape Horn)*, 186n. 22
De Pere (passenger steamer), 71–74
De Tour, Michigan, 119, 181
Detroit: King's Shipyard at, 5; under British control, 3
Detroit Daily Advertiser, 15, 25–26
Detroit Daily Free Press, 25
Detroit, Grand Haven and Milwaukee Railroad Company, 63, 67, 70, 92
Detroit, Grand Rapids and Western Railway, 107
Detroit River, 104, 105, 127
Diamond Alkali (freighter), 115
Dipert, Jack, 128–29, 131
dockwallopers, 14
Door Peninsula, 66, 119
Drew, George C., 57
Dulach, Frank *(Waukesha)*, 11, 44–48, 161, 164, 165–66, 188n. 90, 93
Duluth, Minnesota, 69, 101, 139
Dunbar, J. D. *(R. B. King)*, 31, 159
Duncan Robertson shipyard, 64
Durkee, Truesdell and Company, 10
Durocher, T. L., 123
Durocher, T. L., Company, 119, 123, 181, 183
Dusing, Kenneth, 143

Ecorse, Michigan, 133
Edmunds, James, 33
E. G. Crosby (passenger steamer), 90
E. G. Crosby, 63, 90. *See also Naomi*
E. G. Crosby Company. *See* Crosby Transportation Company
Egelston, Henry, 9
Egg Harbor, Wisconsin, 66
Elberta, Michigan, 110
Eliza (schooner), 37
Emma A. Nelson. See Annie Nelson (schooner)
Empire Cruise Lines, 105
Erickson's Rigging and Millwright Services, 148
Erie L. Hackley (propeller steamer), 12, 20, 64–66, 169

Escanaba, Michigan, 57
Escanaba (U.S. Coast Guard cutter), 129
Eva Fuller, 32
Ezra Stevens (tug), 69

Favorite (steamer), 67–69
Felicity, H. M. S. (sloop), 4–5
Ferry, "Mont," 56
Ferrysburg, Michigan, 56, 67
Fish Creek Transportation Company, 66
Fisher Steel and Scrap Company, 100
Fitzgerald (tug), 119–21, 123, 181
Fjell-Oranje Line, 140, 143
Flint and Pere Marquette Railroad Company, 63
Flower Creek, 36, 37
Footlander, Henry J., 20
Ford, Jonathan H., 9
Foremost. See YP-251
Foss (propeller steamer), 56
Foster, Albert. *See* "Irish"
Foster, Charles, 28
Fox, Lieutenant Commander Joseph *(Woodbine),* 141
Frank Armstrong (ore carrier), 137
Frank Billings (ore carrier), 138–39
Frankfort, Michigan, 110
Franklin, W. E. *(Alabama),* 155
Fred (Waukesha), 45–46, 161, 163, 166
Fred W. Green (sand and gravel carrier), 132–33
Freitag, Richard R. *(Silversides),* 144
French and Indian War, 3
Fringelson, Fingle *(R. B. King),* 187n. 67
Fuller, E. B., 20
fur trade, 2–5

Gartland and Sullivan Steamship Company, 78
Garvey, Dennis, 8, 11
Gary, Indiana, 127
Gatfield, George (U.S. Coast Guard), 120, 123
Gatfield, William (U.S. Coast Guard), 94
Gautier, Charles (H. M. S. *Felicity*), 4
Gayton, Thomas *(Waukesha),* 45, 188n. 93
G. B. Mansfield, 34
George C. Markham (steam barge), 50, 56
George Dunbar (steam barge), 56
George P. Savage (steamer), 69
George R. Roberts (schooner), 8
Georgia (passenger steamer), 59, 61, 76–77
Georgian Bay, 1, 50, 51

Index

Getty (tug), 81
Getty, Henry H., 64
Gill's Rock, Wisconsin, 119, 181
G. J. Truesdell (propeller steamer), 58
Globe Iron Works, Inc., 59
Glover, S. C. *(De Pere)*, 71
Goodman, Autry, 110
Goodman, C. H., 67
Goodrich, Albert E., 57–79, 70, 72–74, 189n. 35
Goodrich, Albert W., 74
Goodrich Steamship Line. *See* Goodrich Transportation Company
Goodrich Transportation Company: bankruptcy of, 78, 98; dock becomes the Mart, 115; early steamships of, 57–59; founding of, 57; renamed, 78, 189n. 36
Goodrich Transit Company, 78, 114, 189n. 36
Gooton, John *(L. J. Conway)*, 37
Goudy, D. M., 51–52
Governor Mason (riverboat), 26
G. P. Kingsbury (tug), 20
Graham and Morton Line, 57, 63, 92, 189n. 36
Graham brothers, 51
Granada (schooner), 27–28, 34, 69, 72, 157
Grand Haven, Michigan: Grand Trunk car ferries in, 108; in post-lumber era, 54
Grand Haven (car ferry), 75
Grand Rapids (car ferry), 109–10
Grand Rapids, Michigan, 26, 54, 67, 75, 89
Grand Rapids and Indiana Railroad. *See* Muskegon, Grand Rapids and Indiana Railroad
Grand Rapids Naval Reserve, 146
Grand River, 4, 26
Grand Trunk Railroad, 67, 108–10, 142; terminal, 63
Grand Valley State University Water Resources Institute, 153
Grandville, Michigan, 25
Great Lakes Clipper Preservation, Inc. *See* S.S. Milwaukee Clipper Preservation, Inc.
Great Lakes Environmental Laboratory, 146, 149
Great Lakes Naval Memorial and Museum, 136, 144–145, 153, 191n. 22. *See also* U.S.S. Silversides and Maritime Museum
Great Lakes Tall Ship Challenge, 152
Great Lakes Transit Corporation, 101

Green, Alfred *(Milwaukee)*, 84, 86
Green, Andrew H., Jr., 132
Green Bay, Wisconsin, 18, 57, 70
Groh, William, 30
G. W. Davis (schooner), 45

Hackley and Hume Company, 82
Hackley and Hume Lumber Company, 12, 13, 16, 17, 39, 40, 43, 67, 185n. 12
Hackley and McGordon Company, 185
Hackley, Charles H., 10, 11, 12, 13, 14, 41–43, 54, 65, 81–83, 185n. 12
Hackley Hospital, 100
Hackley, Joseph, 10
Hackley Transportation Company, 67, 81–82
Halcyon (research vessel), 146–50
Hamilton, Henry (Lieutenant Colonel), 3
Hammond (Indiana) Port Authority, 104
Hanlan's Island, Ontario, 52
Hannah, George, 34
Hansen, Peter, 97
Harbor Springs, Michigan, 98
Harbor Town Marina, 115
Harrington, Dennis *(Milwaukee)*, 86–87
Harris, Fred *(South Haven)*, 33–34
Harry W. Croft (ore carrier), 137
Hartford (steamer). *See Charles H. Hackley*
Hartford and New York Transportation Company, 81
Hartshorn Marina, 137
Harvard (ore carrier), 138
Hattie Hutt (schooner), 50
Havill, C. H., 132
H. B. Moore (schooner), 39
H. C. Albrecht (schooner), 10, 40. *See also Thomas Hume*
Hea, John, 187n. 81
Heering, Peter, 116
Helen (scow-schooner), 32, 34–36, 187
Henderson and Peterson Lumber Company, 36, 187n. 73
Henry Clay (schooner), 8
Henry W. Cort (whaleback), 126–32, 140, 153
Heritage Landing, 152
H. G. Dalton (ore carrier), 136
Highway 16 (auto ferry), 115, 117, 133–36. *See also* LST 393
Hill Transportation Company, 77
History Channel, 104

Index

Hoffman, Albert *(Muskegon)*, 94
Holland Furnace Company, 127
Holland, Michigan, 72, 73, 77, 78, 127, 178; museum, 78
Homans, James T. (Lieutenant), 15, 21, 186n. 29
Honest John (schooner), 8
Hopkins, Barney *(Naomi)*, 89
Houle, Thomas *(Fitzgerald)*, 119
Hubbard (schooner), 12
Hume, George A., 186n. 22
Hume, Thomas, 41, 43, 54, 82, 186n. 22
Hume Home for Assisted Living, 186n. 22
Huron (side-wheel steamer), 53, 57–58
Hutchinson and Company, 136–38
H. Warner (tug), 16

Ida Torrent (steam barge), 39, 56
Illinois (schooner), 8
Illinois (passenger steamer), 90, 98–100, 114, 129, 190n. 61
Indiana (passenger steamer), 59, 78
Indiana Harbor, Indiana, 138–39
Interlakes (Interlake Steamship Company), 136–37
Inter-Urban train, 75, 76, 78
Iowa (passenger steamer), 59, 78–80
Ira O. Smith (tug), 18, 69
"Irish" *(Waukesha)*, 45–48, 188n. 93
Isakson, Isak *(Makefjell)*, 143
"It's Your Money" (television program), 150

Jacobs, Henry, 64
Jacobsen, Ole *(Fred W. Green)*, 133
Jakubovsky, Ransom, 94
James McGordon (tug), 10, 16, 17, 39
James P. Walsh (ore carrier), 137, 139
Jarvis, "Gov" W. B., 171–73
Jaworski, Jed, 111–12
Jay's Treaty, 3
Jessie Boyce, 32
Jessie Martin (schooner), 20
Jessie Philips, 32
J. H. Hackley (tug), 10, 16, 39
Jimmy (L. J. Conway), 37
Jiroch, Frank, 189n. 34
J. J. Sullivan (ore carrier), 137, 139
J. L. Mauthe (ore carrier), 136–37
John Otis (steam barge), 56

John Purves (tug), 142–43
Johnson, Charles E., 114
Johnson, Herbert E., 164
Johnson, John *(South Haven)*, 33
Johnson, John *(Waukesha)*, 45–46
Johnson, Wilhelm *(Rouse Simmons)*, 39
John Stanton (ore carrier), 138–39
Johnston, Brant *(Muskegon)*, 178–79
Johnston, Kate *(Muskegon)*, 179
John T. Hutchinson (ore carrier), 137
John Torrent (tug), 20, 28
Jolliet, Louis, 1
Jolly Inez (steamer), 119. See also *Salvor*
Jones, E. O. *(Muskegon)*, 97
Jones, Guy *(Naomi)*, 89, 175
J. O. Nessen Company, 82
Joy, Morton and Company, 44
Julia B. Merrill (schooner), 51
Juniata (passenger steamer), 101–2, 116. See also *Milwaukee Clipper*

Kansas (passenger steamer), 89, 176
Kate Lyons (schooner), 10, 12, 32, 39
Kelley, Henry, 124
Kelly Bros. (tug), 20
Kenosha, Wisconsin, 9, 10, 15, 19, 39, 58, 72, 135
Kensmann, Edward M. *(L. J. Conway)*, 36–37
Kersman, Jay, 148
Kewaunee, Wisconsin, 50
Keweenaw Peninsula, 119
Kincardine, Ontario, 51
Kingston, Ontario, 51
Kirby, Frank E., 91
Kirby and Carpenter Company, 67
Kirkeby, Axel *(Christel Heering)*, 116
Kohl, Cris, 63
Kremer, Charles R., 48

Lake Michigan Carferry Company, 151, 192n. 3
Lake Ports Shipping and Navigation Company, 127, 132
Lakeside, 20, 27, 33
Lake St. Clair, 3
Lamorandie, E., 4
landing ship/tanks (LSTs), 134, 136, 191n. 22
Lane, Clifford *(Salvor)*, 121–123, 182
LaPlaunt, Alice *(Salvor)*, 119, 121
LaPlaunt, Onney *(Salvor)*, 119, 121

Index

Lassallier, Pierre, 4
Laura Miller (schooner), 33
Lawrence (steamer), 190n. 44
Lee, Kate B., 81
Lee, Seth, 12–13, 41–42, 65, 81
L. E. Simmons (schooner), 43
Levi Grant, 32
Lexington (steamer), 26, 186n. 52
L. G. Mason sawmill, 56
Life Saving Service, 20
Linklater, Angus *(Granada),* 27–28, 157
Linklater, Robert *(Granada),* 27–28
Little Sable Point (Point Solitude), 25, 119, 127, 162, 186n. 49
Livingston Channel (Detroit River), 127
L. J. Conway (schooner), 32, 36–38
Lorain, Ohio, 18, 85, 124, 127
Losby, Peter W., 44, 161, 164
Love Construction and Engineering Company, 118–19
LST 325, 136, 191n. 22
LST 393, 133–34, 136, 153. *See also Highway 16*
Lucia A. Simpson (schooner), 124
lumber: loading of, 14; production of, 14
lumber barges, 14
Lyman, Charles, A. *(Nyack),* 62
Lyman M. Davis (schooner), 20, 21, 48–52, 56, 124, 167–68
Lyons Construction Company, 133
Lytle, Elmer *(Salvor),* 121

Mabel Bradshaw (steamer), 82
Mackinac, Straits of, 5, 51, 80, 124
Mackinac Island, Michigan, 98
Madison (car ferry), 109–10
Magellan (schooner), 42
Majo, A. C., 28, 68–69
Makefjell (freighter), 139–43, 144, 191n. 25
Malone, Pete *(Alabama),* 171–72
Manatra II. See USCGC McLane
Manistee, Lake, 111
Manistee, Michigan, 2, 8, 32, 44, 54, 57, 71, 82, 112, 119
Manistique, Michigan, 39, 57
Manitou Passage (Lake Michigan), 124
Manitowoc, Wisconsin, 36, 40, 44, 58, 61, 76, 89, 103; as shipbuilding center, 18

Manitowoc Shipbuilding Company, 74, 101, 109
Mann Co., A. V., 29, 85
Marine Navigation and Training Association (M.N.T.A.), 145–46
Marine Pollution Control, Inc., 148
Marine Star. See Aquarama
Markle, William *(Lyman M. Davis),* 50
Marquette, Jacques, 1
Mart, the, 99, 100, 102, 104, 115, 117, 136, 140, 147, 151, 153. *See also* West Michigan Dock and Market Corporation
Martin, John, 150
Martin, J. W. *(Roanoke),* 32
Mary Minter (ferry), 65
Mason and Davis Lumber Company, 20, 48
Mason, Lyman G., 24, 48, 56, 67, 83–86
Mathew Wilson (steam barge), 56
Matt *(Granada),* 27–28
Mayer, F. P., 36
Mayflower (paddlewheel steamer/ferry), 65
McCrea, Bruce D., 142
McDermott, Fred *(South Haven),* 33
McDougall Shipyard, 126
McGordon, James, 10
McGraft (tug), 17
McGraft and Montgomery Lumber Company, 27
McGraw, Charles *(Eliza, L. J. Conway),* 37–38
McKee, Max B., 115, 153
McLane (U.S. Coast Guard cutter), 143–46, 153
McMillan, Donald and Dennis, 56
M'Donnell, John, 15
Mees, William, 16
Menominee, Michigan, 66, 67
Menominee (propeller steamer), 59, 71, 74, 79
Mercy Hospital, 100, 122, 183
Michael Groh (propeller steamer), 83
Michigan (naval gunboat). *See Wolverine*
Michigan City, Indiana, 15, 127, 130, 131
Michilimackinac, 3–4
Midvale (freighter), 127
Miller, Edward *(Muskegon),* 93–95, 97–98, 177
Milwaukee, 34, 39, 103, 122; as lumber market, 14–15; immigration to, 18; passenger/auto cross-lake service to, 101–2, 151; railroad cross-lake service to, 67, 107–8
Milwaukee (car ferry), 75
Milwaukee (steam barge), 83–88

Index

Milwaukee Clipper (passenger steamer and auto ferry), 101–4, 105, 114, 115, 116, 117, 135, 151, 153, 190n. 61
Milwaukee 95 (lighthouse tender), 55
Minerva (schooner), 39
Minnie Mueller, 32
Mique, Ted *(Muskegon),* 93, 178–79
Miranda (tug), 69
Mississippi River, 104, 134, 144
Missouri (passenger steamer), 77, 98–100, 114, 190n. 61
Mohr, Charles *(William Nelson),* 124–26
Mona Lake, 16
Montague, Michigan, 2, 35, 54, 65, 126
Montreal, Quebec, 81
Morgan, Sanford "Shanty" *(Wabash Valley),* 70
Morin, Robert G., Sr., 145–46
Morris, Robert W., 17
Morrison, William F. *(Wolverine),* 152
Morro Castle (steamer), 101, 190n. 62
Mouth, the. See Port Sherman
Mullen, Samuel *(Milwaukee),* 84
Municipal Marina, 136
Munroe, Thomas, 51
Murger, Fred *(South Haven),* 34
Muskegon: board of trade, 54; Chamber of Commerce, 54–55; channel, development of, 20–24, 58, 93, 118; common council, 54; customs office in, 20; end of lumbering in, 53–54; jobs in, 8, 54–55; lighthouses in, 21, 24, 118; railroads in, 66–67, 106–7; shipbuilding in, 18, 19, 54–55; State Park, 28, 129; variations in name, 2, 7, 185n. 1
Muskegon (car ferry), 108. See also *Shenango No. 2*
Muskegon (Crosby side-wheel steamer), 63, 91–98, 117, 177
Muskegon (early Goodrich side-wheel steamer), 59, 71
Muskegon (schooner), 8, 9
Muskegon Booming Company, 12, 16–20, 69
Muskegon Chemical Fire Engine Company, 54
Muskegon Chronicle, 62, 80, 95, 97, 117, 129, 137, 139, 142, 149, 150, 167, 175, 177
Muskegon Cracker Company, 54
Muskegon Daily Chronicle, 8, 28, 29, 31, 36–37, 81, 88, 157, 159, 169
Muskegon, Grand Rapids and Indiana Railroad, 63, 67

Muskegon Harbor Company, 23
Muskegon Lake: ferry service on, 63–66; formation of, 2; lumber mills on, 8, 9, 14; trading posts on, 3–4
Muskegon Morning News, 44, 161
Muskegon Railway and Navigation Company, 108
Muskegon Reporter, 53, 58
Muskegon River, 2, 4, 8, 15, 17
Muskegon Steam Mill Company, 9
Muskegon Weekly Chronicle, 29, 48, 68, 107, 165
Myrtle, 32

Nabob (schooner). See *Waukesha*
Naomi (passenger steamer), 63, 89, 90, 91, 175–76. See also *Wisconsin*
Napier, Nelson W. *(Alpena),* 70, 72–73
National Boat and Engine Company. See Racine Boat Company
Navarino (propeller steamer), 59
Nedeau, Harvey, 183
Nedeau, Israel, 181
Nedeau, Lyman *(Salvor),* 121–23, 181–83
Nellie (tug), 18
Nellie Torrent (steam barge), 39, 56
Nelson, Fred *(Our Son),* 124, 126
Nelson, John *(South Haven),* 33
Nelson, Oscar *(Rouse Simmons),* 40
Nelson lumber mill, 23, 107
Neptune (brig), 24–26
Nevada (passenger steamer), 78, 190n. 61
Newall Avery (tug), 28, 69
New Buffalo, Michigan, 43, 57
Newell, Theodore (schooner *Muskegon*), 9
New Hampshire (schooner), 8
Niagara (brig), 152
Nicolet, Jean, 1
NOAA (National Oceanic and Atmospheric Administration), 146, 148–49; field station at Muskegon, 24
Northern Michigan Transportation Company, 98, 190
Northern Transportation Company, 84
North Muskegon, 12, 16, 65, 86, 137
North Muskegon (tug), 20, 39 83
North Shore (passenger and package steamer), 122, 124
Nugent Sand Company, 115

213

Index

Nyack (side-wheel steamer), 62–63, 64, 89, 90, 92

O'Connor, Floyd *(Salvor)*, 121
Octorara (passenger steamer), 101
O'Day, Simon *(C. Hickox)*, 85–88
Ogdensburg, New York, 84
Ojala, Robert A., 149
Old People's Home. *See* Hume Home for Assisted Living
Olmstead, Ida *(Salvor)*, 119, 182
Olmstead, Lornie *(Salvor)*, 119, 120, 123, 182
Olson, Andrew *(R. B. King)*, 187n. 67
O. M. Field (tug), 16, 107
Orion (side-wheel steamer), 59
Oswego, New York, 88
Ottawa (propeller steamer), 58
Ottawa tribe, 2
Our Son (schooner), 124–26

Pabst, Fred, 58
passenger steamers: decline of, 98, 114; development of, 55, 57–59;
Pearson, Paul, 39
Pederson, Ernst *(Makefjell)*, 140
Pennoyer lumber mill, 9
Pentwater, Michigan, 2, 39, 119
Pere Marquette No. 1 (steamer), 82
Pere Marquette No. 4 (car ferry), 78
Pere Marquette 16 (car ferry), 108. *See also* Muskegon (car ferry)
Pere Marquette No. 22 (car ferry), 125
Pere Marquette Car Ferry Line, 78, 108
Pere Marquette Park, 141
Pere Marquette Railroad Company, 82
Pere Marquette Steamer Line, 115, 190n. 61
Petoskey, Michigan, 98
Petrel (revenue cutter), 81
Petries and Company, 86
Pickands-Mather Steamship Company, 136, 137
Pigeon Hill, 2, 115, 117
Pillow, P. *See* Pillow and Cleghorn
Pillow and Cleghorn, 67
Pillsbury (whaleback). See *Henry W. Cort*
Pillsbury Flour Mills Company, 126
Pinchtown, 20
Pioneer Park, 121
Piston Ring Company, 114
Pittsburgh Steamship Company, 126, 136

Pixley, F. A., 97
Pontiac's Rebellion, 3
Pony (tug), 16, 17
Port Huron, Michigan, 50, 105
Port Maitland, Ontario, 110
Port Sheldon, Michigan, 26
Port Sherman, 20, 29, 107, 115, 181, 186n. 41
Port Stanley, Ontario, 105, 108
Port Washington, Wisconsin, 82
Preston, William E., 121–23, 129, 130, 182
Priefer, Robert *(Highway 16)*, 135
Prins Willem V (foreign freighter), 140
Provincial Marine, 3

Racine Boat Company, 55, 114
Racine, Wisconsin, 19, 57, 58, 79, 108, 122, 151
Racine (steamer), 79–80
railroads: transporting lumber, 15, 18. *See also* Muskegon, railroads in
Rattlesnake (scow), 17
Ray, "Doc" Herbert S., 171–73
R. B. King (schooner), 31–32, 159, 187n. 67
Recollect, Jean Baptist, 4
Reedsville. *See* North Muskegon
Reid, David, 149
Rhoades, James M. *(Naomi)*, 89
Rice, Bob *(Carrie Ryerson)*, 44
R. McDonald (steam barge), 39
Roanoke (barge), 32
Robertson, Samuel (H. M. S. *Felicity)*, 4
Robinson, Harry B. *(Muskegon)*, 95–97
Robinson, Thomas, 95
Roen, John J., 133
Rouse Simmons (schooner), 10, 11, 32, 38–40, 41, 43, 186n. 22, 187n. 80
R. P. Easton (tug), 20, 21
Ruddiman, George, 17
Ryerson, Hills and Company (lumber mill), 39, 64
Ryerson, Martin, 17, 58
Ryerson and Morris, 8
Ryerson Creek, 39

Sackville, Fort, 3
Saddle Bag Island (Lake Huron), 119
Sadony, Joseph A., 126
Saginaw, Michigan, 18
Saginaw River Valley, 14

Index

S. A. Irish (schooner), 72
Salvor (stone barge), 117, 119–24, 129, 153, 181–83
Samuel Mather (ore carrier), 137
Sand Products Corporation, 104, 115
Sanford, James, 56
Sarnia, Ontario, 105
Sauble (Sable), Point, 33
Saugatuck, Michigan, 84
Sault Ste. Marie, Michigan, 80
Saxona (freighter), 89
schooners: clipper schooners, 9; "sailing stores," 8; scow schooners, 9
Schuenemann, Herman *(Rouse Simmons)*, 39, 187n. 80
Scotch Bonnet, 36
Seabird (scow), 28
Seabird (side-wheel steamer), 58, 70, 189n. 25
Sealed Power Corporation. *See* Piston Ring Company
Secord, George *(Salvor)*, 121, 181–82
Shaw, A. W., 54
Shaw Walker Company, 54, 114
Sheboygan, Wisconsin, 19, 29
Sheboygan (steamer), 66, 77–78, 169
Shenango No. 2 (car ferry), 107–8. *See also Muskegon* (car ferry)
Shenehon (research vessel), 146–47
Sherman House, 20
shipbuilding, 18, 19
Shurage, Clement *(Salvor)*, 121
Sietsema, Lieutenant Jay, 100
Sills (tug), 41
Silver Inlet (Georgian Bay), 50
Silver Lake (schooner-scow), 108
Sims, John H. *(Neptune)*, 25–26
Sinclair, Patrick (lieutenant governor), 4
Smith, David, 36–37, 187n. 73
Smith, Harry *(Salvor)*, 121–23, 182–83
Smith, James L., 56
Smith, Thomas *(L. J. Conway)*, 36–38
S. M. Stephenson (steam barge), 56
Snider, C. H. J., 51
Society for the Preservation of the City of Milwaukee (S.P.C.M.), 110
Solitude, Point. *See* Little Sable Point
Soo Locks, 139
South Haven, Michigan, 34, 127
South Haven (scow-schooner), 32–34

South Chicago, Illinois, 44, 161, 162
Spartan (car ferry), 151
S.S. Milwaukee Clipper Preservation, Inc., 104
St. Clair River, 1, 3, 58, 105
steam barges, 18, 56
Stearman, Roger, 128
Steffens, Fred *(Muskegon)*, 94–95, 179
St. Ignace, Michigan, 69, 80
Stimson, Fay and Company (lumber mill), 108
St. Joseph, Michigan, 30, 31, 72, 73, 122
St. Lawrence River, 27, 81
St. Lawrence Seaway, 116–17, 139
Stufflebeam, Gerald *(Alabama)*, 74, 75, 78–80
Sturgeon Bay, Wisconsin, 57, 103, 150
Sullivan, Dennis, 47–78
Sultana (freighter), 115
Sunbeam (passenger steamer), 70
Sundew (U.S. Coast Guard cutter), 142
Sunnyside Amusement Association, 51, 167
Sun Shipbuilding and Drydock Company, 104
Superior, Wisconsin, 126
Sutton, Harry *(Henry W. Cort)*, 132
Swain Wrecking Company, 69
Swede *(Waukesha)*, 45, 47, 163

Tall Ships Challenge. *See* Great Lakes Tall Ships Challenge
Temple, A. F., 164
Temple Manufacturing Company, 54
Terry, USQMD. *See Charles H. Hackley*
Thayer Lumber Company, 51, 67
Third Michigan (tug), 18
Thomas Hume (schooner), 10, 32, 38–39, 40–43, 187n. 81, 188n. 88
Thompson, George *(Shenango No. 2)*, 107
Thompson, Michigan, 39
Thompson, Theo *(South Haven)*, 33
Thomsen, Niels P., Lieutenant *(YP-251)*, 145
Thorp, H. W., 155
Tillotson lumber mill, 107
Tionesta (passenger steamer), 101
Titanic, 63
Toledo, Ohio, 127
Toledo, Saginaw and Muskegon Railroad. *See* Grand Trunk Railroad
Toronto, Ontario, 51, 52, 167
Toronto Evening Telegram, 167
Toronto Telegram, 51
Torrent, John, 38, 54, 56

Totten, William D., 155
Trail, Thomas *(Naomi)*, 89
Traverse City, Michigan, 8, 54
Treaty of Paris, 3
Trial (schooner), 28
tugs: booming, 17–18; harbor, 10, 16, 17
Turret Chief (turret steamer), 119, 124. *See also* Salvor
Two Rivers, Wisconsin, 39

Ulster (scow schooner). *See Helen*
United States Gypsum (freighter), 115
U. S. Army Corps of Engineers, 147, 149, 183
U. S. Coast Guard, 78, 94–95, 97, 120–21, 123, 128–32, 133, 142–43, 147–48, 182–83; station at Grand Haven, 95, 121–22, 129; station at Muskegon, 20, 24, 95, 129, 133, 137, 143; station at White River, 129
U. S. Life Saving Service, 20, 28, 29–31, 36, 44, 165, 186n. 20; station at Muskegon, 24, 29, 32, 33, 34, 44
U. S. Navy, 15, 145
U.S.S. Great Lakes Fleet, 151
U.S.S. *Macon,* 105
U.S.S. *Silversides*, 143–146, 153
U.S.S. *Silversides* and Maritime Museum, 136, 144, 146, 191n. 21. *See also* Great Lakes Naval Memorial and Museum

VanDusen, Frank *(J. L. Mauthe)*, 137
Verous, Joseph *(Erie L. Hackley)*, 66, 169
Vickerstown (steamer), 119. *See also Salvor*
Victor (schooner), 9
Vincennes, Illinois, 3
Virginia (passenger steamer), 59–61, 62, 74, 79, 190n. 61
Von Thadden, John *(Helen)*, 34–36
Von Thadden, Mrs. John *(Helen)*, 35–36
voyageurs, 1, 2, 3

Wabash Valley (propeller steamer), 26, 69–70
Waleska (schooner), 29
Walker, Louis C., 54
Walter Smith (schooner), 37
Ward, Ernest E., 100
Ward Line, 57, 58
Waukegan, Illinois, 19, 70

Waukesha (schooner), 11, 44–48, 161, 164, 165, 188n. 93
Wave (schooner), 9
W. C. Kimball, 42
W. C. Walton (schooner), 8
Webster *(Neptune)*, 25
W. E. Fitzgerald (steamer), 115
Welland Canal, 51, 81
West Michigan: dunes, 1–2, 53, 54; settlement of, 7–8
West Michigan Artificial Reef Society, 153
West Michigan Dock and Market Corporation, 115, 153. *See also* Mart, the
W. F. P. Taylor (steamer), 15
Whalen, Edward, 143
Wheelock, Benjamin H., 9
Whitehall, Michigan, 2, 35, 36, 37, 38, 54, 64, 83, 133
White Lake, 8, 32, 35, 37, 57, 171
W. H. McGean (ore carrier), 138–39
Wickham, Tom *(Alabama)*, 172
Willard L. (tug), 142
William A. Paine (ore carrier), 138–39
William McLauchlan (ore carrier), 137
William Nelson (steamer), 124–26
Willow Springs, Illinois, 65
Wilson, Mathew and William H., 56
Windsor, Ontario, 104, 105
Winserowski, Edward *(Salvor)*, 121, 123
Winserowski, Tony *(Salvor)*, 121
Wisconsin, 4, 8, 53; settlement of, 18, 19
Wisconsin (passenger steamer), 63, 67, 189n. 21
Wisconsin and Michigan Steamship Company, 99, 101, 114, 115, 134, 190n. 61
Wisconsin and Michigan Transportation Company, 98, 115, 190n. 61. *See also* Wisconsin and Michigan Steamship Company
Wisconsin Clipper. See Spartan
Witherell, John, 16–17
Wolverine (naval gunboat), 152, 192n. 5
Woodbine (U.S. Coast Guard cutter), 140, 142–43
Woods, Henry J., 30–32, 44
Wyandotte, Michigan, 65, 63, 91

YP-251 (naval vessel), 145

TITLES IN THE GREAT LAKES BOOKS SERIES

Freshwater Fury: Yarns and Reminiscences of the Greatest Storm in Inland Navigation, by Frank Barcus, 1986 (reprint)

Call It North Country: The Story of Upper Michigan, by John Bartlow Martin, 1986 (reprint)

The Land of the Crooked Tree, by U. P. Hedrick, 1986 (reprint)

Michigan Place Names, by Walter Romig, 1986 (reprint)

Luke Karamazov, by Conrad Hilberry, 1987

The Late, Great Lakes: An Environmental History, by William Ashworth, 1987 (reprint)

Great Pages of Michigan History from the Detroit Free Press, 1987

Waiting for the Morning Train: An American Boyhood, by Bruce Catton, 1987 (reprint)

Michigan Voices: Our State's History in the Words of the People Who Lived It, compiled and edited by Joe Grimm, 1987

Danny and the Boys, Being Some Legends of Hungry Hollow, by Robert Traver, 1987 (reprint)

Hanging On, or How to Get through a Depression and Enjoy Life, by Edmund G. Love, 1987 (reprint)

The Situation in Flushing, by Edmund G. Love, 1987 (reprint)

A Small Bequest, by Edmund G. Love, 1987 (reprint)

The Saginaw Paul Bunyan, by James Stevens, 1987 (reprint)

The Ambassador Bridge: A Monument to Progress, by Philip P. Mason, 1988

Let the Drum Beat: A History of the Detroit Light Guard, by Stanley D. Solvick, 1988

An Afternoon in Waterloo Park, by Gerald Dumas, 1988 (reprint)

Contemporary Michigan Poetry: Poems from the Third Coast, edited by Michael Delp, Conrad Hilberry and Herbert Scott, 1988

Over the Graves of Horses, by Michael Delp, 1988

Wolf in Sheep's Clothing: The Search for a Child Killer, by Tommy McIntyre, 1988

Copper-Toed Boots, by Marguerite de Angeli, 1989 (reprint)

Detroit Images: Photographs of the Renaissance City, edited by John J. Bukowczyk and Douglas Aikenhead, with Peter Slavcheff, 1989

Hangdog Reef: Poems Sailing the Great Lakes, by Stephen Tudor, 1989

Detroit: City of Race and Class Violence, revised edition, by B. J. Widick, 1989

Deep Woods Frontier: A History of Logging in Northern Michigan, by Theodore J. Karamanski, 1989

Orvie, The Dictator of Dearborn, by David L. Good, 1989

Seasons of Grace: A History of the Catholic Archdiocese of Detroit, by Leslie Woodcock Tentler, 1990

The Pottery of John Foster: Form and Meaning, by Gordon and Elizabeth Orear, 1990

The Diary of Bishop Frederic Baraga: First Bishop of Marquette, Michigan, edited by Regis M. Walling and Rev. N. Daniel Rupp, 1990

Walnut Pickles and Watermelon Cake: A Century of Michigan Cooking, by Larry B. Massie and Priscilla Massie, 1990

The Making of Michigan, 1820–1860: A Pioneer Anthology, edited by Justin L. Kestenbaum, 1990

America's Favorite Homes: A Guide to Popular Early Twentieth-Century Homes, by Robert Schweitzer and Michael W. R. Davis, 1990

Beyond the Model T: The Other Ventures of Henry Ford, by Ford R. Bryan, 1990

Life after the Line, by Josie Kearns, 1990

Michigan Lumbertowns: Lumbermen and Laborers in Saginaw, Bay City, and Muskegon, 1870–1905, by Jeremy W. Kilar, 1990

Detroit Kids Catalog: The Hometown Tourist, by Ellyce Field, 1990

Waiting for the News, by Leo Litwak, 1990 (reprint)

Detroit Perspectives, edited by Wilma Wood Henrickson, 1991

Life on the Great Lakes: A Wheelsman's Story, by Fred W. Dutton, edited by William Donohue Ellis, 1991

Copper Country Journal: The Diary of Schoolmaster Henry Hobart, 1863–1864, by Henry Hobart, edited by Philip P. Mason, 1991

John Jacob Astor: Business and Finance in the Early Republic, by John Denis Haeger, 1991

Survival and Regeneration: Detroit's American Indian Community, by Edmund J. Danziger, Jr., 1991

Steamboats and Sailors of the Great Lakes, by Mark L. Thompson, 1991

Cobb Would Have Caught It: The Golden Age of Baseball in Detroit, by Richard Bak, 1991

Michigan in Literature, by Clarence Andrews, 1992

Under the Influence of Water: Poems, Essays, and Stories, by Michael Delp, 1992

The Country Kitchen, by Della T. Lutes, 1992 (reprint)

The Making of a Mining District: Keweenaw Native Copper 1500–1870, by David J. Krause, 1992

Kids Catalog of Michigan Adventures, by Ellyce Field, 1993

Henry's Lieutenants, by Ford R. Bryan, 1993

Historic Highway Bridges of Michigan, by Charles K. Hyde, 1993

Lake Erie and Lake St. Clair Handbook, by Stanley J. Bolsenga and Charles E. Herndendorf, 1993

Queen of the Lakes, by Mark Thompson, 1994

Iron Fleet: The Great Lakes in World War II, by George J. Joachim, 1994

Turkey Stearnes and the Detroit Stars: The Negro Leagues in Detroit, 1919–1933, by Richard Bak, 1994

Pontiac and the Indian Uprising, by Howard H. Peckham, 1994 (reprint)

Charting the Inland Seas: A History of the U.S. Lake Survey, by Arthur M. Woodford, 1994 (reprint)

Ojibwa Narratives of Charles and Charlotte Kawbawgam and Jacques LePique, 1893–1895. Recorded with Notes by Homer H. Kidder, edited by Arthur P. Bourgeois, 1994, co-published with the Marquette County Historical Society

Strangers and Sojourners: A History of Michigan's Keweenaw Peninsula, by Arthur W. Thurner, 1994

Win Some, Lose Some: G. Mennen Williams and the New Democrats, by Helen Washburn Berthelot, 1995

Sarkis, by Gordon and Elizabeth Orear, 1995

The Northern Lights: Lighthouses of the Upper Great Lakes, by Charles K. Hyde, 1995 (reprint)

Kids Catalog of Michigan Adventures, second edition, by Ellyce Field, 1995

Rumrunning and the Roaring Twenties: Prohibition on the Michigan-Ontario Waterway, by Philip P. Mason, 1995

In the Wilderness with the Red Indians, by E. R. Baierlein, translated by Anita Z. Boldt, edited by Harold W. Moll, 1996

Elmwood Endures: History of a Detroit Cemetery, by Michael Franck, 1996

Master of Precision: Henry M. Leland, by Mrs. Wilfred C. Leland with Minnie Dubbs Millbrook, 1996 (reprint)

Haul-Out: New and Selected Poems, by Stephen Tudor, 1996

Kids Catalog of Michigan Adventures, third edition, by Ellyce Field, 1997

Beyond the Model T: The Other Ventures of Henry Ford, revised edition, by Ford R. Bryan, 1997

Young Henry Ford: A Picture History of the First Forty Years, by Sidney Olson, 1997 (reprint)

The Coast of Nowhere: Meditations on Rivers, Lakes and Streams, by Michael Delp, 1997

From Saginaw Valley to Tin Pan Alley: Saginaw's Contribution to American Popular Music, 1890–1955, by R. Grant Smith, 1998

The Long Winter Ends, by Newton G. Thomas, 1998 (reprint)

Bridging the River of Hatred: The Pioneering Efforts of Detroit Police Commissioner George Edwards, by Mary M. Stolberg, 1998

Toast of the Town: The Life and Times of Sunnie Wilson, by Sunnie Wilson with John Cohassey, 1998

These Men Have Seen Hard Service: The First Michigan Sharpshooters in the Civil War, by Raymond J. Herek, 1998

A Place for Summer: One Hundred Years at Michigan and Trumbull, by Richard Bak, 1998

Early Midwestern Travel Narratives: An Annotated Bibliography, 1634–1850, by Robert R. Hubach, 1998 (reprint)

All-American Anarchist: Joseph A. Labadie and the Labor Movement, by Carlotta R. Anderson, 1998

Michigan in the Novel, 1816–1996: An Annotated Bibliography, by Robert Beasecker, 1998

"Time by Moments Steals Away": The 1848 Journal of Ruth Douglass, by Robert L. Root, Jr., 1998

The Detroit Tigers: A Pictorial Celebration of the Greatest Players and Moments in Tigers' History, updated edition, by William M. Anderson, 1999

Father Abraham's Children: Michigan Episodes in the Civil War, by Frank B. Woodford, 1999 (reprint)

Letter from Washington, 1863–1865, by Lois Bryan Adams, edited and with an introduction by Evelyn Leasher, 1999

Wonderful Power: The Story of Ancient Copper Working in the Lake Superior Basin, by Susan R. Martin, 1999

A Sailor's Logbook: A Season aboard Great Lakes Freighters, by Mark L. Thompson, 1999

Huron: The Seasons of a Great Lake, by Napier Shelton, 1999

Tin Stackers: The History of the Pittsburgh Steamship Company, by Al Miller, 1999

Art in Detroit Public Places, revised edition, text by Dennis Nawrocki, photographs by David Clements, 1999

Brewed in Detroit: Breweries and Beers Since 1830, by Peter H. Blum, 1999

Detroit Kids Catalog: A Family Guide for the 21st Century, by Ellyce Field, 2000

"Expanding the Frontiers of Civil Rights": Michigan, 1948–1968, by Sidney Fine, 2000

Graveyard of the Lakes, by Mark L. Thompson, 2000

Enterprising Images: The Goodridge Brothers, African American Photographers, 1847–1922, by John Vincent Jezierski, 2000

New Poems from the Third Coast: Contemporary Michigan Poetry, edited by Michael Delp, Conrad Hilberry, and Josie Kearns, 2000

Arab Detroit: From Margin to Mainstream, edited by Nabeel Abraham and Andrew Shryock, 2000

The Sandstone Architecture of the Lake Superior Region, by Kathryn Bishop Eckert, 2000

Looking Beyond Race: The Life of Otis Milton Smith, by Otis Milton Smith and Mary M. Stolberg, 2000

Mail by the Pail, by Colin Bergel, illustrated by Mark Koenig, 2000

Great Lakes Journey: A New Look at America's Freshwater Coast, by William Ashworth, 2000

A Life in the Balance: The Memoirs of Stanley J. Winkelman, by Stanley J. Winkelman, 2000

Schooner Passage: Sailing Ships and the Lake Michigan Frontier, by Theodore J. Karamanski, 2000

The Outdoor Museum: The Magic of Michigan's Marshall M. Fredericks, by Marcy Heller Fisher, illustrated by Christine Collins Woomer, 2001

Detroit in Its World Setting: A Three Hundred Year Chronology, 1701–2001, edited by David Lee Poremba, 2001

Frontier Metropolis: Picturing Early Detroit, 1701–1838, by Brian Leigh Dunnigan, 2001

Michigan Remembered: Photographs from the Farm Security Administration and the Office of War Information, 1936–1943, edited by Constance B. Schulz, with Introductory Essays by Constance B. Schulz and William H. Mulligan, Jr., 2001

This Is Detroit, 1701–2001, by Arthur M. Woodford, 2001

History of the Finns in Michigan, by Armas K. E. Holmio, translated by Ellen M. Ryynanen, 2001

Angels in the Architecture: A Photographic Elegy to an American Asylum, by Heidi Johnson, 2001

Uppermost Canada: The Western District and the Detroit Frontier, 1800–1850, by R. Alan Douglas, 2001

Windjammers: Songs of the Great Lakes Sailors, by Ivan H. Walton with Joe Grimm, 2002

Detroit Tigers Lists and More: Runs, Hits, and Eras, by Mark Pattison and David Raglin, 2002

The Iron Hunter, by Chase S. Osborn, 2002 (reprint)

Independent Man: The Life of Senator James Couzens, by Harry Barnard, 2002 (reprint)

Riding the Roller Coaster: A History of the Chrysler Corporation, by Charles K. Hyde, 2003

Michigan's Early Military Forces: A Roster and History of Troops Activated prior to the American Civil War, rosters compiled by Le Roy Barnett with histories by Roger Rosentreter, 2003

Beyond the Windswept Dunes: The Story of Maritime Muskegon, by Elizabeth Sherman, 2003

For an updated listing of books in this series, please visit our Web site at http://wsupress.wayne.edu

www.ingramcontent.com/pod-product-compliance
Lightning Source LLC
Chambersburg PA
CBHW081946230426
43669CB00019B/2935